Canadian Copyright

"*Canadian Copyright* is an indispensable, layperson's guide through the practical, legal, and philosophical copyright maze...a much needed book."

—**Paul Whitney,** City Librarian, Vancouver Public
Library, and Chair of the Canadian Urban
Library Council Copyright Committee

"At long last! We now have a lively and engaging primer on Canadian copyright law for those who most need it—the people who actually create and consume cultural goods in this country. Murray and Trosow clarify Canadian law, and make an exciting and incisive contribution to Canadian cultural policy debates."

—**Rosemary J. Coombe,** Canada Research Chair in Law,
Communication and Culture, York University

Canadian Copyright

A Citizen's Guide

Laura J. Murray and Samuel E. Trosow

Between the Lines

TORONTO

Canadian Copyright
© 2007 by Laura J. Murray and Samuel E. Trosow
First published in 2007 by
Between the Lines
720 Bathurst Street, Suite #404
Toronto, Ontario M5S 2R4
Canada
1-800-718-7201

Library and Archives Canada Cataloguing in Publication
Murray, Laura Jane, 1965-
    Canadian copyright : a citizen's guide / Laura J. Murray and Samuel E. Trosow ; illustrator, Jane Burkowski.
Includes bibliographical references and index.
ISBN 978-1-897071-30-4
1. Copyright—Canada—Popular works. I. Trosow, Samuel E.
II. Title.
KE2799.2.M87 2007   346.7104'82   C2007-905230-4   KF2995.M87 2007

Illustrations by Jane Burkowski
Cover and text design by George Kirkpatrick
Printed in Canada

Between the Lines gratefully acknowledges assistance for its publishing activities from the Canada Council for the Arts, the Ontario Arts Council, the Government of Ontario through the Ontario Book Publishers Tax Credit program and through the Ontario Book Initiative, and the Government of Canada through the Book Publishing Industry Development Program.

Canada Council Conseil des Arts
for the Arts du Canada

Canadä

ONTARIO ARTS COUNCIL
CONSEIL DES ARTS DE L'ONTARIO

Contents

PART IV: POLICY

Tables

Preface

THE AUTHORS of this book come to a common interest from different directions. One of us, Sam Trosow, is an Associate Professor at the University of Western Ontario; he is jointly appointed in the Faculty of Law and in the Faculty of Information and Media Studies (FIMS). He previously worked in California as a practising lawyer and later as a law librarian. His academic research focuses on the political economy of information and knowledge: that is to say, where information and knowledge come from, how they circulate, and how they intersect with political and social processes. Beyond his work on copyright in the digital environment, he also has strong interests in legal theory and in the role of libraries as public information services.

The other author, Laura Murray, is an Associate Professor in the English Department of Queen's University. Her background is in literary theory, Aboriginal studies, and eighteenth- and nineteenth-century American literature. She was first drawn to learn about copyright issues upon hearing Aboriginal artists speak of the mismatch between copyright and their way of thinking about cultural custodianship. As she later followed American debates over the constitutionality of copyright reform and the effects of digital technology on culture, she decided that a Canadian literary critic could offer something missing from the discussion. In 2003, concerned that there seemed to be few sources of information about emerging legislative reform in Canada, she started the website www.faircopyright.ca.

The book emerges from an enormously rich and dynamic conversation amongst a wide range of people. On the law and policy end we thank Jody Ciufo, David Fewer, Michael Geist, Paul Jones, Elizabeth Judge, Howard Knopf, Wallace McLean, Russell McOrmond, Ira Nadel, Myra Tawfik, Paul Whitney, and all the members of the faircopy Listserv. The thoughts and expertise of artists and writers were important to the genesis of this book: we thank especially Karl Beveridge, Susan Crean, John Degen, Richard Fung, John Greyson, Christopher Moore, and the participants of Copycamp, September 2006, even and especially when our opinions differ from theirs. Comments and inquiries from many Canadians that came in via the faircopyright.ca website over the past three years have been invaluable prompts about what ordinary people want to know about copyright. Special thanks to the artists and others who agreed to be interviewed on their experiences with copyright, and to Kirsty Robertson, who managed the intellectual and logistical dimensions of interviewing with admirable poise. Linda Quirk did invaluable library and editing work up to the eleventh hour, and we are grateful to Shannon Smith for her rigorous yet down-to-earth comments on the manuscript. Jane Burkowski proved a tolerant as well as talented illustrator.

Laura's grants from the Social Science and Humanities Research Council and Sam's from the University of Western Ontario Academic Development Fund provided much appreciated research funding; Laura is also grateful to Queen's University for a sabbatical that enabled the writing of the book. Working with Paul Eprile, Jennifer Tiberio, and Robert Clarke of Between the Lines has been a pleasure. Marie Blosh was an excellent troubleshooter and sounding board. Finally, Laura would like to thank Sergio Sismondo for his many dimensions of generosity, and Alison Gowan and Richard Day for explorations in the musical public domain.

Laura Murray and Sam Trosow

Introduction

COPYRIGHT LAW is an imperfect but ingenious policy mechanism. In its regulation of ownership arrangements for works of human expression, it has profound effects on culture, democracy, and economics. Over the years, and in different countries, it has been adapted and diversified to many new situations and technologies. Its pieces shift like coloured shards in a kaleidoscope: in any given situation, we see something different. The panorama is endlessly fascinating and dynamic.

We admit that this is an unconventional way of looking at copyright law. Most people don't think of it as beautiful or translucent—they see it as black and white or sometimes all too grey. They try to blow it up, hit other people over the head with it, or run the other way. Most people also see copyright law, along with law in general, as static: some things are illegal, some things are legal, and the judge will tell us which is which. If it isn't static, many people think it ought to be: that with the right tools we can immobilize copyright law and make it more certain. But in fact all law is always developing in a complex and fitful way—

through changing legislation, through legal precedents from case law, and through the practice and beliefs of ordinary citizens. Law is not a thing, but a process based on a set of social relationships.

For many people this aliveness of the law produces confusion, but in copyright, as in other areas of law, we think it also produces opportunities. If ordinary people educate themselves about the history and various incarnations of copyright around the world, they can glimpse principles, costs, and possibilities often masked by the misleading self-evidence of the here and now. Widespread knowledge of existing law can enable people to make more effective use of it—in our terms, to *practise fair copyright*. Widespread knowledge of proposed laws can help us make sure that the kaleidoscope doesn't get clouded over or locked in one position.

These days copyright is becoming part of just about everybody's life. That's why you are reading this book. Whether you are a parent, artist, business person, blogger, teacher, student, or music fan, questions about copyright law have popped into your head or landed in your lap. You may have encountered copy protection on a CD you bought—and after a brief tantrum, you may have wondered if it's possible or legal to disable it. You may wonder if your children's file-sharing will get them, or you, in trouble with the law. You may want to stop people from ripping off your screenplay or photograph. You may wonder whether you should read all that legalese on a software licence or a publishing contract, and whether you'd understand it if you did. You may want to know if it's okay to capture an image from somebody else's website and post it on your own. You may wish you knew how to argue with a boss, a teacher, or a lawyer who says, "You can't do that."

You need information. But what are you getting? If you are a writer or musician, you are being told that as a "content provider," you should be grateful for small mercies: just sign here, shut up, and be glad the big corporations are fighting the pirates on your behalf. If you are a consumer, you are being bombarded with messages that you are a pirate, that pirates are evil, and that pirates will face legal liability if they don't stop their nefarious activities. If you are a teacher or student, your school board or institution is warning you about the evils of piracy with a vehemence formerly associated with anti-drug campaigns.

We think that pirate talk, together with threats of lawsuits against consumers and promotion of law reform to limit consumers' rights, is a *cause* of a serious legitimacy crisis in copyright law—not a productive solution. True, digital technologies allow easier copying and can increase copyright infringement. Rights holders have reason for concern. But new technologies also allow easier monitoring and control of reasonable and customary consumer use. Consumers notice that digital rights management (DRM) is getting in the way of the enjoyment of materials they buy. They see the big profits of the media conglomerates; they see the vain attempts of the music industry to sustain old approaches to business; and they wonder why they are being cast as the bad guys.

Ironically, creators may be collateral damage in the war against so-called pirates. As journalist John Lorinc has pointed out, "The views of the creators themselves have been overwhelmed by those of producers, publishers and media conglomerates, and assumed to always coincide."[1] Some consumers have become so incensed at the hypocrisy and greed of the music, film, software, and media industries that they routinely disregard copyright law. Facing strong-arming or indifference from broadcasters, labels, museums, or other distributors, and a blunt sense of entitlement from consumers, creators often feel caught between the frying pan and the fire.

Meanwhile, other consumers are afraid to engage with the cultural objects around them, which limits their ability to become creators themselves. The climate of fear is not only frustrating for individuals, but also detrimental to the broader cultural and political environment.

In fact, most day-to-day activities of most Canadians do not constitute actionable copyright infringement, and they certainly do not constitute theft or pillage. Canadian copyright law is actually much more nuanced than the piracy-as-theft metaphor suggests. The law distinguishes between large-scale commercial infringement, which is indeed damaging to all stakeholders, and the ordinary use of legitimately purchased, borrowed, or viewed materials, which contributes to the growth of culture and democracy.

To recognize and assert such distinctions is, in our view, to practise copyright responsibly. As the Supreme Court declared in *Théberge v. Galerie d'Art du Petit Champlain* (2002), "Excessive control by holders of copyrights and other forms of intellectual property may unduly limit the ability of the public domain to incorporate and embellish creative innovation in the long-term interests of society as a whole, or create practical obstacles to proper utilization."[2] The court also noted, "Once an authorized copy of a work is sold to a member of the public, it is generally for the purchaser, not the author, to determine what happens to it."[3] In 2004, in *CCH v. Law Society of Upper Canada*, the Supreme Court was even more explicit about the importance of users' rights.

The relative balance of Canada's current copyright situation may be temporary. The Canadian government is under considerable domestic and diplomatic pressure to fortify copyright owners' rights. As a culmination of consultation beginning in 2001, the Liberal government under Paul Martin introduced Bill C-60 in 2005, although the bill was abandoned when that government fell. The minority government of Stephen Harper, which has engaged in no public consultation, has claimed that new legislation is imminent. When new legislation is introduced the complexity of the issues, the intensity of lobbying efforts, and the fragility of minority governments may slow the process. But slowness is not a bad thing. In 1998 the United States moved quickly to respond to digital technology with new legislation, and Canada can learn from the problems that have arisen from that haste. If Canadian policy-makers manage to maintain users' rights through the next rounds of copyright reform, they may be able to ease the growing legitimacy crisis in copyright law. This will serve Canada well.

This book has a strong Canadian focus because Canadians are short on practical and accurate information about what we can and can't do within the framework of our own copyright law. Canadians tend to know more about U.S. law. Copyright litigation in the United States is more frequent and often more notorious; U.S. law has moved fast and controversially in a "maximalist" direction; U.S. copyright warnings and ads preface almost every movie and DVD we watch; and U.S. public interest watchdogs such as the Electronic Frontier Foundation are fighting back with vigour. But there are many important differences between Canadian and U.S. copyright law. We need to know those differences. Canadian law is what we live under, whatever the origin of the materials in question.

We have organized the book into four parts.

In Part I we survey the major philosophical and economic justifications for copyright (chapter 1) and Canadian copyright's origins in British, U.S., and French traditions (chapter 2). While a discussion of philosophical concepts such as utilitarianism may seem intimidating, time spent here may help you to place and assess the copyright claims you hear around you on an everyday basis. The thumbnail early history of copyright has many fascinating resonances with present-day problems and controversies. Canadian copyright law particularly has always been caught between international forces, and it still is: it helps to know where we've come from.

Part II takes us to and through the Copyright Act. Reading the act systematically and understanding its context in case law provide the necessary groundwork for analyzing and crafting solutions in particular situations. In this spirit, we survey (chapter 3) the requirements for copyright to "subsist" in a work (or in some other subject matter), and look at the differences between different classes of works, explaining certain basic requirements such as originality and fixation in a tangible medium. We then enumerate (chapter 4) the rights held by an owner of copyright. While people usually think of copyright as the right to prohibit the making of copies, it is really much broader than that. Chapter 5 addresses the question of *who* owns copyright—it isn't always the author. Chapter 6, on users' rights, explains the scope and details of limitations on owners' rights. Copyright law has often privileged the owners' rights to the detriment of users' rights, but here we review a series of recent Canadian court cases that give more weight to the rights of users of copyrighted materials. Finally, we need to look at what happens if you or someone else wants to act against infringement (chapter 7). This chapter covers practicalities such as statutory damages, cease and desist letters, and the difference between civil and criminal infringement.

Part III covers more specific terrain, considering the issues that copyright presents for people creating and using particular media, or working in certain creative communities, institutions, or industries: from the areas of craft and design and digital rights through education, film, and journalism to websites, among others. In each case we identify special circumstances, real-life examples, and important case law, exploring sometimes thorny issues of both owners' rights and users' rights. You can dip into these chapters according to your particular needs and interests. They don't have to be read completely or in order, but they do presume that you've read Part II and are comfortable with the basic terms, principles, and building blocks of copyright.

We have three groups of readers in mind for these chapters—as indeed for the book as a whole: independent or freelance creators, amateur creators, and consumers. While the interests of these groups are often distinct, we believe that in the larger context of corporate capitalism they have much in common.

Needless to say, we can't anticipate or answer all of your copyright questions. We don't specifically address many artistic or craft practices—dance, theatre, and video-game design, for example. And in a book of this nature we can't cover all the myriad details of the Copyright Act and case law. When it comes to a particular practice, the law evaluates each fact situation individually, and it isn't often possible to extrapolate with certainty from an analogous situation. So if you have a worrying legal dilemma, you will need to conduct further research or consult a lawyer. But if you have read this book first, you will at least be armed with basic terminology and good questions. You might even get some pleasure in seeing the look of surprise on the lawyer's face when you ask, "But what about Section 14.1?"

Part IV outlines some alternatives and counterparts to copyright, starting with the provocative pairing of Aboriginal customary law and the "free culture" movement, and discussing other ways of supporting creative activity such as grants and tax incentives. We argue that copyright has too prominent a role as "*the* solution" in cultural policy when in fact it functions best as only one policy tool among many others. In the final chapter we present a number of recommendations for reform of Canada's Copyright Act, which is likely to come hard on the heels of this book's publication.

We hope that you will find some answers to your questions in this book. But even more, we hope that once you have read the book, you will be able to "practise copyright" attuned to the big issues of culture and democracy that it raises.

PART I: IDEAS

General Resources

- James Boyle, *Shamans, Software, and Spleens: Law and the Construction of the Information Society*, 1996.

- William W. Fisher, "Theories of Intellectual Property," 2000.

- Carla Hesse, "The Rise of Intellectual Property, 700 B.C.–A.D. 2000: An Idea in the Balance," 2002.

- Lawrence Lessig, *Free Culture: How Big Media Uses Technology and the Law to Lock Down Culture and Control Creativity*, 2004.

- Lyman Ray Patterson, *Copyright in Historical Perspective*, 1968.

- Edward Samuels, *The Illustrated Story of Copyright*, 2000.

For further details about sources listed here and elsewhere, please see the Bibliography.

1: Copyright's Rationales

COPYRIGHT IS so entrenched in popular thinking about the production and dissemination of culture that we may think of it as natural or inevitable. We may even drape it with mystical ideas about the creative process. To be sure, authors and artists have always had a special connection to their work. The seventeenth-century poet John Milton wrote that books "preserve as in a vial the purest efficacy and extraction of that living intellect that bred them." An anonymous author declared to the British Parliament in 1735, "If there be such a Thing as Property upon Earth, an Author has it in his Work."[1]

These claims were made, however, as polemical assertions in the midst of raucous debate, not as statements of established fact. In exalting authors as sources or owners, Milton and the anonymous author spoke against the "common sense" of their time, according to which an artist was most often honoured as a custodian and animator of collective tradition. Artistic and intellectual production understood in this collective way tended to be supported by a patronage system rather than by a system of individual rights or property. Alternative models do exist for

8

encouraging and supporting cultural production (see chapter 18). We need therefore to think twice about copyright's logic.

Established Philosophies of Copyright

Why should copyright holders have exclusive rights in their works? Copyright laws relate to two major lines of philosophical justification: rights-based theories and utilitarianism. Both of these approaches have advantages and limitations, and both of them are explicitly or implicitly represented in today's copyright debates.[2] The economic analysis that holds sway in many quarters today can be seen as a descendant of both lines of thought.

Rights-Based Theories

Rights-based theories are rooted in ideas of natural law. Proponents of natural law believe that the law exists independently, separate and apart from legislation that has been posited by any particular state. While natural law may be associated with a religious world view, it can also appeal to an abstract moral authority, such as justice. The principles of natural law are expressed in documents such as the Magna Carta and the French Declaration of the Rights of Man. The claim from the American Declaration of Independence "that all men are created equal, that they are endowed by their Creator with certain unalienable Rights" is a good example of natural law philosophy. More generally, the idea of "human rights" is derived from a natural law approach: rights come from "nature or nature's God," as the Declaration of Independence puts it, not from a particular ruler or government.

A natural law approach to property would hold that a person has a natural entitlement to his person and to the fruits of his labours. The most well-known expositor of this philosophy is John Locke, who in his *Second Treatise of Government* (1690) set out a theory that justifies the private appropriation of public resources.[3] While Locke was writing about the appropriation of physical resources (that is, land and things), his work has come to be applied to intellectual labour as well. Locke begins with the premise that "the 'labour' of [a person's] body and the 'work' of his hands, we may say, are properly his." Then he says that whatever a person "removes out of the state that Nature hath provided and left it in, he hath mixed his labor with it and joined to it something that is his own and thereby makes it his property."[4]

In a Lockean view of copyright, the labour supplied by the author provides a justification for a claim to exclude others—even if the author is working with materials previously available to all. A claim that copyright ought to be perpetual could also be justified by reference to Locke, because property rights in physical resources are perpetual.

Interestingly, Locke also specified two limitations on the right to appropriate from the commons. First, he stated that the appropriation must leave as much and as good for others; second, he did not consider ownership legitimate when individuals appropriated more than they could use.[5] Locke was also explicitly opposed to perpetual copyright.[6] Thus, whether we are talking about tangible property or intellectual property, Locke may provide justification both for owners' rights *and* for limitations to them.

On some level many people may think of copyright as a "natural" right because it just seems "fair" that authors should hold rights in work

---

Is Disney's copyright in *Beauty and the Beast* legitimate, according to Lockean thinking?

Yes: Disney created private property by taking a story from the public domain and adding its labour to that story. But Locke was talking about a world of limitless resources. In his *Second Treatise of Government* (chapter 5, section 33), he wrote: "No body could think himself injured by the drinking of another man, though he took a good draught, who had a whole river of the same water left him to quench his thirst."

Are fairy tales a limitless resource? Does Disney's taking of them leave less for others? Those are questions that Locke invites us to ask. Copyright law has developed distinctions between "rival" and "non-rival" goods, and between ideas and expression, in order to answer questions such as these. While Disney can "own" its version of the story, copyright law holds that such ownership only extends to the new elements that the studio adds. The story itself has to be left free for others to use as well.

they have created. But the courts, in the Anglo-American tradition, do not see it this way. In the seventeenth century, English courts held that acts of Parliament were subject to the constraints of natural law, often understood to be embodied in "common law," or the accumulated collection of precedent from specific legal cases. In *Dr. Bonham's Case* (1610), the court said that the "common law will control Acts of Parliament, and sometimes judge them to be utterly void: for when an Act of Parliament is *against common right and reason*, or repugnant, or impossible to be performed, the common law will control it, and adjudge such an Act to be void."[7] But after 1688 acts of Parliament were thought to be supreme: in other words, the law was understood to lie in what the government had expressly promulgated, enacted, or "posited." In the realm of copyright, this "positive law" viewpoint was confirmed in the 1774 case *Donaldson v. Becket*.[8] In this case a divided House of Lords affirmed the limited copyright term of the Statute of Anne over claims of common-law perpetual copyright, rejecting the notion of a "natural" copyright separate and apart from the statute.[9] Thus, while today's justifications for copyright law are often rooted in the thinking of natural law, Anglo-American law now operates predominantly according to positive law principles.

Still, rights-based or natural law theories do continue to play a more central role in the civil law systems that originated in Continental Europe, brought to Canada through French law.[10] Civil law systems place more emphasis on the individual rights of the author as a person, and tend to

[Philosopher Robert] Nozick asks: If I pour my can of tomato juice into the ocean, do I own the ocean? Analogous questions abound in the field of intellectual property. If I invent a drug that prevents impotence, do I deserve to collect for twenty years the extraordinary amount of money that men throughout the world would pay for access to the drug? If I write a novel about a war between two space empires, may I legitimately demand compensation from people who wish to prepare motion-picture adaptations, write sequels, manufacture dolls based on my characters, or produce t-shirts emblazoned with bits of my dialogue? How far, in short, do my rights go?

—William Fisher, "Theories of Intellectual Property," 188–89.

view copyright as an extension of the personality of the author. Canadian law represents a blending of English and French traditions, and Supreme Court cases in particular often reflect a combination of the two.

Utilitarianism

Utilitarianism is another major stream of justification of copyright. As a general school of thought, utilitarianism is generally attributed to the nineteenth-century English philosopher Jeremy Bentham. According to Bentham, people can make decisions in a situation of competing interests by measuring the total amount of "happiness" produced. "A measure of government," he wrote, "may be said to be conformable to or dictated by the principle of utility, when ... the tendency which it has to augment the happiness of the community is greater than any which it has to diminish it."[11]

The so-called "Copyright Clause" of the U.S. Constitution might be taken as an example of utilitarianism: it does not appeal to a higher power, as in natural law thinking, but rather empowers Congress to enact intellectual property laws as a tool for general benefit—that is, "to promote the progress of science and the useful arts." While Canada's copyright principles are not articulated at the constitutional level, our

---

Like many since, the eighteenth-century English writer Samuel Johnson combined natural law and utilitarian thinking in his approach to copyright:

> There seems ... to be in authours a stronger right of property than that by occupancy; a metaphysical right, a right, as it were, of creation, which should from its nature be perpetual; but the consent of nations is against it, and indeed reason and the interests of learning are against it; for were it to be perpetual, no book, however useful, could be universally diffused amongst mankind, should the proprietor take it into his head to restrain its circulation.... For the general good of the world, therefore, whatever valuable work has once been created by an authour, and issued out by him, should be understood as no longer in his power, but as belonging to the publick.

Source: Johnson quoted in Boswell, *Boswell's Life of Johnson*, 546.

courts and legislators have often and increasingly used a rhetoric of public or national interest that could be said to be utilitarian.[12]

As a legal philosophy, utilitarianism is associated with legal positivism—the approach that locates the law not in established practice and custom, but in the statute alone. Sometimes positivism can be democratic in spirit, privileging the visible "black letter" law over invisible entrenched interests. However, the classical formulation of legal positivism, as stated by John Austin in his 1832 work *The Province of Jurisprudence Determined*, shows a harsher side of the doctrine: "The matter of jurisprudence is positive law; law strictly and simply so called: or law set by political superiors to political inferiors."[13] Most legal education today is based on a modified positivist approach to learning black-letter law. We take a more "realist" approach, locating legal authority not only in the written laws, and not only in general practices and understandings of the good, but in their interaction.[14]

Economic Analysis

In today's debates, copyright is most often justified in economic terms: we are living in a "knowledge-based economy," the claim goes, and we need a particular vision of copyright to drive that economy. Classic economic analysis of copyright law rests on three general assumptions: that the free market system is the appropriate allocation device to guide the creation and dissemination of "information and knowledge-based products"; that information- and knowledge-based goods and services will be underproduced without a guarantee of sufficient market-based financial incentives to creators and owners; and that the expansion of exclusive intellectual property rights is necessary to protect these market-based incentives from being undermined by acts of appropriation.

Within the limitations of these assumptions, economic analysis seeks to promote the efficient allocation of resources in a market setting. In its sacralization of property rights, it is underpinned by natural law philosophies; but it is also essentially utilitarian in nature, in that it recognizes the existence of a trade-off between limiting access to works and providing economic incentives to create works. After all, an economy in which every single transaction with a copyrighted work were "monetized" or metered in some way would carry great financial and bureaucratic costs, which might slow down its growth (economists call these "transaction costs"). The trade-off is often referred to as the "balancing" of interests between the rights of owners and the rights of users.

Such cost-benefit analysis is open to criticism on a number of grounds. One central problem is that the losses that come from limiting access are not as susceptible to precise measurement as are the financial benefits accruing to the owners of exclusive copyright interests. Henry Richardson argues that cost-benefit analysis "makes no room for intelligent deliberation about how to best use our resources," and that it thus "defeats its own aims."[15] The balancing approach also does not seem to adequately consider how different stakeholders come to the table with different resources, different backgrounds, and different levels of political power. But while it may be argued that the discourse of "balancing of interests" fails to address several problems, it is certainly better than the one-dimensional approach of arguing that protections are good, and more protections are better, without regard to the losses on the other side.

The argument is often made that copyright protections need to be

> The Internet does lower the cost of copying and, thus, the cost of illicit copying. Of course, it also lowers the costs of production, distribution, and advertising, and dramatically increases the size of the potential market. Is the net result, then, a loss to rights-holders such that we need to increase protection to maintain a constant level of incentives? A large, leaky market may actually provide more revenue than a small one over which one's control is much stronger. What's more, the same technologies that allow for cheap copying also allow for swift and encyclopedic search engines—the best devices ever invented for detecting illicit copying. It would be impossible to say, on the basis of the evidence we have, that owners of protected content are better or worse off as a result of the Internet. Thus, the idea that we must inevitably strengthen rights as copying costs decline doesn't hold water. And given the known static and dynamic costs of monopolies, and the constitutional injunction to encourage the progress of science and the useful arts, the burden of proof should be on those requesting new rights to prove their necessity.
>
> –James Boyle, "Second Enclosure Movement and the Construction of the Public Domain."

expanded because of changes in technology, or because new cultural practices threaten existing business models. But looking at copyright only from the standpoint of protections overlooks the reality that one person's additional rights are just further restrictions for someone else. Rather than thinking about rights in a vacuum, we prefer to think also about the corresponding duties and disabilities that the rights impose on others. In other words, it makes just as much sense to speak of copyright *restrictions* as of copyright *protections*.

The Problem of Intellectual Property

So far we have introduced two major paths of philosophical justification for copyright, and suggested how they underlie modern economic analysis. While we pointed out some of their pitfalls, we generally followed the tendencies of both approaches to gloss over the distinction between tangible property (land, chattels, goods, widgets) and intangible intellectual property (expression, knowledge, information). However, the differences between tangible and intellectual goods are fundamental, and any fully convincing justification of copyright (or, for that matter, patent, although we will not get into that here) must recognize these differences. The traditional rationales for copyright, then, can be challenged—and if copyright is to maintain its legitimacy this challenge must be acknowledged.

Copyright laws attempt to regulate the flow of intellectual and information goods—or at least the particular ways in which ideas, information, and knowledge are expressed. Talk about the importance of flows of information and knowledge is ubiquitous: Canadians are constantly being told that we live in an "information society." But little attention has been paid in the policy context to understanding the nature and characteristics of information, ideas, and knowledge. Copyright policy typically proceeds from the assumption that intellectual goods are "things" without further analysis.

In fact, intellectual goods exhibit two major differences from private goods, or commodities: they are generally *non-rival* in consumption, and they *do not inherently possess exclusion mechanisms*. We would class intellectual goods, then, as *public goods*.

If a good is rivalrous in its consumption, it is depleted or used up when one person consumes it. Physical consumer goods that populate store shelves are rivalrous in consumption. When a widget is purchased it is no longer on the shelf for the next shopper. Depletable energy resources are another classic example of rivalry in consumption. When we say that public goods are *non-rival* in consumption, we mean that the consumption of the good by one person does not reduce the amount of the good available for consumption by others. If you walk down a street illuminated by a street light, the light is not depleted because you enjoyed its benefit. The bulb in the lamp will be depleted through use and is itself a private good with rivalry in consumption. But the service of street lighting is a public good and exhibits non-rivalry in consumption. The act of breathing does not significantly reduce the air available for everyone else, so it too is non-rivalrous in consumption. (Locke said the same about water, so we can see that goods can change, depending on circumstance, from non-rival to rival or vice versa.)

In the context of copyright analysis, we can distinguish a book or a CD (physical goods with rivalry in consumption) from the information contained in the book or CD. Until recently, information was necessarily distributed in physical containers, so the differences between rivalry and non-rivalry in consumption were not as noticeable as they are today. With advances in digital technology, content is now routinely severed from its container. A digital file is non-rival in consumption and can be distributed to ten thousand persons just as well as ten. One could even

If nature has made any one thing less susceptible than all others of exclusive property, it is the action of the thinking power called an idea, which an individual may exclusively possess as long as he keeps it to himself; but the moment it is divulged, it forces itself into the possession of everyone, and the receiver cannot dispose himself of it. Its peculiar character, too, is that no one possesses the less, because every other possesses the whole of it. He who receives an idea from me, receives instruction himself without lessening mine; as he who lights his taper at mine, receives it without darkening me.

–Thomas Jefferson to Isaac McPherson, Monticello, Aug. 13, 1813, in Jefferson, *Writings of Thomas Jefferson*, 13, 333–34.

say that the essence of information as information is that it is non-rival in consumption.

There are certainly exceptions to this general observation. For example, hot market information and other types of proprietary data might become less valuable with wider distribution.[16] But we could also note that much information or expression becomes *more* valuable as more people use it, by the phenomenon known by economists as "network effects." The telephone system provides an apt analogy: it would not be very valuable to you if you were the only person with a telephone, but the more people using the system, the more value it has. A similar thing happens in the cultural marketplace with bestsellers, fads, and trends.

The second aspect of a public good that distinguishes it from a private good is that it does not have an *exclusion mechanism*. A tollgate is an example of an exclusion mechanism. So is a cash register: when you go to the store, you don't get to enjoy a new shirt or bicycle unless you pay for it. Public goods are different. Anyone can use them, regardless of whether they express a preference for them in the marketplace. People who walk down a street at night get the benefit of the streetlight whether or not they helped pay for it. No shield emerges to block the light from those who have not paid taxes in that jurisdiction (or at least not yet: maybe somebody will think of a way to do it). National defence, policing, roads, and schooling are other common examples of goods that lack an exclusion mechanism. You enjoy the "benefits" of national defence expenditures whatever your opinion on how tax revenues should be spent.

Whether or not a good has an effective exclusion mechanism can be a question of public policy, a question of technology, or both. The law of theft is an exclusion mechanism that has long been imposed as a matter of public policy. It is against the law to take an item out of a store without paying for it, and it is against the law to sneak into a theatre without buying a ticket. The exclusion mechanism may also be a technological device. The automated tollgate is an older such technology, and consumers are now becoming familiar with a vast array of new digital locks or gateways, known as technological protection measures (TPMs). But exclusion mechanisms are often hybrid: that is, the law often acts to reinforce a technological exclusion mechanism. Think of cable television.

Table 1. Comparison of Pure Public Goods and Pure Private Goods

	Consumption	Exclusion Mechanism
pure public good	non–rival (joint) consumption; use does not result in depletion of the good	exclusion mechanism is not present
pure private good	rival consumption; use results in depletion of the good	exclusion mechanism is present

It used to be that television airwaves were pure public goods. By turning on your television and viewing a broadcast, you were not depleting the airwaves available for others to enjoy. Cable companies introduced an exclusion mechanism: you had to pay to get the system hooked up. If you "fix" the cable box so that you can view programs without subscribing to the service (or create a device to do so), you are likely to be in violation of a law, and subject to sanctions. The same double exclusion mechanism could be layered onto TPMs, even though there are many legitimate reasons to defeat a TPM: making a backup copy of a computer program, for example, or accessing public domain content (see chapter 9).

We have seen how intellectual goods are inherently non–rival in consumption as they are not naturally subject to an exclusion mechanism. The container holding the information (the book, the CD) is rivalrous in consumption and is subject to an exclusion mechanism and rivalry in consumption, but the information contained therein is not. Public goods present a problem for market-oriented economists because if an item has public good characteristics, people will be able to use and enjoy it without having to pay for it. Lack of exclusion means you can obtain the benefit of the good whether or not you are willing to pay for it. The price system, which is based on rules of supply and demand, cannot operate for public goods, and we have in this an instance of what economists call total market failure.

While many people see the public goods quality of digital information and expression as an exciting phenomenon, mainstream economists and large-content owners see public goods as a problem that needs to be cured. They desperately need the price system to work. A fix is needed, and the cure is to create some sort of exclusion mechanism. In the case of intellectual goods, the laws of intellectual property can be layered on top of technology to create artificial scarcity and impose constraints on free flows of information.

These artificially created exclusion mechanisms are powerful policy tools. They may well be justifiable on natural law or utilitarian grounds: we may say, for example, that it isn't fair that an author not be paid for her work, or that it is in the public interest that she be paid. Or we may think that only the individuals who need a certain good ought to pay for it. But the exclusion mechanisms should be used carefully, because they have the potential to unduly restrict the transfer of information and knowledge. We can think of this dilemma in terms of "balancing" different interests. But the public goods analysis also raises a wider question that cannot be properly analyzed within the constraints of conventional cost-benefit analysis. Should we be cautious, as a society, about subjecting information goods to the analytical and policy approaches typically applied to tangible goods? Legislators and courts have most often treated them differently: perhaps we should heed this history.

2: Copyright's Histories

WHERE DOES Canadian copyright law come from? Like so many Canadian institutions, it is the product of a long history of imposed and adapted British law and competing French traditions, complicated by the weighty proximity of U.S. markets and cultural influence. British, French, and U.S. law are all quite different, and to understand Canada's situation fully we need to know something about the early histories of each of them, as well as the history of copyright in Canada through the twentieth century. Within copyright's early history—and in particular within the eighteenth-century and nineteenth-century book trade—we find familiar versions of many of today's debates and dilemmas, including the challenges posed by digital technologies. While we may or may not resolve these issues in the same way now, the historical comparisons can alert us to a range of possibilities and forces that we may not see by gazing only at our present situation—the international dimensions of which are laid out at the conclusion of the chapter.

First, though, there are three overall observations to keep in mind. One is that copyright's history is quite short—action-packed, but short.

All art created before the late eighteenth century was enabled not by any concept of owners' rights, but by some version of patronage, commission, and employment. Second, although copyright does indeed benefit many authors, authors have not been its main concern or driving force. Throughout history, it is the larger book trade—today the "cultural industries" or "tech sector"—that has demanded expansion of copyright, often using the rhetoric of authors' rights to do so.

Third, copyright is a pragmatic policy tool that exists in widely differing forms. How sharp or blunt the tool should be, how broad its application should be, who it should benefit, and how long it should exist—these have been and will continue to be matters for public policy to sort out.

Canada's Three Copyright Legacies

The United Kingdom

Modern Anglo-American copyright is usually said to begin with Britain's 1710 Statute of Anne, titled in full "An Act for the Encouragement of Learning, by Securing the Copies of Printed Books in the Authors or Purchasers of such Copies, during the Times Therein Mentioned."[1] The Statute of Anne marked a departure from the printing regulations of the hundred and fifty years preceding it. With the introduction of the printing press to England in the sixteenth century, the Crown had feared the spread of seditious works. To aid in controlling a dangerous new technology, it granted a publishing monopoly in 1557 to the Stationers' Company, a group of London printers and booksellers who could be relied upon to censor works in exchange for large profits. Although the Stationers' Company kept a register of books and pamphlets licensed, it did so mainly to document its gatekeeping function, not to record property ownership as we would know it today. During this period, authors' main support came through patronage: their expenses would be lightened by wealthy supporters. They could sell their "copy" once, but could not benefit from or set the terms for its reprinting.[2]

During and following the Civil War of the mid-seventeenth century, the licensing system fell into disarray, and in 1692 Parliament let the Licensing Act lapse. This was no act of political openness: as Joseph

Loewenstein puts it, "The licenser's judgment was ... to be displaced by the more methodical constraints of the laws of libel, seditious libel, and treason."[3] It is partly out of this situation that a sense of authors' rights began to emerge. Novelist (and journalist) Daniel Defoe declared, "If an Author has not a right of a Book, after he has made it, and the benefit be not his own, and the Law will not protect him in that Benefit, 'twould be very hard the Law should pretend to punish him for it."[4] During the unregulated period, printing enterprises began to spring up in the provinces, to meet growing market demand. Panicked at the prospect of losing its monopoly, the Stationers' Company wrote to Parliament with the dire warning that, as copyright historian Mark Rose frames it, "If Parliament failed to confirm [their] literary property, thousands of mechanics and shopkeepers would be deprived of their livelihoods, and 'Widows and Children who at present Subsist wholly by the Maintenance of this Property' would be reduced to extreme poverty."[5]

In 1710 Parliament did move to regulate the book trade, but without reinstating the Stationers' monopoly and perpetual rights. In the Statute of Anne it limited the term of copyright to fourteen years, renewable for another fourteen if the author was still living. It allowed parties outside

In 1663 Sir Roger L'Estrance helpfully laid out the range of parties involved in the production of a book:

The Instruments for setting the work [of promotion] afoot are These. The Adviser, Author, Compiler, Writer, Correcter, and the Persons for whom, and by whom; that is [to] say, the Stationer (commonly), and the Printer. To which may be Added, the Letter-Founders, and the Smiths, and Joyners, that work upon Presses. The usual Agents for Publishing, are the Printers themselves, Stitchers, Binders, Stationers, Hawkers, Mercury-women, Pedlers, Ballad-singers, Posts, Carryers, Hackney-Coachmen, Boat-men, and Mariners.

In today's publishing, music, film, and broadcast industries, just as many professions have a stake in the business, and hence in copyright.

Source: McKeon, *Secret History of Domesticity*, 51.

the Stationers' Company—authors and their assignees—to own those rights. While modern copyright acts have added complexity and nuance to copyright's operation, applied it to media other than books, and extended its term (tying it to the length of the author's life), the core of copyright comes down to us from the Statute of Anne: that is, the author is given a monopoly to exploit the work, and to restrict others from doing so, for a limited time.

The limited time period in the Statute of Anne presented difficulties for booksellers used to a perpetual monopoly.[6] They accepted the idea of authors' rights fairly quickly, partly because the courts made it clear that publishers' rights were based on authors' rights, and partly because rhetorically authors' rights were (and remain) a more powerful rallying cry than publishers' or booksellers' rights.[7] Publishers even argued that authors' rights were perpetual under common law, and it was not until 1774 that this line of argument was rejected. In *Donaldson v. Becket*, the House of Lords ruled that the Statute of Anne cancelled any existing common-law copyright.[8] This decision leaves us with the principle that has underpinned Anglo-American copyright ever since: that copyright is a creature of statute alone, not common law.

> ... for the encouragement of learned men to compose and write useful books; may it please your Majesty, that it may be enacted ... That from and after [April 10, 1710], the author of any book or books already printed, who hath not transferred to any other the copy or copies of such book or books ... shall have the sole right and liberty of printing such book and books for the term of one and twenty years, to commence from ... [April 10, 1710], and no longer; and That the author of any book or books already composed, and not printed and published, or that shall hereafter be composed, and his assignee, or assigns, shall have the sole liberty of printing and reprinting such book and books for the term of fourteen years.... Provided always, That after the expiration of the said term of fourteen years, the sole right of printing or disposing of copies shall return to the authors thereof, if they are then living, for another term of fourteen years.
>
> –Statute of Anne, 1710.

The United States

As U.S. legislators established a body of law for their new nation, they started with the British Statute of Anne as a model but soon developed different legal principles better suited to their particular stage of cultural and economic development. Although Canada's law is based on British law, we need to understand early U.S. law to grasp the origins of Canadian copyright in the nineteenth century; the debates in Canada in this period lay very much in the shadow of the burgeoning U.S. book industry and its particular legal and philosophical underpinnings. Early U.S. copyright is also interesting because of the contrast it presents to present-day U.S. law.

Certain key elements of an approach to copyright are embedded in the U.S. Constitution. Article I, Section 8 grants Congress power to enact legislation "to promote the progress of science and useful arts, by securing for limited times to authors and inventors the exclusive right to their respective writing and discoveries." This clause enables various forms of intellectual property law, including patent and copyright.[9] Note the similarity between the language of "promotion" and the Statute of Anne's stated purpose of "Encouragement": both are examples of the utilitarian justification for copyright. Exclusive rights are not in themselves the constitutional goal: they exist to enhance a long-term goal of public benefit, that is, the promotion of science and the arts.[10] Beyond the so-called "copyright clause" of the Constitution, another section speaks to related issues. The framers were concerned that government not be permitted to undermine the robust exchange of ideas necessary for a democracy. In response to the history of censorship in England, they developed the First Amendment to the Constitution, which guarantees freedom of speech.[11]

The first U.S. copyright act, set down in 1790, is notable for its refusal to grant copyright protection to non-American works or authors.[12] As Meredith McGill argues, this omission was not an oversight but a matter of principle, and Congress repeatedly refused to grant copyrights to foreign authors through the 1850s. McGill writes, "Not only was the mass-market for literature in America built and sustained by the publication of cheap reprints of foreign books and periodicals, the primary vehicles for the circulation of literature were uncopyrighted newspapers and magazines."[13] Scholars have often lamented the disadvantage that this regime imposed upon U.S. authors, who had to compete with cheap British blockbusters for audiences. British authors, notably Charles Dickens, were in turn incensed at the cheap circulation of their work in the United States. However, the availability of cheap books clearly contributed to the building of a hungry and educated American reading audience.

As U.S. markets developed, the rhetoric of authors' rights did begin to emerge in the country. But—partly because of the treaty's strong authors' rights provisions—the United States did not sign the 1886 Berne Convention (indeed, it signed this treaty only in 1988), and it was not until 1891 that the U.S. government developed a reciprocal copyright treaty with Great Britain. By 1903, as the United States came to be a major player in the international cultural trade, the *Bleistein v. Donaldson* case articulated an idea of natural authors' rights. In a case concerning copied circus posters, Justice Oliver Wendell Holmes of the Supreme Court argued that any image was "the personal reaction of an individual upon nature. Personality always contains something unique. It expresses its singularity even in handwriting, and a very modest grade of art has in it something irreducible, which is one man's alone."[14] As Carla Hesse points out, "Through the Holmes decision the rhetoric of authorial originality and natural rights ... made its way into American jurisprudence at the very moment when America began to supplant Europe as the hegemonic global economic power."[15] But even with this shift in perspective, U.S. lawmakers continued (with some limited exceptions) to steadfastly refuse any idea of rights vested by nature in the author.

France

Today it is a truism to say that Canadian copyright law derives from both French and British law—by which people usually mean that there is a (hopefully productive) tension between a "*droit d'auteur*" tradition deriving from natural law, and a "copyright" tradition that is more utilitarian in its philosophical underpinnings. However, utilitarianism has almost as long a history in France as it does in England. In a lively debate in the 1760s and 1770s, two philosophers—Denis Diderot and the Marquis de Condorcet—articulated contrasting views. Diderot held that products of the mind were even more like property than land itself, whereas Condorcet argued that literary property was "not a property derived from the natural order ... it is a property founded in society itself. It is not a true right; it is a privilege."[16] The Crown agreed with Condorcet, but the Revolution revoked all existing legislation and protocol for the book trade. In 1791 Condorcet was involved in drafting a law that recognized works as property, but property that could only be held ten years past the death of the author. In 1793 the National Convention passed a version of this act—based, like British law, on the idea of a limited property right. This statute governed copyright in France until 1957.[17]

In her survey of French case law and scholarship, Gillian Davies shows that throughout the nineteenth century authors' rights were not thought to arise directly out of natural law. The change in thinking seems to have occurred in the first half of the twentieth century. In the consulting and documentation associated with the new law of 1957, which was intended to codify existing practice, she finds a strong leaning towards natural rights thinking and very few mentions of the public interest. The

> The most sacred, most legitimate, most unassailable, and if I may put it this way, the most personal of all properties, is a work which is the fruit of the imagination of a writer; however, it is a property of a kind quite different from other properties. When an author has delivered his work to the public, when the work is in the hands of the public at large, so that all educated men may come to know it, assimilate the beauties contained therein and commit to memory the most pleasing passages, it seems that from that moment on the writer has associated the public with his property, or rather has transmitted it to the public outright; however, during the lifetime of the author and for a few years after his death nobody may dispose of the product of his genius without consent. But also, after that fixed period, the property of the public begins, and everybody should be able to print and publish the works which have helped to enlighten the human spirit.
>
> —Isaac Le Chapelier, Report to the French Parliament, 1791, in Davies, *Copyright and the Public Interest*, 137.

rapporteur of the committee drafting the new law mentioned the public interest only to subsume it in authors' rights when he wrote that the goal of the new law was to "effect the synthesis of the author's rights and the interests of the public, in the preeminence of the creator."[18] Indeed, the very first article of the 1957 act, still in place, explicitly repudiates a utilitarian philosophy of copyright:

> The author of a work of the mind shall enjoy in that work, by the mere fact of its creation an exclusive incorporeal property right which shall be enforceable against all persons. The legislator does not intervene to attribute to the writer, the artist, the composer, an arbitrary monopoly, under the influence of considerations of expediency, in order to stimulate the activity of men of letters and artists in the interest of the collectivity; the author's rights exist independently of his [the legislator's] intervention.[19]

French law does contain a number of exceptions that indicate a recognition of citizens' needs—it permits quotations for critical, informational, polemical, scientific, or educational purposes; parody, pastiche, and caricature; and some recordings of broadcasts for the purposes of preservation. Its philosophical orientation, like its name, *droit d'auteur*, is clearly centred on the author. But this single focus represents the ascendance of one of two strands of French copyright thought—and when we speak of the French tradition in Canadian law, we may be speaking of a tradition that developed alongside Canadian law, rather than prior to it.[20]

The Beginnings of Copyright in Canada

Although the British North America Act of 1867 named copyright as an area of Canadian federal jurisdiction, the so-called Imperial Copyright Act of 1842 remained in force in Canada until 1911, fifty-seven years after Confederation, and Canada did not pass its own Copyright Act until 1924. Why?

Copyright history in Canada up to its first Copyright Act can be understood as a story about the grip of British law and the weight of U.S. market forces on a cluster of small colonies. As such, it offers a resonant foundation for thinking about Canada's copyright interests today, during a time when we still have to craft a position in the context of huge American cultural imports—although the British legal framework has now been replaced with pressures from the World Trade Organization (W T O) and the World Intellectual Property Organization (W I P O).[21] The question remains now, as it was then: are Canada's interests the same as those of the major cultural exporters? If not, to what extent is Canada free to develop its own policy directions and mechanisms?

In the nineteenth century Canadians mainly read British books in U.S. reprint editions. Books printed in Britain were expensive, with high shipping charges as well, whereas U.S. printers were producing large numbers of cheap unauthorized reprints—which were not illegal under U.S. law. British publishers were not amused at what they perceived as a lost British North American market. Some in Britain were also concerned that Canadians' access to U.S. books might be "sapping the principles and loyalty of the Subjects of the Queen."[22] As a result, in 1842 the Imperial Copyright Act outlawed importation of reprints into Britain and its possessions and put a 35 per cent duty on U.S.-originated publications, provoking a huge outcry in British North America. After all, was it not Britain's duty to facilitate the education of its subjects? As writer Susanna Moodie stated, "Incalculable are the benefits that Canada derives from cheap [U.S.] reprints of all the European standard works, which in good paper and in handsome bindings, can be bought at a quarter the price of the English editions."[23] In 1847 the Foreign Reprints Act permitted imports once again, for a duty of 12.5 per cent that was in practice seldom collected.

By the 1860s printers had joined in a discussion previously dominated by booksellers. With Confederation and broader economic development, they saw the prospect of national markets, and they lobbied for the repeal of the Foreign Reprints Act: the Canadian market was too small to enable prices as low as the ones that U.S. printers could charge, and Canadian printers wanted exclusive access to it. Furthermore, the Canadian printers wanted a licensing scheme that would put them on a par with the Americans by allowing them to reprint British books without permission for a standard royalty, and in 1872 the Canadian Parliament passed a copyright act containing such a provision.[24] But

Canadian legislation required British approval, which was not forthcoming. As the Canadian printer John Lovell recalled after participating in a diplomatic mission to England, "The English publishers would not yield an inch. They said they would not allow any colonial to publish

In 1843 a parliamentary committee was struck in Ottawa to study copyright's effects on the Canadian book trade. It made it clear that what we now call "access" to printed material was necessary to the cultural and economic development of Canada, and it even argued that U.S. reprints were necessary to ensure Canadians' loyalty to the Queen:

2nd. that the free admission into this Province of American Reprints of English Works of Art and Literature, could not lessen the profits of English Authors and Publishers; because, although the reading population of the Province is great in number, yet the circumstances of the population generally are so limited in their means, that they are unable to enjoy English Literature at English prices; that owing to that inability to pay for such Work of Art and Literature there has never been a demand for those Works, and consequently no supply.

3rd. That the exclusion of American Reprints of English Literature, if possible, would have a most pernicious tendency on the minds of the rising generation, in morals, politics, and religion; that American Reprints of English Works are openly sold, and are on the tables or in the houses of persons of all classes in the Province; that a law so repugnant to public opinion cannot and will not be enforced; that were that exclusion possible, the Colonists would be confined to American literary, religious, and political Works, the effect of which could not be expected to strengthen their attachment to British Institutions, but, on the contrary, is well calculated to warp the minds of the rising generation to a decided preference for the Institutions of the neighboring States, and a hatred deep rooted and lasting of all we have been taught to venerate, whether British, Constitutional, or Monarchical, or cling to, in our connection with the Parent State.

Source: English Copyrights Act: Report of the Select Committee, Canada (Province), Legislative Assembly, 1843, in Parker, *Beginnings of the Book Trade in Canada*, 110–11.

one of their books. Their ignorance of Canada was profound. They treated Canada as if it was part and parcel with the United States."[25] Nonetheless, printers went on with various other approaches. For example, in 1879 the Canadian Parliament imposed a duty on imported U.S. books by weight—a duty by price would have provided little barrier because the books were so cheap.[26]

As the Europeans moved towards the agreement that in 1886 became the Berne Convention for the Protection of Literary and Artistic Works, and the British and Americans laboured to come to a reciprocal agreement finally signed in 1891, Canadians grew more concerned. Although Berne did for the first time give authors publishing first in Canada copyright throughout the Empire and beyond, it threatened Canadians' access to reprints, and Canadian publishers' ability to ground their business in reprinting—which would be, indeed, the only way they could ever afford to publish Canadian authors. Another major problem for the Canadian book trade was the British publishers' habit of selling North American rights to U.S. printers, thus shutting out the possibility of a Canadian edition—or of flooding the Canadian market themselves with cheap "colonial editions." In 1889 Canada passed a Copyright Act that required books and periodicals to be manufactured in Canada in order to obtain copyright there—thus in effect removing itself from the Berne Convention. But British power was bluntly applied. Canada passed this bill again in 1890, 1891, and 1895, but every time it was turned back by the Colonial Office. Canadian publishing continued to get by through a combination of individually arranged reprints and tariffs on U.S. imports until 1899, when approval was given for a bill that prohibited importation of foreign-produced editions of books that were already printed in Canada.

Canada's lack of power to develop copyright law suited to its situation clearly hampered the development of its publishing industry in the nineteenth century. When the United Kingdom passed a new Copyright Act in 1911, Canada finally won the right to make its own law—which for various reasons did not come into force until 1924. The 1924 Canadian act was almost identical to the U.K. act of 1911.

Canadian Copyright Since 1924—and Its International Context

Although representatives of the large cultural industries are fond of saying that the Canadian Copyright Act is outdated, the 1924 Act was amended ten times between 1931 and 1997.[27] Since 1984 the government has commissioned many studies of copyright policy.[28] The two most significant series of amendments, in 1988 and 1997, are referred to by today's policy-makers as Phase I and Phase II of copyright reform, respectively.[29] In addition the government has amended the act as part of implementing particular international agreements. For example, the North American Free Trade Implementation Act of 1993 and the World Trade Organization Agreement Implementation Act of 1994 both contained provisions amending the Copyright Act.[30]

Some critics say the copyright reform process has been too slow. The U.S. government, the Department of Canadian Heritage, and the Canadian Recording Industry Association (CRIA) in particular are eager to see Canada move ahead with legislation to make circumvention of digital locks illegal, to make downloading and file-sharing illegal, and to make various other changes.[31] One factor in the delay has been the nature of the parliamentary system: especially with the recent spate of minority governments, parliaments end suddenly, and a new government always entails startup time. But there are reasons for slowness beyond foot-dragging or logistics. In Canada the copyright portfolio is shared between the departments of Industry and Canadian Heritage, which tend to have very different views of the subject. The Department of Industry, concerned with facilitating innovation, may be more concerned with ensuring the "right to tinker" and minimizing transaction costs of rights clearance, whereas Canadian Heritage, essentially Canada's arts ministry, sees its role as defending owners' rights. Asking these two departments to work together slows matters down, but leaving the job to one of them would be unlikely to produce good results. Furthermore, it seems appropriate to take time in responding to technologies so new that it is not clear what effects they are having on markets, creators, or consumers. Some countries rushed into implementation of the treaties fashioned by the World Intellectual Property Organization in 1996, and others implemented the treaties with much more draconian provisions than necessary. Canada has no need to repeat these mistakes given the opportunity to study the effects of laws that other countries have passed.

Canadian copyright policy, then, has an important international dimension. Just as Canada's copyright laws in the nineteenth century were formed in the context of pressures of international markets and political relationships, so too are those of the twenty-first century.

Historically, international copyright rules were harmonized for the first time through the Berne Convention of 1886.[32] Berne sets certain minimum standards, provisions that the signators are expected to comply with. For example, the agreement requires that certain sorts of works be covered, and that moral rights be granted; it also states that copyright must exist whether or not a work is registered. But Berne has no effective enforcement mechanism, and recently efforts have been made towards

In its 2001 "Framework for Copyright Reform," the Canadian government usefully reviews the recent history of legislation. Significantly, according to the document, Canada is already compliant with its international obligations:

Modernization of the *Copyright Act* was achieved most recently through two massive phases of reform. Phase I, passed in 1988, included:
- statutory protection for computer programs
- clarification and extension of moral rights
- the elimination of the compulsory licence for the reproduction of musical works and the substitution of a right of negotiation
- the introduction of a new procedure to licence works where the owner could not be located
- new rights for visual artists to exhibit their works in public
- increased criminal sanctions, and the enactment of rules under which collective organizations could form and operate under the supervision of a revamped Copyright Board.

In 1997, the Government introduced another large package of amendments known as Phase II (Bill C-32). It included:
- new remuneration rights to producers and performers of sound recordings when their sound recordings are broadcast or publicly

incorporating intellectual property agreements within international trade agreements. The W T O Agreement includes an understanding on trade-related aspects of intellectual property (T R I P S).[33] T R I P S contains standards for the protection of intellectual property, including copyright, that go well beyond the standards contained in the Berne Convention. The agreement is enforceable as part of the overall apparatus of the W T O and is subject to the same dispute settlement provisions as other trade agreements such as the General Agreement on Tariffs and Trade (G A T T) and General Agreement on Trade in Services (GATS).

In addition to the W T O framework, various other treaties and agreements also include sections on intellectual property.[34] N A F T A contains a chapter on intellectual property, although it is generally similar in its provisions to those found in T R I P S. In 1996 the World Intellectual Property Organization promulgated two treaties dealing with copyright,

performed by radio stations and in public places like bars and restaurants;

- a compensation system for private copying, in the form of a levy on blank audio recording media, benefitting eligible composers, lyricists, performers and producers of sound recordings for the making of recordings;
- provisions granting exclusive book distributors legal protection in the Canadian market;
- a number of new exceptions to non-profit educational institutions, libraries, archives, museums, broadcasters and persons with perceptual disabilities allowing them to reproduce or use copyright material in specific circumstances without paying royalties or obtaining authorization from rights holders; and,
- statutory damages and wide injunctions to enhance the enforcement of copyright.

In the intervening years, the Government also adopted a series of smaller legislative amendments, mainly to conform with our international trade agreements. As a result of all these amendments, Canada's *Copyright Act* is now consistent with our international obligations.

Source: Canada, Industry Canada/Canadian Heritage, Copyright Policy Branch, "A Framework for Copyright Reform."

the WIPO Copyright Treaty (WCT) and WIPO Performances and Phonograms Treaty (WPPT).[35] While Canada has signed these agreements, known together as the WIPO Internet Treaties, it has not ratified or implemented them. Technically, Canada has no obligation to do so, and the treaties are written in a manner that enables different forms of implementation. Despite pressures being brought to bear from south of the border, then, Canada has choices as it approaches WIPO issues. Given that the WIPO copyright treaties were penned in 1996, perhaps *they* are outdated. Indeed, despite all the attention paid to the WIPO Internet Treaties over recent years, it is trade-related treaties that will bring the greatest pressure on Canada to follow U.S. copyright agendas.

Along with those of forty-eight other countries, Canada's intellectual property rights (IPR) practices are being monitored by the Office of the United States Trade Representatives (USTR), an arm of the U.S. government's executive branch, responsible for international trade policy. The tenor of a 2006 USTR report makes it clear that the United States is determined to enforce its vision of copyright beyond its own borders:

> Canada is being retained on the Watch List in 2006, and the United States will conduct an Out-of-Cycle Review to monitor Canada's progress on IPR issues under the leadership of its new government. Due to the dissolution of Canada's Parliament in late 2005 and elections in early 2006, Canada's legislative progress on IP issues in 2005 was interrupted. The United States looks to the new government to make progress on IPR issues a priority in the coming year. Key areas for action include the ratification and implementation of the WIPO Internet Treaties, amendment of the copyright law to provide adequate and effective protection of copyrighted works in the digital environment.... The United States will use the Out-of-Cycle review to monitor Canada's progress in providing an adequate and effective IPR protection regime that is consistent with its international obligations and its advanced level of economic development, including improved border enforcement, ratification and implementation of the WIPO Internet Treaties, and strong data protection.

Source: Office of the United States Trade Representative, *Special 301 Report*, 2006.

PART II: LAW

General Resources

- Copyright Act — http://laws.justice.gc.ca/en/C-42/.

- Canadian Intellectual Property Office, "A Guide to Copyrights," http://strategis. ic.gc.ca/sc_mrksv/cipo/cp/copy_gd_main-e.hmtl.

- David Vaver, *Copyright Law*, 2000.

3: Copyright's Scope

COPYRIGHT IS only one of the "big four" intellectual property devices. The others are patent, trademark, and the law of confidential information and trade secrets.[1] Patent law protects inventions, and trademark law provides a system of avoiding consumer confusion by protecting logos, brand names, and other identifiers used in the course of trade. Trade secrets law protects information closely held within an organization from damaging unauthorized disclosure. While sometimes the subject matter of these regimes may overlap with that of copyright—for example, a trademarked image might also be protected by copyright, and a piece of software might represent part of a patentable device and a copyrighted sequence of code—the principles, laws, and regulatory arrangements of each form of intellectual property (IP) are distinct (see Table 2). All of these types of IP have been generating lively and even impassioned debate around the world in recent years—debates analogous to those provoked by copyright.[2]

But just what does copyright law cover? Chapter 4 will consider which rights copyright owners actually hold, and chapter 5 will examine how

	Copyright	Patent	Registered Trademark	Confidential Information
purpose of rights	to protect forms of expression (does not protect ideas or facts)	to protect inventions (does not protect ideas, algorithms, or scientific theorems)	to protect distinguishing marks from use by others that would create consumer confusion	to protect against unauthorized disclosure of information held as confidential
basis for law	Copyright Act [R.S.C. 1985, c. C-42] (purely statutory)	Patent Act [R.S.C. 1985, c. P-4] (purely statutory)	Trademarks Act [R.S.C. 1985, c. T-13] + common law	no statute; based on common-law precedents
types of interests protected	literary, dramatic, musical, and artistic works; performers' performances; sound recordings; broadcast signals	inventions—meaning any new and useful art, process, machine, manufacture, or composition of matter, or any new and useful improvement in any art, process, machine, manufacture, or composition of matter	marks used for the purpose of distinguishing certain wares or services from others; certification marks; and distinguishing guise	information held within a firm
requirement for creation of interest	fixation of an original expression in a tangible medium (no formalities required)	application and examination	application and examination	no formalities
term of protection	general rule for works is life of author plus 50 years	20 years from date of filing	15 years from date of registration; can be renewed over and over	as long as the information remains confidential
maintenance during term	protection lasts whether or not the copyright is defended	protection lasts whether or not the patent is defended	can be lost through non-use, non-defence, or failure to renew registration	can be lost through disclosure or failure to take reasonable measures to protect from disclosure

these are modified and limited by the rights of users. But before we get there we need to understand what types of materials can be the subject of copyright protections in the first place, what are the requirements for copyright to begin to exist, and how long the copyright interest lasts.

Copyright's umbrella covers only certain things:

- Copyright subsists in works and other subject matter.
- For copyright to subsist in a work, an original expression must be fixed in some tangible form.
- Copyright applies to original expressions, not to facts or ideas.
- Formalities are not required for a copyright interest to arise; the interest exists at the moment of fixation in a tangible medium of expression.
- Copyright interests are limited in duration, and at the end of the copyright term the materials enter the public domain.

Copyright Subsists in Works and Other Subject Matter

The first copyright act, the Statute of Anne, applied only to particular types of literary works. But as William Hayhurst observes, "During the eighteenth and nineteenth centuries in England, engravers, textile designers, sculptors, dramatists, music publishers, artists and photographers managed to have a succession of statutes enacted.... Added to rights to prevent copying were rights to prevent unauthorized public performances of dramatic and musical works."[3]

As new representational technologies and cultural practices developed, the category of works continued to expand. The current Canadian Copyright Act recognizes four different categories of works—literary, dramatic, musical, and artistic—and they are all very inclusive. Furthermore, since 1997 copyright applies to performers' performances, sound recordings, and broadcast signals. This "other subject matter" carries with it slightly different constellations of rights than what the act deems "works"; rights in non-traditional subject matter are often known as "neighbouring rights." (See Table 3.)

Many objects containing intellectual property actually comprise several distinct works. For example, a poetry anthology is a "compilation" in which every poem is also a distinct work with its particular copyright status. Similarly, a photograph of a sculpture is itself a work, but use of it would in some cases require permission of the owner of copyright in the sculpture. Disputes sometimes arise from this layering of interests. The *Robertson v. Thomson* case of 2006 split the Supreme Court over the issue of the relation between the newspaper publisher's ownership of copyright in the compilation and the freelance writer's ownership of copyright in the individual article.

For Copyright to Subsist in a Work, an Original Expression Must Be Fixed in Some Tangible Form

Originality

A work must be original in order to gain copyright protection. But "original" is obviously a very slippery term: it can mean everything from "truly novel" (never seen before in all human history) to a much more pedestrian "not expressly copied."

For many years the legal test for originality in Canada was that "for a work to be original it must originate from the author; it must be the product of his labour and skill and it must be the expression of his thoughts."[4] Courts had some difficulty in arriving at consistent conclusions based on these principles. In *B.C. Jockey Club v. Standen* (1986), a court held that the compilation of information in horse-racing forms could be protected. In *CCH v. Law Society of Upper Canada* (1999), the trial court held that headnotes summarizing reported court cases lacked a sufficient amount of imagination or "creative spark" to satisfy the originality requirement.[5] Some cases set the bar too low, allowing copyright for works of questionable originality that didn't amount to much more than the laborious collection of data, while others seemed to be setting it too high.

In *Tele-Direct v. American Business Information* (1998), the Federal Court of Appeals tried to articulate a new standard in a case involving a telephone directory—a type of compilation that combines elements that are clearly not under copyright (the raw listing data) and some that clearly are (the layout and presentation of the directory as a whole). The court

Table 3. Works and Other Subject Matter Covered by Copyright

Category	Definition
	WORKS
every original literary, dramatic, musical, and artistic work	includes every original production in the literary, scientific, or artistic domain, whatever may be the mode or form of its expression, such as compilations, books, pamphlets and other writings, lectures, dramatic or dramatico-musical works, musical works, translations, illustrations, sketches and plastic works relative to geography, topography, architecture, or science
artistic work	includes paintings, drawings, maps, charts, plans, photographs, engravings, sculptures, works of artistic craftsmanship, architectural works, and compilations of artistic works
architectural work	any building or structure or any model of a building or structure
book	a volume or a part or division of a volume, in printed form, but does not include (a) a pamphlet, (b) a newspaper, review, magazine or other periodical, (c) a map, chart, plan or sheet music where the map, chart, plan or sheet music is separately published, and (d) an instruction or repair manual that accompanies a product or that is supplied as an accessory to a service
choreographic work	includes any work of choreography, whether or not it has any story line
cinematographic work	includes any work expressed by any process analogous to cinematography, whether or not accompanied by a soundtrack
collective work	(a) an encyclopedia, dictionary, yearbook, or similar work, (b) a newspaper, review, magazine, or similar periodical, and (c) any work written in distinct parts by different authors, or in which works or parts of works of different authors are incorporated
compilation	(a) a work resulting from the selection or arrangement of literary, dramatic, musical, or artistic works or of parts thereof, or (b) a work resulting from the selection or arrangement of data
computer program	a set of instructions or statements, expressed, fixed, embodied, or stored in any manner, that is to be used directly or indirectly in a computer in order to bring about a specific result
dramatic work	includes (a) any piece for recitation, choreographic work or mime, the scenic arrangement or acting form of which is fixed in writing or otherwise, (b) any cinematographic work, and (c) any compilation of dramatic works

lecture	includes address, speech, and sermon
literary work	includes tables, computer programs, and compilations of literary works
musical work	any work of music or musical composition, with or without words, and includes any compilation thereof
performance	any acoustic or visual representation of a work, performer's performance, sound recording or communication signal, including a representation made by means of any mechanical instrument, radio receiving set, or television receiving set
photograph	includes photo-lithograph and any work expressed by any process analogous to photography
plate	includes (a) any stereotype or other plate, stone, block, mould, matrix, transfer, or negative used or intended to be used for printing or reproducing copies of any work, and (b) any matrix or other appliance used or intended to be used for making or reproducing sound recordings, performer's performances, or communication signals
sculpture	includes a cast or model
work of joint authorship	a work produced by the collaboration of two or more authors in which the contribution of one author is not distinct from the contribution of the other author or authors
	NON-TRADITIONAL SUBJECT MATTER
communication signal	radio waves transmitted through space without any artificial guide, for reception by the public
performers' performance	any of the following when done by a performer: (a) a performance of an artistic work, dramatic work, or musical work, whether or not the work was previously fixed in any material form, and whether or not the work's term of copyright protection under the Act has expired; (b) a recitation or reading of a literary work, whether or not the work's term of copyright protection under the Act has expired; or (c) an improvisation of a dramatic work, musical work, or literary work, whether or not the improvised work is based on a pre-existing work
sound recording	a recording, fixed in any material form, consisting of sounds, whether or not of a performance of a work, but excludes any soundtrack of a cinematographic work where it accompanies the cinematographic work

Source: Adapted from the Copyright Act.

Why does it matter whether the standard for originality is too high or too low?

- If it is too low, facts or ideas could become effectively unavailable for others to use freely or reuse. Copyright extended to an alphabetical directory listing or the collection of publicly available data into an "obvious" chart or table would effectively confer ownership on the data itself.
- If the standard is too high, courts find themselves in the role of evaluating artistic merit, which is not appropriate. Also, works that as a practical matter ought to have copyright protection—pamphlets and instruction manuals, for example—might not meet the requirement.

sought a middle ground: "For a compilation to be original, it must be a work that was independently created by the author and which displays at least a minimal degree of skill, judgment and labor in its overall selection or arrangement. The threshold is low, but it does exist."[6] But this pronouncement too was subject to various interpretations. What exactly is meant by "skill, judgment and labor"? Can the requirement be met by an abundance of one or two of the three, or is some of each required?

In 2004 the Supreme Court provided needed clarification in its decision in *CCH v. Law Society of Upper Canada*, the case in which the trial court had set a standard of creative spark for originality. The Supreme Court followed the Appeals Court in rejecting that approach. "For a work to be 'original,'" it stated, "it must be more than a mere copy of another work. At the same time, it need not be creative, in the sense of being novel or unique."[7] While noting that "creative works will by definition be 'original' and covered by copyright"—in other words, "creativity is not required to make a work 'original'"—Chief Justice McLachlin went on to provide a more precise articulation of the originality test, which is now the standard:

> What is required to attract copyright protection in the expression of an idea is an exercise of skill and judgment. By skill, I mean the use of one's knowledge, developed aptitude or practised ability in producing the work. By judgment, I mean the use of one's capacity for discernment or ability to form an opinion or evaluation by comparing different possible options in producing the work.[8]

Many scholars have criticized copyright law's originality requirement, arguing that it implies an overly individualistic "Romantic" idea of authorship. Surely, they argue, originality is impossible, given that we all work within shared traditions and languages. Many years ago, Canada's own Northrop Frye blamed copyright for readers' tendency to exalt an author's contribution over the rich tradition from which it sprang. Mark Rose sums copyright up as "an institution built on intellectual quicksand: the essentially religious concept of originality, the notion that certain extraordinary beings called authors conjure works out of thin air." But as Jessica Litman puts it, "The very act of authorship in any medium is more akin to translation and recombination than it is to creating Aphrodite from the foam of the sea."

In Canada as elsewhere, though, the courts have not generally understood originality to mean novelty in the strict sense. The law is concerned with which "head" produced the work, and thus refuses copyright to a copied work, but it does not require that the work has no antecedents: it does not demand that a work should "rise spontaneously from the vital root of genius," as the Romantic poets would see it. If it did—if authors had to *prove* originality—copyright law could not function at all. We tend to agree with Paul Saint-Amour, who argues: "The phenomenon of 'copyright creep,' however much one might regret its reapportioning of public and private domains, appears to have resulted from the influence of the private sector on the legislative climate, rather than from some privatizing drive inherent in copyright's metaphysics."

Sources: Frye, *Anatomy of Criticism*, 96; Rose, *Authors and Owners*, 142; Litman, "Public Domain," 966; Young, "Conjectures on Original Composition," 11; Saint-Amour, *The Copywrights*, 6.

The court further noted that the "exercise of skill and judgment will necessarily involve intellectual effort" and "the exercise of skill and judgment required to produce the work must not be so trivial that it could be characterized as a purely mechanical exercise."[9] In this statement, the court explicitly rejected the "sweat of the brow" doctrine, which accords originality to works simply by virtue of the labour that went into them.

Fixation

Copyright only subsists in works fixed in some tangible form. Interestingly, there is no fixation requirement on the face of the Canadian statute.[10] The fixation requirement comes from case law, and it is related to the principle that ideas are not covered by copyright: according to what is known as the "idea-expression dichotomy," only the embodiment of the ideas is protected. But where is the boundary between idea and expression? What constitutes fixation?

The most often-cited Canadian case about the fixation requirement is *Canadian Admiral v. Rediffusion* (1954), involving televised Montreal Alouettes football games. The gist of the case, at least insofar as fixation is concerned, was that the transmission of a live broadcast of a game did not meet the fixation requirement. The court contrasted simultaneous, unedited transmission with the broadcast of a taped game, which it did recognize as a fixation. (Since this case, communication signals have been added to the act as a category in which copyright can subsist—even though they are not fixed—but the case still offers guidance on the nature of fixation.)

In his book *Copyright Law* David Vaver takes a sceptical view of fixation as a requirement for copyright, arguing that it is better thought of as a rule of convenience than as a fundamental principle.[11] Indeed, the requirement is especially fraught in the digital age, when the distinction between

Is a joke covered by copyright?

It depends. A good line or two, spontaneously if aptly delivered, would probably not be covered. In *Glenn Gould Estate v. Stoddart* (1998), the court found that the interviewer who elicited Gould's unscripted words owned the copyright in them. But a more prolonged piece in a public venue, even if improvised, would probably count as a performer's performance under section 15 of the act—according to which the performer alone has the right to "fix" the performance in any form or to authorize such fixation. But if comics are working from somebody else's written material rather than generating their own material in performance, they need permission, because that material, like all written matter, is "born copyrighted."

fixation and lack of fixation seems arbitrary. It also seems as if some forms of contemporary art in which the work's essence lies in its changeability— with media such as melting ice, shifting light, or even, notoriously, rotting meat—might have difficulty meeting the fixation requirement.[12]

But this is not a new problem: an older challenge comes in the case of an oral presentation. If a speaker is speaking from notes, clearly the notes are fixed works in which copyright subsists. But what if the words exist only in spoken form? The Copyright Act contains a special definition for "lecture" that includes a speech, address, or sermon (see Table 3)—a definition that seems to constitute an exception to the requirement of fixation. But not all oral presentations are speeches, addresses, or sermons, and this has left storytellers, for example, vulnerable to having their work appropriated by listeners bearing tape recorders or notepads. The relatively new category of "performers' performance" would cover many oral presentations. In the case of a performers' performance, the Copyright Act is explicit that there is no requirement for fixation.[13]

Copyright Applies to Original Expressions, Not to Facts or Ideas

Copyright does not apply to ideas or facts: it applies to the way they are put into place. This is the crucial distinction of the idea-expression dichotomy. If we allowed parties to claim ownership rights over facts or ideas, cultural innovators would be constrained by lack of access to raw materials. Also, of course, ownership of facts and ideas would have various deleterious effects on democracy and public discourse. Copyright's recognition of the right to an exclusive claim to a particular *expression* of an idea or fact is a sort of compromise, permitting both reward and foundation for innovation.

Weather reports in a newspaper, for example, might be arranged in a table with the date in one column, the city in the next, and the temperature in the next. No one can own these facts, even if someone puts expertise and expense into collecting them. But a more original presentation format might attract copyright: an animated artistic map, for instance, with moving clouds and a distinctively dressed announcer reading a script that includes the weather forecast. Although a third party can still use the facts presented therein without permission, a full studio production is a different matter from the bland weather table, and it crosses the line from unprotected facts to copyrightable subject matter.

The location of the idea-expression line is often difficult to pinpoint (many of the major thinkers of the twentieth century would say the distinction between ideas and expressions does not exist),[14] but the courts have developed principles for doing so. In *Cuisenaire v. South West Imports* (1969), the plaintiff attempted to apply copyright to a set of coloured rods used for teaching math to young children, as described in a book he had published. The court rejected this claim, noting that copyright applied to the book, but not to the rods themselves—the idea embodied in the book.[15]

Where is the boundary between "idea" and "expression" in a fictional work? In their abstract form, dramatic plots are "ideas," not "expressions." For example, the "boy meets girl and their families are outraged" plot is not in itself copyrightable. But fill things out a bit with character names, specific wording, and plot twists, and an author may be able to claim copyright. In *Anne of Green Gables Licensing Authority v. Avonlea Traditions* (2000), the defendant, a manufacturer of "Anne" souvenirs, relied on *Cuisenaire* for the proposition that copyright should not extend beyond a book to cover three-dimensional objects described therein. But the court held that a literary work includes "any of its characters whose descriptions are distinctive, thorough, and complete." It rejected the defendant's parallel with *Cuisenaire*, stating that the "Anne" merchandise required licensing as an expression of the "detailed verbal portrait" in the literary work.[16] So here we have, in a sense, copyright upheld in an idea—the idea of the characters in a book.

Courts have sometimes recognized that dangers to innovation can arise from understanding "expression" too expansively. In a recent dispute between two computer software companies, *Delrina v. Triolet Systems* (2002), the court noted, "If there is only one or a very limited number of ways to achieve a particular result in a computer program, to hold that that way or ways are protectable by copyright could give the copyright holder a monopoly on the idea or function itself."[17] This case shows how the idea-expression dichotomy will act as a limit on the scope of copyright in a case in which a particular idea can only be expressed in one way (or only a very few ways). In this situation, it is said that the idea "merges" with the expression of the idea, and copyright cannot be applied.

The idea-expression dichotomy also provides the basis for withholding copyright protection from the elements in a database. In Europe, special legislation provides statutory protection for databases, and the North American database industry has been clamouring for similar legislation for many years. It seems unlikely that database legislation will have much of a chance in Canada, although it remains on the wish list of some entrepreneurs in the information industry.

Formalities Are Not Required for a Copyright Interest to Arise; the Interest Exists at the Moment of Fixation in a Tangible Medium of Expression

One of the persistent myths about copyright is that in order to exist, a copyright must be registered, and the work marked with the copyright symbol ©. In fact, copyright exists at the moment an original expression is fixed into some tangible medium (or, for copyright's other subject matter, at the moment of performance, broadcast, or sound recording). It does not matter whether the work is marked with a ©, and it does not matter whether or not the copyright is subsequently registered, at least insofar as the initial question of validity of copyright is concerned.

A day can hardly go by in the life of most members of modern society without the creation of many works in which copyright subsists: grocery lists, emails, doodles, unfinished love notes, and voice memos with some small modicum of originality are covered automatically by copyright—along with novels, rock operas, and scientific treatises. You probably do not assert copyright in your everyday creations, but you could. In using

How do I register copyright in my work?

Go to http://cipo.gc.ca—the website of the Canadian Intellectual Property Office—and follow the instructions. The process is straightforward and does not require the assistance of a lawyer. In 2007 the registration fee was $50. Your work will be listed in the publicly available database of registered Canadian copyrights.

works created by others, then, you should never assume that you do not have to worry about infringement just because there are no apparent markings. You may be just as guilty of infringement of copyrighted materials that lack such a marking and that are unregistered.[18]

Even though a copyright mark is not required, you may have reason to affix one, or even to go to the trouble and expense of registering a copyright. Copyright marking puts the whole world on notice of your copyright interest. Short of litigation, it reminds other users that the materials are subject to copyright even though they may be readily accessible in a library or on the Internet. You can mark your work with a © whether or not you have registered it.

Registration goes even further to create a presumption of ownership. If you ever have to defend your copyright in court, registration will prevent an infringer from claiming not to know that your work was copyrighted.[19] Registration also sets a creation in a time frame that could be important if a priority dispute arises with another party. However, the vast majority of copyright owners never register their copyrights. As the Canadian Intellectual Property Office states on its website:

> Registration is no guarantee against infringement. You have to take legal action on your own if you believe your rights have been violated. Also, registration is no guarantee that your claim of ownership will eventually be recognized as legitimate. Note too, that the Copyright Office does not check to ensure that your work is indeed original, as you claim. Verification of your claim can only be done through a court of law.[20]

A growing number of people simply don't want to assert all the rights that copyright automatically grants them. If this is how you feel, you can register your work with Creative Commons (www.creativecommons.ca) instead of the Copyright Office. This process, which is free, allows you to choose a licence reserving some or none of the rights granted to you by the Copyright Act.

Copyright Interests Are Limited in Duration, and at the End of the Copyright Term the Materials Enter the Public Domain

Many people think of copyright as a form of private property, similar to personal goods or real estate. But unlike the ownership interests in personal property, real estate, or even other intangible goods, the duration of a copyright interest is limited in time. In Canada the term of protection for copyright is generally the life of the author plus fifty years—or as section 6 of the act puts it, "The term for which copyright shall subsist shall, except as otherwise expressly provided by this Act, be the life of the author, the remainder of the calendar year in which the author dies, and a period of fifty years following the end of that calendar year." The idea here is that the children and grandchildren of the author or copyright owner have a chance to benefit from his or her estate. Thus the term of copyright in the work of Paul Kane, who died in February 1871, ended at midnight on December 31, 1921; the term of copyright in the work of Lucy Maude Montgomery, who died in April 1942, ended at midnight on December 31, 1992.

At the end of the copyright period, the copyright interest automatically lapses and the work enters the public domain. All works in which copyright subsists are destined to become part of the public domain: it is just a matter of time. You can think of copyright term as a moving wall between today's creators and a shared heritage: the constant renewal of the public domain ensures that creators have a constantly growing mass of resources with which they can work freely—in both senses of the word.

Different countries have different copyright terms: in the United States, copyright generally lasts for the life of the author plus seventy years, and in Mexico the term is life of the author plus one hundred years. But because copyright is national in application (its jurisdiction is limited to the territory of the country that enacts it), Canadians in Canada follow the term stipulated in the Canadian act, no matter what the origin of the material in question.

Within the Canadian Copyright Act, there are special cases for copyright term in certain classes of works or other subject matter (see Table 4).

Table 4. Duration of Copyright Term in Special Cases

Subject	Copyright term	Copyright Act Section
author is known	life of author + 50 years	6
author is unknown	earliest of (a) a term consisting of the remainder of the calendar year of the first publication of the work and a period of 50 years following the end of that calendar year, and (b) a term consisting of the remainder of the calendar year of the making of the work and a period of 75 years following the end of that calendar year (but where, during that term, the author's identity becomes commonly known, the general rule of life + 50 then applies)	6.1
joint authors all known	life of last surviving author + 50 years	9(1)
all joint authors are unknown	same as 6.1 except that if identity of one or more of the authors becomes known, the term is then life of the last surviving author + 50 years	6.2
photograph (where first owner is a corporation)	remainder of year of making + 50 years	—
photograph (where first owner also owns majority of corporation)	general rule of section 6	6
photograph (where first owner is an individual)	general rule of section 6	6
works owned by Crown	remainder of year of making + 50 years	12
performers' performance	end of calendar year of first fixation + 50 years, or date of performance + 50 years if not fixed in a recording	23(1)(a)
sound recording	end of calendar year of making + 50 years	23(1)(b)
broadcast	end of calendar year of broadcast + 50 years	23(1)(c)

Unpublished works represent another case of specific copyright term issues. Prior to 1999 the copyright duration for unpublished works was perpetual. If a work was eventually published—with permission of the heirs or estate, if they could even be identified—the term would last for fifty years from that point. Since many important works (such as manuscripts, works in progress, and private correspondence) remain unpublished during the life of an author, perpetual copyright created serious problems for historians and other scholars. The 1997 amendments to the act improved this situation, but they are bafflingly complex, and furthermore they created a lamentable and anomalous waiting period for archival materials whose authors died between 1949 and 1998. In these cases, strangely, the author's published works will enter the public domain before their unpublished works (see Table 5).[21]

Table 5. Duration of Copyright for Unpublished or Posthumously Published Works

Category of Work	Date of Expiration of Copyright
work published after author's death but before Jan. 1, 1999	end of calendar year of publication + 50 years
unpublished work of author who died before Jan. 1, 1949	Dec. 31, 2003
unpublished work of author who died between Jan. 1, 1949 and Jan. 1, 1999	Dec. 31, 2049
unpublished work of author who died after Dec. 31, 1998	year of author's death + 50 years

Every January 1, blogger Wallace McLean celebrates Public Domain Day by listing authors, composers, architects, and other creators whose work has entered the Canadian public domain. On January 1, 2007, the inductees included playwright Bertolt Brecht, painter Jackson Pollock, and journalist H.L. Mencken—along with a host of others. The moment of entrance into the public domain may mark a cessation of income for descendants or heirs, but it brings riches to others, as the theatre director Craig Walker explains:

> I don't want to characterize myself in an unpleasant way, but a theatre artist of my sort does a little bit sit like a vulture, watching for the fifty year period to expire after the author's death, because there are different things that one is then able to do in creating a new work out of that. *The Master Builder* [by Henrik Ibsen, 1892], that I'm doing right now, I've written my own adaptation of it and I've changed it quite a bit actually. There's reasons why it's not staged very often. If you tried to do it as it is on the page, even with a modern translation, it's cumbersome and it's turgid, but there's some exciting drama underneath there, so my adaptation streamlined it.
>
> Plus it's my opinion, and I think that many audience members would share it, that the central female character is kind of a sexist construction: she doesn't seem like a real woman. But by altering it so that she's a projection from the main character's mind it becomes interesting in itself, and that very fact that she's not well rounded makes sense. She's this middle-aged man's fantasy. So the work suddenly gains a new kind of relevance and appeal.
>
> My job as a director with any play is to provide a kind of conduit between the author's imagination and the audience, and the art demands a certain amount of freedom in how I judge is best to do that. And yeah, I could screw it up … I could make an utter piece of shit out of the thing, and people would say it's lamentable what the man did with Ibsen. But on the other hand, I'm certainly not trying to do that, and I'm not trying to be nasty towards Ibsen: I'm trying to make Ibsen work for this audience.

Directors can make changes to works still under copyright, but by convention, not one word of a play may be altered or cut without permission of the creator, estate, or copyright owner—which is sometimes difficult to obtain. That is why creative productions tend to blossom after the expiration of copyright: think of all the wild and wonderful versions of Shakespeare on screen or on stage.

Sources: Wallace McLean, "Public Domain Day 2007," posting to CopyrightWatch.ca, Jan. 1 2007, http://www.copyrightwatch.ca/; Craig Walker, interview with Laura Murray, Kingston, Ont.

4: Owners' Rights

ASSUMING THAT all of the conditions for copyright to subsist have been met, the first owner has not one "copyright" but rather a series of distinct rights—or in the usual copyright metaphor, a bunch of sticks in a bundle. Each of these rights is enumerated in the Copyright Act. Each confers the ability to do some specific thing with the material in question, and also to exclude other people from doing so without permission. The economic rights can be separately deployed: an owner might keep some, sell or license others to distinct purchasers under particular conditions, and give one or two away. Authors' moral rights, in contrast, can be waived, or bequeathed upon death, but not assigned to others.

The key section of the Copyright Act for purposes of determining the economic rights of the owner of a work is section 3(1), which sets out thirteen rights: reproduction, performance, publication, authorization, and nine others listed in subsections (a) through (i). While each of those rights is different, and many apply only to certain types of works, in every instance the right is a "sole right." This means that the owner of the right not only can do the thing specified, but also can exclude others

Table 6. Rights in Works and Other Subject Matter

Subject Matter	Pertinent Section of the Act
works	3(1)
performers' performance	15(1)
sound recording	18(1)
communication signal	21(1)

from doing it. For example, the right of reproduction does not just grant the owner the right to make reproductions of the work: it excludes the rest of the world from doing so without the consent of the owner. The word "sole" is why copyright is referred to as a sort of monopoly.

Keep in mind too that each of these rights is severable and freely assignable on its own. People often use the term "derivative rights" to refer to an owner's right to control follow-on use of her or his work, but this umbrella term does not appear in Canadian law, which in fact specifies rights one by one.

The Reproduction Right

Section 3(1) starts with the "sole right to produce or reproduce the work or any substantial part thereof in any material form whatever." In questions of copyright, the reproduction right is usually the first thing that comes to mind. When you use a photocopy machine, copy and paste on your computer, or make a digital copy of a CD, you are implicating the reproduction right. (By using the word "implicating," we mean that you are in a position where you ought to ask whether you are infringing—though as we will see, you can implicate a right without infringing it.)

What exactly does it mean to "produce or reproduce" a work? Or to put it another way, what activity or conduct is required to trigger the operation of this section? Usually, the situation is straightforward. If you put a book on a photocopy machine and press START, you are implicating the reproduction right.

For the purposes of this Act, "copyright," in relation to a work, means
the sole right to produce or reproduce the work or any substantial part
thereof in any material form whatever, to perform the work or any substantial part thereof in public or, if the work is unpublished, to publish
the work or any substantial part thereof, and includes the sole right

(a) to produce, reproduce, perform or publish any translation of the
    work,

(b) in the case of a dramatic work, to convert it into a novel or other
    non-dramatic work,

(c) in the case of a novel or other non-dramatic work, or of an artistic
    work, to convert it into a dramatic work, by way of performance in
    public or otherwise,

(d) in the case of a literary, dramatic or musical work, to make any
    sound recording, cinematograph film or other contrivance by means
    of which the work may be mechanically reproduced or performed,

(e) in the case of any literary, dramatic, musical or artistic work, to
    reproduce, adapt and publicly present the work as a cinematographic
    work,

(f) in the case of any literary, dramatic, musical or artistic work, to com-
    municate the work to the public by telecommunication,

(g) to present at a public exhibition, for a purpose other than sale or hire,
    an artistic work created after June 7, 1988, other than a map, chart
    or plan,

(h) in the case of a computer program that can be reproduced in the
    ordinary course of its use, other than by a reproduction during its
    execution in conjunction with a machine, device or computer, to rent
    out the computer program, and

(i) in the case of a musical work, to rent out a sound recording in which
    the work is embodied,

and to authorize any such acts.

— Copyright Act, Section 3(1).

Sometimes the border between what is or is not a production or reproduction is less clear. The 2002 Supreme Court case *Théberge v. Galerie
d'Art du Petit Champlain* wrestled with the copyright implications of a

chemical process that can remove an image from a piece of paper and transfer it to a canvas. In a split decision, the majority of the judges decided that transferring the image from one medium to another did not constitute a reproduction. For them, the important question was whether the number of works increased: at both the start and end of the process, there was one work. For the minority, the important point was that there was a new and independent fixation of the work even though the source was destroyed: a new work was "produced."[1]

A more common source of controversy is the substantiality requirement. The act says that the owner of the reproduction right has an exclusive right to reproduce the whole work "or any substantial part thereof." This means that the owner's right to exclude does not extend to reproductions that are *not* substantial. The act does not define what is meant by "substantial." Where is the line between a non-substantial snippet, and a substantial reproduction that implicates the reproduction right? In determining whether the threshold of substantiality has been met, courts have looked to both quantitative and qualitative factors, and they have not laid out any "magic number." If anyone tells you that without permission you can safely use 5 per cent or three seconds or two column inches—or any such handy formula—they are simply wrong.

Two Copyright Board cases demonstrate the inadequacy of analysis based on quantitative factors alone. While Copyright Board rulings are not usually cited with much authority, they give an idea of how the court's principles may be interpreted. In one case a Montreal museum sought a licence to reproduce and display twelve quotations. (The museum had not been able to locate the owner of the copyright, and section 77 of the Copyright Act gives the Copyright Board responsibility to license reproduction in such situations.) The Board dismissed the application on the grounds that it was not required. Applying a *quantitative* standard, the Board noted that the four hundred words that the museum intended to use represented less than 1 per cent of the 175 or so pages of the relevant books. The Board also found the *qualitative* aspect of the proposed use to be insignificant because the quotations did not constitute the central element of the work; because the proposed use was different from that contemplated by the original author; and because the resulting material was not a substitute for the original work.

Hager v. ECW Press (1999)

The situation:
Barbara Hager wrote a book, *Honour Song: A Tribute*, that was published in 1996 by Raincoast Books in Vancouver. The book, about well-known Aboriginal Canadians, contained a chapter on country singer Shania Twain based on Hager's interviews. A subsequent book, *Shania Twain: On My Way*, published by ECW Press in 1997, reproduced sixteen passages from Hager's interviews with Twain, comprising about one-third of the *Honour Song* chapter. This second work used direct quotes from Twain taken from Hager's book, rearranged Hager's own words, and interposed additional materials. Neither author nor publisher obtained permission for the material reproduced.

The result:
One of the issues raised in this case was whether the copying was substantial or insubstantial. The court stressed that substantiality is a "question of fact" and looked at several factors to make its determination:

- the quality and quantity of the material taken;
- the extent to which the defendant's use harms the plaintiff's activities and diminishes the value of the plaintiff's copyright;
- whether the material taken is the proper subject matter of a copyright;
- whether the defendant intentionally appropriated the plaintiff's work to save time and effort; and
- whether the material taken is used in the same or a similar fashion as the plaintiff's material.

Weighing all of these factors, the court found that the threshold of substantiality had been met and assessed damages at $9,000 (an estimate of the fee that the second author would have paid to Hager) plus 10 per cent of ECW's profit on the book.

However, in a case concerning a documentary film about World War Two, the Board ruled that use of eight excerpts comprising 325 words out of a 342-page veteran's memoir *was* a substantial use requiring a licence: the Board decided that it constituted "from a qualitative standpoint, an appropriation ... of Sergeant Johnson's 'knowledge, time and talent' and therefore, of a substantial part of his work."[2]

Hager v. ECW and the Copyright Board cases suggest that obtaining permission or paying a licensing fee is not required if the requisite threshold of substantiality is not met. Given the indistinctness of this threshold, however, many potential users are unsure of what is permissible, and rights holders have been using intimidation tactics to assert their preferred norm for substantiality. If you are afraid of being sued, you won't sample a big label record without permission, or quote more than a few lines of a high-profile poet's work. While these uses might well be considered "non-substantial" by the courts, they are routinely policed by means of letters from lawyers demanding immediate cessation of the allegedly infringing activity. (We call these letters "nasty-grams.") Substantiality is an area in which the law in practice seems to come as much from industry clout as from statute or case law.

The Public Performance Right

The second copyright, also contained in the first sentence of section 3(1), is "the sole right ... to perform the work or any substantial part thereof in public." But what does it mean to "perform the work," and when is that performance deemed to be "in public"?

The Copyright Act defines "performance" as "any acoustic or visual representation of a work ... including a representation made by means of any mechanical instrument, radio receiving set or television receiving set." You can perform a work by singing it or acting it out, but also by playing a "performer's performance" of it on a CD player or other device—because the work is contained within the performance of the work. The act uses the clumsy term "performer's performance" to differentiate a performance by a human from a performance by a radio, television, or other technology.

The leading Canadian case discussing the public performance right is *Canadian Admiral v. Rediffusion* (1954)—the same case cited earlier on questions of fixation (see chapter 3). In this case revolving around televised football games, the court concluded that the rebroadcast of the games was not a matter of public performance because it was done in the private homes of cable subscribers, not in "public." The court rejected the argument that a large number of private performances, because of their numbers, become public performances. It reasoned that the character of the individual audiences remained the same; each being private and domestic and therefore not "in public."[3]

Showing a work in a public theatre where admission is being charged is clearly an instance of a public performance, and viewing a video in the privacy of your home is clearly not. But in between these two extremes are all sorts of grey areas. One interesting example is the classroom setting, where it is understood that only a number of students registered for a course will be in the room to see the performance of the work. Passers-by would not be invited in. Is this more analogous to the public theatre or the private home? The courts have never been asked. (For more on this question, see chapter 10.)

The First Publication Right

The opening paragraph of section 3(1) concludes with a clause about the first publication right. In the case of a work that is unpublished, the owner has the sole right "to publish the work or any substantial part thereof." This simply means that the owner has the right to publish a work for the first time—or to withhold it from publication.

Unlike other section 3 rights, which are persistent, the first publication right is exhausted upon publication. The act provides that a work is considered published when copies of the work are made available to the public.[4]

The Translation Right

According to section 3(1)(a), the first owner also has the sole right "to produce, reproduce, perform or publish any translation of the work." It has long been understood that a translation of a work is an original literary work of which the translator is the author. However, the rights of the original author stand: translation requires permission.

In recent years, computer code has produced the main question about translation rights. Is it a translation within the meaning of the translation

In the nineteenth century, authors did not have translation rights. When Harriet Beecher Stowe went to court in 1853 over an unauthorized translation of *Uncle Tom's Cabin* into German, the court said that while she retained the "exclusive right to print, reprint and vend ... 'copies of her book,'" a translation was to be considered "a transcript or copy of her thoughts or conceptions, but in no correct sense ... a copy of her book."

Source: *Stowe v. Thomas.*

right to rewrite a computer program in a different programming language? In *Apple Computer v. Mackintosh Computer* (1986) the federal trial court held that conversion from one code to another did not constitute a translation.[5] But in another case, *Prism Hospital Software v. Hospital Medical Records Institute* (1994), a B.C. court ruled that the conversion of a program into a different programming language did constitute a translation. There still seems to be quite a bit of uncertainty in this area.

The Conversion Rights

Although works are categorized as literary, dramatic, musical, or artistic, a work often starts out in one category and is later adapted into another. Thus a poem becomes a song, a movie becomes a novel, or a novel becomes a play. In each case, the adapter would require a licence because such conversions are the sole right of the owner under sections 3(1)(b) through (e).[6]

The Public Communication Right

Of increasing importance in the networked environment is section 3(f), which sets forth the right "to communicate the work to the public by telecommunication." While this right once mainly regulated the behaviour of broadcasters, in the era of fax machines and computer networks it potentially affects many more people.

In *SOCAN v. CAIP* the court was called on to harmonize the owners' right set out in section 3(f) with the express limitation on that right set out in section 2.4(1)(b). While this complex case grappled with many different issues (including the question of the differences between

SOCAN v. CAIP (2004)

The situation:
The Society of Composers, Authors and Music Publishers of Canada (SOCAN) collects tariffs for the performance or communication to the public of music. Its Tariff 1, for example, is for music played on the radio, and its Tariff 3 is for cabarets, cocktail lounges, and bars. In 1999 SOCAN proposed Tariff 22 for music performed or communicated to the public via the Internet.

SOCAN argued that a communication to the public occurs when the end user can gain access to a musical work from a computer connected to a network—and thus that virtually everyone involved in the Internet transmission chain is liable for the communication, including those who provide transmission services, operate equipment or software used for transmissions, provide connectivity, provide hosting services, or post content. The Canadian Association of Internet Providers (CAIP) argued the opposite.

The result:
The Copyright Board rejected SOCAN's holding that according to the "common carrier" exemption of Section 2.4(1)(b), a person whose only act is to provide the means of communication does not communicate that work to the public. Liability must be assessed as a function of the role that the entity plays in that transmission, and not as a function of what it generally does. In other words, while a person who posts music on an open server authorizes its communication to the public, the typical activities of an Internet service provider (ISP) do not constitute communication by telecommunication to the public. As a result, there would be no liability for an ISP to pay a royalty. Upon appeal, the Copyright Board's decision was mostly upheld at the Federal Court of Appeal, and entirely upheld at the Supreme Court.

uploading and downloading), it stands for the broad proposition that owners' rights cannot be read in an overly broad manner.

The Exhibition Right

Section 3(1)(g) stipulates a public exhibition right for certain artistic works created after June 7, 1988. This means that even if a gallery or an individual owns a work of art, a fee must be paid upon exhibition for as long as its copyright subsists. The artist may negotiate that fee individually or through a collective such as Canadian Artists' Representation Copyright Collective (CARCC).

The Rental Rights

Generally speaking, the exclusive rights of an owner do not include the right to rent out the work. In *Théberge v. Galerie d'Art du Petit Champlain* (2002), the Supreme Court described an established rule when it noted, "Once an authorized copy of a work is sold to a member of the public, it is generally for the purchaser, not the author, to determine what happens to it." One of the things the purchaser might choose to do with a work is to rent it out. This is what allows libraries and video stores to exist. (This does not mean making copies of a tape and renting it out: that would violate the reproduction right. It refers to renting out the lawfully purchased copy itself.)

But section 3(1) contains two specific exceptions in which the owner is granted exclusive rental rights. Section 3(1)(*h*) applies to reproducible computer programs, and section 3(1)(*i*) applies to sound recordings that embody a musical work. This means that if you rent out computer programs or sound recordings without the permission of the owner, you will be in violation of one of the owner's rights.

The Authorization Right

Last among the economic rights, but certainly not least, is the authorization right. Section 3(1) closes with the words "and to authorize any such acts." *Any such acts* refers to all of the rights set out in 3(1), and in essence incorporates the entire section.

Unfortunately, the term authorization is nowhere defined in the act. What does it mean to authorize someone to do something? Telling your assistant to go to the photocopy machine, punch in your copy code, and make a copy of an article for everyone in your workplace is probably authorization to reproduce a work. But what if you just provide a copy machine for others to use as they wish? The overarching question here is where to draw the line between being a significant enabler of a particular result, and doing something that is merely part of a causal chain.

Fortunately, recent case law has placed some constraints around the potentially enormous scope of the authorization right. In *CCH v. Law Society of Upper Canada* (2004), the Supreme Court rejected the publishers' line of argument that a library's provision of free-standing photocopiers constituted a violation of publishers' authorization right. "A person does not authorize infringement by authorizing the mere use of equipment that could be used to infringe copyright," wrote the majority. "Courts should presume that a person who authorizes an activity does so only so far as it is in accordance with the law."[7] Absent evidence of particular knowledge or involvement, a court would not hold that a person who lends a neighbour a chainsaw authorizes its use for murder or destruction of property. The same holds for copying devices: VCRs, computers, cameras, or copy machines have significant productive and non-infringing uses, and the law would not presume that making them available to others constitutes authorization to infringe copyright. Libraries and other providers of such technology usually make this explicit by reminding users of the existence of copyright law.

Moral Rights

Section 3 only describes copyright owners' economic interests. But there is a whole other realm of rights that are personal to *the author*—a term that in the Copyright Act refers not only to writers but to artists, composers, and all other creators of works. Moral rights, as they are called, exist separate and apart from economic rights, and are presented in sections 14 and 28 of the Copyright Act. They can only be held by creators and their heirs—not by corporations or contracting parties. They can be waived, but they cannot be assigned in the same way as economic rights.

Moral rights are essentially three: the right of integrity, the right of attribution, and from section 28.2(1)(b), the right of association. The main question about the right of integrity is: How do we tell whether a modification to a work has prejudiced the honour or reputation of the author?

A couple of Canadian cases have engaged with this question. In *Snow v. Eaton Centre* (1982), the court accepted the artist's subjective opinion that his reputation had been damaged; in *Prise de Parole v. Guérin* (1996), the court would have required some objective evidence to make a finding for moral rights infringement.

Painting, sculpture, and engraving aside—they are treated specially in section 28.2(2)—a claim to violation of moral rights will more likely be successful in court if backed up by objective evidence, perhaps in the form of an independent expert witness, linking the change to the artwork with damage to the artist's reputation or honour.

On the right of attribution, we might ask when mentioning the source is "reasonable in the circumstances," a limitation stated in section 14.1(1). This could be interpreted to mean that an artistic practice such as collage, which by convention does not feature attribution, does not infringe the right of attribution. But there is no case law on this question in Canada. We might also ask, what constitutes association? The answer is clear, perhaps, when a song is used to advertise a product or promote a political cause, but what if a piece of art is put on the same wall as the logo for a company sponsor? Again, the courts have not spoken on this subject.

> 14.1(1) The author of a work has, subject to section 28.2, the right to the integrity of the work and, in connection with an act mentioned in section 3, the right, where reasonable in the circumstances, to be associated with the work as its author by name or under a pseudonym and the right to remain anonymous....
>
> 28.2(1) The author's right to the integrity of a work is infringed only if the work is, to the prejudice of the honour or reputation of the author,
> (a) distorted, mutilated or otherwise modified; or
> (b) used in association with a product, service, cause or institution.
> (2) In the case of a painting, sculpture or engraving, the prejudice referred to in subsection (1) shall be deemed to have occurred as a result of any distortion, mutilation or other modification of the work.
> (3) For the purposes of this section,
> (a) a change in the location of a work, the physical means by which a work is exposed or the physical structure containing a work, or
> (b) steps taken in good faith to restore or preserve the work
> shall not, by that act alone, constitute a distortion, mutilation or other modification of the work.
>
> — Copyright Act, Sections 14 and 28.

Notably, U.S. copyright law does not include a general moral rights provision—apart from some special provisions in the Visual Artists Rights Act.[8] In fact, the United States has been quite hostile to the whole idea of moral rights, which does after all sometimes get in the way of maximum exploitation of a market for a work. On this issue, Canada lies somewhere between France (in which moral rights are perpetual) and the United States.

Snow v. Eaton Centre (1982)

Toronto's Eaton Centre commissioned artist Michael Snow to create a sculpture of sixty Canada geese in flight. It held all economic copyright in the work. As part of its Christmas decorations for 1982, the management festooned the geese with red ribbons. Snow went to court, seeking an injunction to have the ribbons removed. He argued that the ribbons made his otherwise naturalistic work look ridiculous and constituted a modification that damaged his honour and reputation. The court accepted his argument. In other words, the court deemed that an artist's subjective opinion about the effect of a change to his work on his reputation is sufficient so long as it is arrived at reasonably. (This case was decided before the addition of Section 28.2[2] to the act: today, a sculptor would not have to make a claim about honour and reputation.)

Prise de Parole Inc. v. Guérin (1996)

In 1992 the book publisher Guérin published an anthology for schools entitled (ironically, it turns out) *Libre Expression* (Free expression). The book included an unauthorized extract consisting of about one-third of Doric Germain's young adult novel *La Vengeance de l'orignal* (The vengeance of the moose). Sales of the novel plummeted, and Germain's publisher sued for infringement. Germain claimed that the abridgement of the novel—for example, the removal of descriptions of hunting and fishing methods—was also an infringement of his moral rights.

The court found that Guérin had infringed the reproduction right, and awarded damages. But on the issue of moral rights, the court did not find the author's distress at the abridgement of his novel sufficient to prove damage to his reputation and honour. It dismissed the moral rights claim.

5: Determining Ownership

ONE OF the most daunting challenges of working with copyright material is identifying its owner. We have seen that copyright interests are multiple, but that together they (the whole bundle of sticks, as it were) generally do start out in the possession of one owner. It might seem that finding the first owner at least would be easy. But in many cases, it isn't. Initial ownership can turn on the terms of employment or contract, the origin of the material, or the nature of the work in question. Once the rights have been transferred to others, things become more difficult still. There is no central registry of copyright. Librarians, copyright collectives, and the Copyright Board can help you in a search for downstream rights holders, but your own research skills are your main tool.

First Ownership

Who is the initial owner of the economic copyrights set out in section 3? We might presume that it would be "the author"—a term that the Copyright Act uses to refer not only to writers but also to creators of all types of works. Indeed, section 13(1) provides that "the author of a work shall be the first owner of the copyright therein."

Yet in many cases the author is not the first owner of the economic rights in the work. Section 13(3) states:

> Where the author of a work was in the employment of some other person under a contract of service or apprenticeship and the work was made in the course of his employment by that person, the person by whom the author was employed shall, in the absence of any agreement to the contrary, be the first owner of the copyright.

In terms of copyright as policy, this is an important part of the act: many of the policy justifications for copyright are based on the idea of just desserts for the author-as-copyright-owner, but this section reminds us that most copyrighted works in the world do not even start out under the ownership of the person who made them. Memos, promotional material, manuals, company artwork, and the like are all owned by the businesses whose employees generated them. For workers and freelancers, this subsection raises three practical issues. What does "employment under a contract of service or apprenticeship" mean? How do we determine whether work is done within the "course of employment"? And what does "any agreement to the contrary" mean? Can agreements to the contrary be implied, or do they need to be in writing?

As it turns out, the practical applications of section 13 differ in various employment situations (as we shall see in Part III of this book), but we need to mention a couple of general points here. First, the default rules are only that. In many cases, the parties have decided to order their affairs in a different manner—either through industry practice, or through specific terms of contract. You may need to read through quite a lot of fine print before you can be sure who owns the rights.

Second, other areas of law inform some of the legal questions that arise in the context of employment. Questions from fields as diverse as tort liability, taxation, and agency often turn on whether or not someone was employed and whether they were acting in the scope of their employment when a particular incident or event occurred. These precedents can be applicable to the issues raised under section 13. For example, "freelancers" are not considered to be employees even if they are working under a contract. University faculty, by industry custom, own the copyright in their work, even though this may not always be formalized in writing.

Even when the economic rights pass to the employer under section 13(3), the first owner of *moral* rights is always the author. However, since many employers require that moral rights be waived, moral rights often do not exist in work produced in the course of employment.

Table 7. Rules Governing First Ownership

Subject Matter	Owners' Right	First Owner
works	section 3	general rule: author, section 13(1) exception for engraving, photograph, or portrait person who ordered and paid for the plate, absent agreement to contrary, section 13(2) exception for works made in scope of employment: employer, absent agreement to contrary, section 13(3)
performers' performance	sections 15 and 26	performer, section 24(a)
sound recording	section 18	maker, section 24(b)
communication signal	section 21	broadcaster, section 24(c)

One final possibility for first ownership is the Crown. Under section 12 of the Copyright Act, where any work has been prepared or published by or under the direction or control of Her Majesty (or any government department), the copyright in the work belongs to Her Majesty. This ownership rule is a default rule, and can be altered by contract (freelancers doing research for the government may sometimes retain copyright to their work, for example). Where copyright is owned by the Crown, its duration is fifty years following the end of the calendar year of its first publication.

In recent years the potential severity of Crown copyright has been lessened somewhat by grants of public licences to use certain types of government documents such as acts, regulations, and court cases.[1] But Crown copyright is increasingly criticized on the grounds that taxpayers who have already paid for work produced by the government ought not to face any costs or hurdles to use it. In the United States, copyright does not subsist in federal government works.[2]

Preparing a Canadian edition of a guide to writing style in 2004, Professor Ira Nadel at the University of British Columbia wanted to include Pierre Trudeau's 1970 address to the nation announcing the War Measures Act and imposing martial law to contain the FLQ crisis. But who owned the rights? His first thought was that a public speech by a prime minister would be public domain. When a colleague told him about Crown copyright, he diligently contacted—in turn—the Prime Minister's Office, the Library of Parliament, the National Archive, and Trudeau's law firm. Nobody at any of these places knew how he could go about clearing copyright. Finally, through the Trudeau Foundation, and more or less by accident, he heard from an executor of Trudeau's will, who gave him permission to publish.

The irony is that, according to Elizabeth Judge, assistant professor of law at the University of Ottawa, and an expert on Crown copyright, such a speech is almost undoubtedly owned by the Crown, and not the Trudeau estate. Had the speech been given in a less clearly formal capacity, it might have been Trudeau's copyright. But the text of a prime ministerial speech such as this would most likely belong to the Crown.

Assigned Rights

For creators the various ways in which the first owner can redeploy his or her "bundle of rights" are bread-and-butter information. But these points are equally important for users of copyrighted material. There is, alas, no central registry where you can find the owner of copyright in a given work you want to use or license: mandatory registration of copyright is not permitted in countries that are members of the Berne Convention. Finding copyright owners can require considerable detective work, but it helps to start with knowledge of the ways in which the rights—the sticks in the bundle—can be dispersed.

Although moral rights, understood to be an extension of the persona of the creator, cannot be assigned, they can be passed on to heirs (for the duration of fifty years after the death of the author), and they can also be waived. In identifying the layers of rights in any work, it is important to know if moral rights exist, and to keep analysis of them distinct from analysis of economic rights. Unfortunately, the only way of being sure if they exist or not is to see the author's or employee's contract.

Economic or section 3 rights, though, are freely assignable because the law favours a fluid and flexible system of multiple transactions with respect to even the same work. Section 13(4) of the act provides:

> The owner of the copyright in any work may assign the right, either wholly or partially, and either generally or subject to limitations relating to territory, medium or sector of the market or other limitations relating to the scope of the assignment, and either for the whole term of the copyright or for any other part thereof, and may grant any interest in the right by licence, but no assignment or grant is valid unless it is in writing signed by the owner of the right in respect of which the assignment or grant is made, or by the owner's duly authorized agent.

Again, interests may be assigned in whole—that is, the entire interest can be transferred to another party—or in part. A partial assignment may apply to a specific territory, to a particular period of time, to a particular medium, or to a particular aspect of the interest. For example, just because a textbook publisher or a website has permission to reproduce a work does not mean that it can authorize further uses of that work.

As we've seen, performers' performances, sound recordings, and broadcast signals are also covered by copyright law. To determine the copyright in, say, a DVD of a televised concert, it is helpful to think of the metaphor of an onion. Let's start near the centre of the onion. When a performer performs a work, we are dealing with two distinct copyrightable objects: the performer's performance and the work. The performer has economic rights in his performance, as set out in section 15 of the act. If the work (a song, for example) is within copyright, we have to analyze its rights ownership situation apart from that of the performance—and there may be both economic and moral rights to consider. Now let's add two more layers as we consider the recording of the broadcast of the performer's performance of the work. We now have two more owners: the maker of the recording, and the broadcaster. Each participant in the chain requires permission of those holding rights in prior links, and some uses of the DVD might require separate fees or permissions at each level.

Collectives

Although no central registry of all copyrights and their holders exists in Canada—or in any Berne Convention country—section 70.1 of the Copyright Act provides for the functioning of copyright collective societies, usually known simply as "collectives." Canada has some thirty-four copyright collectives, each representing authors and owners in certain media for certain different types of use. Collectives do not *own* rights, but they are authorized by rights owners to license them. So for example, Audio Ciné represents a stable of international film studios, CCLI (Christian Copyright Licensing Inc.) serves the licensing needs of Christian publishers, SCAM (Société civile des auteurs multimédias) negotiates broadcast rights on behalf of international francophone creators, and DRTVC (the Direct Response Television Collective) licenses the retransmission of infomercials.[3] In many areas of licensing, two collectives exist, one for Quebec and one for the rest of Canada.

Collectives can streamline both the process of finding the owner(s) and setting the fee for use. For example, if you want to record your rendition of a copyrighted song, you might contact the Canadian Musical Reproduction Rights Agency (CMRRA) and see if your chosen song is in their "repertoire"—that is, if they represent its composer and lyricist. Through reciprocal relationships, Canadian collectives represent rights owners in many countries besides Canada. But they do not represent *all* rights owners—so you might have to pursue your search for the owner by more creative means.

Collectives also negotiate "blanket" licences in situations in which users are working with many different works, performances, sound recordings, or broadcasts. So, for example, most schools, colleges, and universities have licences with Access Copyright, a Canadian agency founded by groups of creators and publishers to license "reprography" or photocopying. These licences cover many routine copying uses in those institutions. Radio stations have licences with SOCAN for airplay of recordings.[4] Fees for these licences are set by the Copyright Board. The collectives should funnel royalties back to rights owners according to established formulas.

One music collective, the Canadian Private Copying Collective (CPCC), has generated special public controversy. The CPCC, as authorized in sections 81 to 86 of the Copyright Act, collects levies on blank recording media on the premise that they are being used for "private copying" of music.

Consumer discontent here has a number of dimensions. A consumer who pays ninety-nine cents for an iTunes song, and then a levy for the privilege of copying that music onto a CD, is paying twice, and probably doesn't like that. Then too, although the blank media levy was introduced at the record labels' behest in 1997 as a payment scheme for private copying, the labels have been (unsuccessfully) trying to sue downloaders for doing exactly what the levy is supposed to legitimize.

Consumer resentment has also built up because purchasers of such media must pay a levy to the CPCC for redistribution to music rights owners, even if they are using the media for computer backups or storing non-copyrighted work. Finally, because of the nature of the music marketplace most of the money leaves Canada—and other countries do not have equivalent levies that send money back our way.

Sources: http://www.cb-cda.gc.ca/news/c20032004fs-e.html; www.cpcc.ca; *BMG Canada v. Doe* (2005); Howard Knopf, Testimony to the Canadian Heritage Committee, Ottawa, April 20, 2004,

Ideally, collectives make things easier for creators, other rights owners, and users alike. They may be a special help to non-corporate rights holders or rights seekers, who have neither the time nor the expertise to pursue independent searches and negotiations. However, payment formulas can sometimes put independent creators at a disadvantage. For example, the music collectives remunerate rights holders based on radio play and album sales, which may mean underpayment to musicians whose work circulates on the Internet or is broadcast on college radio. The collective Access Copyright has both publisher and creator members, and it is not always clear that the creators get a fair shake.[5] On the user side, there is a widespread trend of "upward creep" in tariff levels with collectives: when collectives request a raise in the tariff level, the Copyright Board may give them less than they ask, but will rarely give them nothing—even if there is little justification for an increase. Pricing for tariffs has also reflected a narrow interpretation of fair dealing and other users' rights.

Unlocatable Copyright Owners

Many types of works are not clearly marked with their author's name. Other works may be clearly labelled, but it may be impossible to find the author or his heirs. Alternately, the copyright in a given work may have been resold several times and the path may be too faint or convoluted to trace. If you have searched libraries, bibliographies, phone books, and other sources and have not been able to find the copyright owner of a work that you want to reproduce or adapt in some way, what do you do?

In Canada, the Copyright Board manages a clearance system for published works whose copyright owners are unlocatable. In order to qualify for such a licence, a user must have made a "reasonable effort" to locate the rights owner.[6] In some cases royalties may be assessed, usually to be paid through the pertinent collective society.

The United States and Europe have no such system in place, and have been studying how to approach the barrier to access and research posed by "orphan works."[7] Some critics consider Canada's system cumbersome or unfair. Why, they ask, should one pay royalties to others when a rights holder cannot be found? And how do we deal with "orphaned" unpublished works, which lie outside Canada's system and yet pose some of the greatest problems for researchers?

6: Users' Rights

IF THIS book had been written even just a few years earlier, the title of this chapter would probably not be "Users' Rights." It would be something like "Exceptions to Infringement: Fair Dealing and Other Defences." But the Supreme Court's *CCH v. Law Society of Upper Canada* decision of 2004 changed the copyright landscape in Canada by declaring, "The fair dealing exception, like other exceptions in the Copyright Act, is a user's right. In order to maintain the proper balance between the rights of a copyright owner and users' interests, it must not be interpreted restrictively."[1] The term "users' rights" names a weighty counterpart to owners' rights and allows us effectively to imagine copyright as a system of relationships and interests. In the post-*CCH* era, Canadians should be just as familiar with the idea of fair dealing as they are with the idea of copyright infringement.

The Statutory Nature of Fair Dealing

Section 29 of the Copyright Act states, "Fair dealing for the purpose of research or private study does not infringe copyright." Sections 29.1 and

29.2 also list criticism or review and news reporting as other allowable purposes—with the added requirement of naming the source. The five categories, then, that fall under the fair dealing provision are research, private study, criticism, review, and news reporting.

The list is categorical: that is, before a user can rely on the fair dealing doctrine, that use must fall within one of those five areas set out in the act. This requirement runs counter to popular belief. People often invoke fair dealing in conversation by noting that they have used only a very little of the source, that they have substantially altered it, or that they were not making any money from the use. These factors do come into fair dealing analysis, but they are only relevant if the use first falls within one of the five enumerated categories.

Some of the confusion may well come from the difference that exists between U.S. "fair use" and Canadian "fair dealing." Canada's categorical requirement contrasts with the open-ended nature of fair use in United States. Section 107 of the U.S. statute begins:

> Fair use of a copyrighted work, including such use by reproduction in copies or phonorecords or by any other means specified by [section 106], for purposes *such as* criticism, comment, news reporting, teaching (including multiple copies for classroom use), scholarship, or research, is not an infringement of copyright. (Emphasis added.)

Use of the term "such as" in legislation indicates that the details listed are meant to be merely illustrative, not exhaustive. It is because of the phrase "such as" that case law in the United States has come to recognize parody as a legitimate purpose for fair use. The specific mention in the U.S. statute of "multiple copies for classroom use" is also markedly absent from the Canadian definition of fair dealing.

Whereas the Canadian statute does nothing to define "fair dealing" beyond the enumerated categories in which it falls, section 107 of the U.S. statute provides a test for fairness:

> In determining whether the use made of a work in any particular case is a fair use the factors to be considered *shall include*—
>   (1) the purpose and character of the use, including whether such

use is of a commercial nature or is for nonprofit educational purposes;

(2) the nature of the copyrighted work;

(3) the amount and substantiality of the portion used in relation
to the copyrighted work as a whole; and

(4) the effect of the use upon the potential market for or value of
the copyrighted work.

The fact that a work is unpublished shall not itself bar a finding of fair use if such finding is made upon consideration of all the
above factors. (Emphasis added.)

Here again the language is open-ended. The four factors set forth are
preceded by the important signal words "shall include," leaving judges
free to consider other factors they deem pertinent.

Still, despite the apparently expansive nature of statutory fair use
in the United States, the doctrine has been constrained in practice.
Aggressive litigation on the part of an overreaching content industry
recognizes that risk-averse users will probably back down before taking
on a well-financed lawsuit from a corporate entity. The doctrine has
also been constrained by a markedly conservative judicial attitude that
places a heavy emphasis on the economic interests of corporate owners
at the expense of the other fair use factors.[2] In this climate self-censor-
ship also plays a role. Many scholars and public interest advocates have
noted the pronounced "chilling effect" produced by the mere threat of
litigation, whatever the outcome in court might be. Users' rights advo-
cate Siva Vaidhyanathan has gone so far as to declare that in practice fair
use is altogether useless.[3]

From Limited Defence to Users' Right

Copyright litigation is less common in Canada than in the United States,
which means that we might expect there to be a less powerful "chilling
effect" operating on users' rights here. However, throughout the twentieth century fair dealing was consistently viewed in Canadian courts and
legal circles as nothing more than a limited defence to infringement. In
1999 a standard casebook on Canadian intellectual property law suc-

cinctly stated the gist of the difference between Canadian fair dealing and U.S. fair use:

> In Canada there is little scope for judicial discretion. The Canadian "fair dealing" exception is very limited and relatively explicit. Any copying must fall within one of the specified categories (research, private study, criticism or review, or news reporting). These categories are exclusive; no additional purposes can be recognized.
>
> The "fair use" provision in the United States, on the other hand, involves considerable judicial discretion in applying broad principles or theories underlying copyright protection as well as specifically stipulated factors, and without any limit as to categories or purposes.[4]

Several cases exemplified the notion that fair dealing was a limited defence that should be construed narrowly. In 1990 the Supreme Court reiterated the view from a 1934 case, *Performing Right Society v. Hammonds*, in which it was stated that the Copyright Act "was passed with a single object, namely, the benefit of authors of all kinds."[5]

This approach was also followed in *Michelin v. CAW* (1997). Michelin sued the Canadian Auto Workers for using an image of the Michelin Man (whose name, it turns out, is "Bibendum") on unionization posters. The court noted the categorical nature of fair dealing and concluded that its provisions "should be restrictively interpreted as exceptions." In the section of *Michelin* dealing with the union's claim that its freedom of expression had been impinged in violation of section 2(b) of the Charter of Rights and Freedoms, the court even went so far as to state:

> [Michelin] argues that using another's private property is a prohibited form of expression or else qualifies as a special circumstance warranting the removal of the expression from the protected sphere. I agree with the plaintiff's submission that the defendants are not permitted to appropriate the plaintiff's private property—the "Bibendum" copyright—as a vehicle for conveying their anti-Michelin message. Thus, the defendants' expression is a prohibited form or is subject to what Justice Linden ... called

a "special limitation" and is not protected under the umbrella of paragraph 2(b).[6]

The court found the CAW to be infringing Michelin's copyright. This 1996 judgment reflected the standard textbook wisdom about the nature and scope of the fair dealing defence, in keeping with the 1934 case. But within a very short time this approach was cast aside by no less than the Supreme Court of Canada—illustrating just how much the principle of users' rights as an offset to the notion of copyright as private property had developed in recent years. It seems unlikely that a court today would reach such a harsh conclusion.[7]

The shift began in 2002 with *Théberge v. Galerie d'Art du Petit Champlain*, when the Supreme Court held that the proper balance in copyright "lies not only in recognizing the creator's rights but in giving due weight to their limited nature. In crassly economic terms it would be as inefficient to overcompensate artists and authors for the right of reproduction as it would be self-defeating to undercompensate

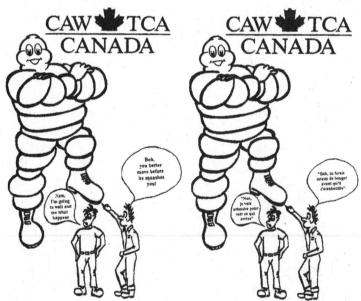

Don't Wait until it's too late! Because the job you save may be your own. Sign today for a better tomorrow. CAW Granton Office: 752-7415

«N'attendez pas qu'il soit trop tard» parce que l'emploi que vous préservez peut être le vôtre. Signez aujourd'hui pour un avenir meilleur. Bureau des TCA à Granton: 752-7415

them." While not faced with a case focusing directly on fair dealing, the *Théberge* court announced what amounted to a new policy framework for copyright analysis, stating, "Excessive control by holders of copyrights and other forms of intellectual property may unduly limit the ability of the public domain to incorporate and embellish creative innovation in the long-term interests of society as a whole, or create practical obstacles to proper utilization."[8]

As the federal government's consultation on copyright reform continued through 2003,[9] there was no sign that the *Théberge* framework was being given any serious consideration. Meanwhile, a long-standing dispute between the Law Society of Upper Canada (LSUC) and a group of commercial publishers of law-related materials (including CCH Canadian Ltd.) was working its way through the courts. The Law Society's Great Library had been faxing articles and other research materials to members off-site and allowing in-house patrons to use self-service photocopiers; the case was to decide whether this practice constituted copyright infringement. In 1999 the Federal Court Trial Division had rejected the defence of fair dealing raised by the Law Society, holding that the then-current interpretation of fair dealing did not encompass the activities of the custom photocopy service of the Great Library. This court once again cited the 1934 *Performing Right Society v. Hammonds* case to assert that authors' rights alone were a sufficient mechanism for serving the public good through copyright.[10]

But the trial court's logic was rejected by the Federal Court of Appeal, which reversed the first *CCH v. Law Society of Upper Canada* ruling in part, holding:

> The Trial Judge erred in law when he stated that exceptions to infringement must be "strictly construed" (at paragraph 175). There is no basis in law or in policy for such an approach. An overly restrictive interpretation of the exemptions contained in the Act would be inconsistent with the mandate of copyright law to harmonize owners' rights with legitimate public interests.[11]

While the Court of Appeal found that the trial court had made a mistake in applying a restrictive view to the fair dealing defence, because of

Many Canadians understand users' rights in terms of the practice of their community or trade, rather than in terms of the law. Sometimes this "common sense" is in tension with the law—many people will tell you, for example, that using the work of another but *changing* it a lot is not infringement, or that if the work is foisted on you without your choice (as in the case of advertising) you have the right to reproduce it. Despite such misconceptions, non-lawyers often apply impressive amounts of self-consciousness and reason to users' rights. Consider the thoughts of art gallery curator Jan Allen:

> I feel in a way, even though we're a public institution, we have a mandate for research and we push those limits. We take certain risks and we work with things that we think are meaningful ... and part of that is flirting with those edges around the interpretation of copyright. Again, I'm really going by what is common practice and feeling that that is where I have to draw the line. Otherwise ... if you are too legalistic about it I think you could get off in some weird pristine edge of things and it would be very lonely. Like we've got the painting that came into the collection in the last year that makes reference to Captain Nemo's underwater cave ... are we going to get permission for that? No, we're not. We're in a place in culture where culture feeds on itself ... its own codes ... so you can't start excluding all those codes ... they are part of the language ... so I think that you have to trust that the interpretation of the law and that its enactment, its practice, does play itself out so that there's some leeway.

Source: Jan Allen, Curator of Contemporary Art,
Agnes Etherington Art Centre, Kingston, Ont., interview with Kirsty Robertson.

an inadequate factual record its judges were unwilling to grant a declaration that the library was protected by fair dealing.

In its 2004 decision in *CCH v. Law Society of Upper Canada*, the Supreme Court did declare the use to be fair dealing. More significantly, the Supreme Court made a number of points that clearly expanded the scope of fair dealing. First, the court clarified the nature and character of the fair dealing defence:

Procedurally, a defendant is required to prove that his or her dealing with a work has been fair; however, the fair dealing exception is perhaps more properly understood as an integral part of the *Copyright Act* than simply a defence. Any act falling within the fair dealing exception will not be an infringement of copyright. The fair dealing exception, like other exceptions in the *Copyright Act*, is a user's right. In order to maintain the proper balance between the rights of a copyright owner and users' interests, it must not be interpreted restrictively.[12]

The court went on to quote, and adopt, legal scholar David Vaver's observation: "User rights are not just loopholes. Both owner rights and user rights should therefore be given the fair and balanced reading that befits remedial legislation."[13]

The same year, in *SOCAN v. CAIP*, the Supreme Court noted, "The capacity of the Internet to disseminate 'works of the arts and intellect' is one of the great innovations of the information age." To which it added, "Its use should be facilitated rather than discouraged, but this should not be done unfairly at the expense of those who created the works of arts and intellect in the first place."[14] In these three major cases (*Théberge*, *CCH*, and *SOCAN*), the Supreme Court articulated the idea of users' rights, while also demonstrating the need for careful balancing of interests.

A Six-Part Test for Fair Dealing

The Canadian statute does not contain any protocol for distinguishing a "fair" instance of reproduction for criticism purposes from an "unfair" instance. As the Supreme Court put it in *CCH v. Law Society of Upper Canada*, "The *Copyright Act* does not define what will be 'fair'; whether something is fair is a question of fact and depends on the facts of each case."[15] In *CCH*, however, the Supreme Court followed the Court of Appeal, and to a striking degree the four-part test of the U.S. statute, in laying out a number of criteria for making such a decision. Parliament may want to consider incorporating these criteria into the Copyright Act, but for now the tests in *CCH* constitute the most authoritative guide to the question of fair dealing.

The first question, then, is the **purpose** of the use. Does it constitute research, private study, criticism, review, or news reporting? Neither the act nor *CCH* defines these terms, so it would seem that their definitions would come from ordinary practice and usage. (For discussion of the scope of the "criticism" category, see chapter 16.) The *CCH* court stated, "These allowable purposes should not be given a restrictive interpretation or this could result in the undue restriction of users' rights." While it noted that commercial purposes might tend to be less "fair" than non-commercial purposes, it did not disqualify them from this first test, stating, "Lawyers carrying on the business of law for profit are conducting research within the meaning of s. 29 of the *Copyright Act*."[16]

Is it fair dealing?

1. The purpose of the dealing: Does the use fall under one of the five catego-ries of research, private study, criticism, review, or news reporting?
   - If no, it's not fair dealing.
   - If yes, proceed to the following five tests and make a judgment based on the cumulative weight of all results.
2. The character of the dealing
3. The amount of the dealing
4. Alternatives to the dealing
5. The nature of the work
6. The effect of the dealing on the work.

If the use is not deemed to fall into one of the five categories, that is the end of the matter: there is no fair dealing defence. If it does fall into one of the categories, the analysis can continue.

CCH glosses the second consideration, the **character** of the dealing:

If multiple copies of works are being widely distributed, this will tend to be unfair. If, however, a single copy of a work is used for a specific legitimate purpose, then it may be easier to conclude that it was a fair dealing. If the copy of the work is destroyed after it is used for its specific intended purpose, this may also favour a find-ing of fairness.[17]

These sentences suggest a focus within the "character" criterion on the number of copies made, and a fairly narrow conception of fair dealing. But the Court goes on:

> It may be relevant to consider the custom or practice in a particular trade or industry to determine whether or not the character of the dealing is fair. For example, in *Sillitoe v. McGraw-Hill Book Co. (U.K.)*, [1983] F.S.R. 545 (Ch. D.), the importers and distributors of "study notes" that incorporated large passages from published works attempted to claim that the copies were fair dealings because they were for the purpose of criticism. The court reviewed the ways in which copied works were customarily dealt with in literary criticism textbooks to help it conclude that the study notes were not fair dealings for the purpose of criticism.

This is a key part of the *CCH* decision: it reminds people in diverse "trades or industries" that their practice has a role in determining the law. It would follow that if we narrow our practice, asking permission for every tiniest use, we narrow our users' rights in the law. Instead, we could heed this passage and use past practice, "common sense," and a little courage about the habits of use in our particular circles. If, for example, journalists can quote certain portions of printed texts without permission, why can't they do the same with digital texts? If they do not, they are effectively participating in a narrowing of fair dealing.

With the third criterion laid out in *CCH*, the **amount** of the dealing, the court begins by reminding us of the substantiality requirement for infringement: "If the amount taken from a work is trivial, the fair dealing analysis need not be undertaken at all because the court will have concluded that there was no copyright infringement." The substantiality requirement effectively functions as a user's right. The court observes, "The quantity of the work taken will not be determinative of fairness, but it can help in the determination. It may be possible to deal fairly with a whole work. As Vaver points out, there might be no other way to criticize or review certain types of works such as photographs."[18] This will surprise many readers: there is *no absolute measure or formula* for how much or what portion of a work can be used under fair dealing. In this holistic approach to analysis, you simply need to be able to show that you needed to use the amount you used.

In its rules governing thesis submission, Simon Fraser University tells graduate students that they can quote no more than five hundred words or 2 per cent of copyrighted works. This rule is completely unworkable for normal scholarly practice: for example, to abide by it a literature student would have to ask permission to quote more than three or four words from a fourteen-line sonnet. Instead, SFU should be instructing its students to perform a full fair dealing analysis, following *CCH*, in which quantity is only one component.

University libraries often post notices above their photocopy machines, indicating permitted quantities of copying. These amounts represent the terms of the Access Copyright licence, not the principles of fair dealing. Fair dealing may sometimes extend beyond the Access licence; for more on this, see chapter 10.

Source: Simon Fraser University Library, http://www.lib.sfu.ca.

Criterion four is **alternatives** to the dealing. Did you really need to use this *particular* piece for your purpose? The court says, for example, "If there is a non-copyrighted equivalent of the work that could have been used instead of the copyrighted work, this should be considered by the court."[19]

Next the court turns to the **nature** of the original work. The examples used all have to do with publicity and exposure:

> Although certainly not determinative, if a work has not been published, the dealing may be more fair in that its reproduction with acknowledgement could lead to a wider public dissemination of the work—one of the goals of copyright law. If, however, the work in question was confidential, this may tip the scales towards finding that the dealing was unfair.[20]

These comments, in which wide dissemination is seen as a public benefit, sharply contrast with the court's comments on character of the work, in which multiple copies are viewed suspiciously. In any case, this criterion offers a place for an argument about the desirability of further dissemination: users could argue, for example, that reproduction of some portion of an out-of-print book for an enumerated purpose serves the public interest.

In its discussion of the final criterion, the **effect** of the dealing on the work, the court is insistent that "although the effect of the dealing on the market of the copyright owner is an important factor, it is neither the only factor nor the most important factor that a court must consider in deciding if the dealing is fair."[21] This will also come as a surprise to most readers: competition in the original's market is only one in the long list of issues. If a use does compete in the market with the original, but is legitimate criticism and only takes what it needs to achieve its purpose, for example, there may well be a finding of fair dealing. Commercial use is not a nail in the fair dealing coffin; the *CCH* case, after all, concerned use by lawyers in private practice who might otherwise have bought more materials from the publishers, and yet the court considered their use fair dealing.

When it comes to the basics of fair dealing, then, for most purposes you will be able to think through the factors and issues yourself—whether you want to know what uses you can make without permission, or whether you need to know if someone else is infringing on your copyright. If you do have to consult a lawyer, this initial independent analysis will get you off to a good start.

Other Limitations on Owners' Rights

Other sections in the Copyright Act limit the enforceability of owners' rights to various degrees. In addition to the general fair dealing provisions, there are a number of special provisions for qualifying educational institutions, libraries, museums, and archives; we outline these in chapters 10 and 13.

The act also provides various other specific limitations and exceptions to owners' rights. While two of these items pertain to broadcasting, another applies only to the Librarian and Archivist of Canada, and yet another allows copies or transmission of information for compliance with other laws.[22] Other exceptions of more general interest include backing up computer programs; conversion for people with perceptual disabilities; various art, reporting, and performance activities; and copying music recordings for private use (see Table 8). Many of these items also contain counterexceptions, so that the user's right described is often quite narrow. Some of these exceptions might also overlap with fair dealing.

Table 8. Additional Limitations and Exceptions to Owners' Rights

Common Name of Exception	It is not an infringement of copyright …	Section of Copyright Act
backup of computer programs	… in a computer program for a person who owns a copy of the computer program that is authorized by the owner of the copyright to	30.6
	(a) make a single reproduction of the copy by adapting, modifying or converting the computer program or translating it into another computer language if the person proves that the reproduced copy is	
	(i) essential for the compatibility of the computer program with a particular computer,	
	(ii) solely for the person's own use, and	
	(iii) destroyed immediately after the person ceases to be the owner of the copy; or	
	(b) make a single reproduction for backup purposes of the copy or of a reproduced copy referred to in paragraph (a) if the person proves that the reproduction for backup purposes is destroyed immediately when the person ceases to be the owner of the copy of the computer program.	
incidental use	… to incidentally and not deliberately	30.7
	(a) include a work or other subject matter in another work or other subject-matter; or	
	(b) do any act in relation to a work or other subject matter that is incidentally and not deliberately included in another work or other subject matter.	
perceptual disabilities	… for a person, at the request of a person with a perceptual disability, or for a non-profit organization acting for his or her benefit, to	32

	(a) make a copy or sound recording of a literary, musical, artistic, or dramatic work, other than a cinematographic work, in a format specially designed for persons with a perceptual disability;	
	(b) translate, adapt, or reproduce in sign language a literary or dramatic work, other than a cinematographic work, in a format specially designed for persons with a perceptual disability; or	
	(c) perform in public a literary or dramatic work, other than a cinematographic work, in sign language, either live or in a format specially designed for persons with a perceptual disability.	
	(2) Subsection (1) does not authorize the making of a large print book.	
	(3) Subsection (1) does not apply where the work or sound recording is commercially available in a format specially designed to meet the needs of any person referred to in that subsection, within the meaning of paragraph (a) of the definition "commercially available."	
use of plans or models	... for an author of an artistic work who is not the owner of the copyright in the work to use any mould, cast, sketch, plan, model, or study made by the author for the purpose of the work, if the author does not thereby repeat or imitate the main design of the work.	32.2 (1)(a)
buildings and public art	... for any person to reproduce, in a painting, drawing, engraving, photograph or cinematographic work	32.2 (1)(b)
	(i) an architectural work, provided the copy is not in the nature of an architectural drawing or plan, or	
	(ii) a sculpture or work of artistic craftsmanship or a cast or model of a sculpture or work of artistic craftsmanship, that is permanently situated in a public place or building.	
lecture reporting	... for any person to make or publish, for the purposes of news reporting or news summary, a report of a lecture given in public, unless the report is prohibited by conspicuous written or printed notice	32.2 (1)(c)

Table 8. (continued)

public reading	affixed before and maintained during the lecture at or about the main entrance of the building in which the lecture is given, and, except while the building is being used for public worship, in a position near the lecturer.	
	… for any person to read or recite in public a reasonable extract from a published work.	32.2 (1)(d)
political speech reporting	… for any person to make or publish, for the purposes of news reporting or news summary, a report of an address of a political nature given at a public meeting.	32.2 (1)(e)
performance at agricultural fairs	… for a person to do any of the following acts without motive of gain at any agricultural or agricultural-industrial exhibition or fair that receives a grant from or is held by its directors under federal, provincial, or municipal authority:	32.2(2)
	(a) the live performance in public of a musical work;	
	(b) the performance in public of a sound recording embodying a musical work or a performer's performance of a musical work; or	
	(c) the performance in public of a communication signal carrying	
	(i) the live performance in public of a musical work, or	
	(ii) a sound recording embodying a musical work or a performer's performance of a musical work.	
religious, educational, or charitable performance	No religious organization or institution, educational institution and no charitable or fraternal organization shall be held liable to pay any compensation for doing any of the following acts in furtherance of a religious, educational or charitable object:	32.2(3)
	(a) the live performance in public of a musical work;	
	(b) the performance in public of a sound recording embodying a musical work or a performer's per-	

(c) the performance in public of a communication signal carrying

(i) the live performance in public of a musical work, or

(ii) a sound recording embodying a musical work or a performer's performance of a musical work.

private music copying Subject to subsection (2), the act of reproducing all or any substantial part of

(a) a musical work embodied in a sound recording,

(b) a performer's performance of a musical work embodied in a sound recording, or

(c) a sound recording in which a musical work, or a performer's performance of a musical work, is embodied

onto an audio recording medium for the private use of the person who makes the copy does not constitute an infringement of the copyright in the musical work, the performer's performance or the sound recording.

(2) Subsection (1) does not apply if the act described in that subsection is done for the purpose of doing any of the following in relation to any of the things referred to in paragraphs (1)(a) to (c):

(a) selling or renting out, or by way of trade exposing or offering for sale or rental;

(b) distributing, whether or not for the purpose of trade;

(c) communicating to the public by telecommunication; or

(d) performing, or causing to be performed, in public.

7: Enforcement of Owners' Rights

COPYRIGHT CASES can emerge from either civil or criminal proceedings. Civil cases are lawsuits brought by one private party on another. Criminal cases are prosecuted by the government (the Crown). In the realm of copyright civil cases are much more common. Both kinds of cases can move up through the courts if they are appealed and cross-appealed. (See Table 9.)

In general terms, the law recognizes two sorts of civil infringement: general (or primary) infringement and secondary infringement. Section 27(1) of the Copyright Act sets out the definition of primary infringement: "It is an infringement of copyright for any person to do, without the consent of the owner of the copyright, anything that by this Act only the owner of the copyright has the right to do."

If an aggrieved copyright holder files suit, and if one of the basic owners' rights is implicated, a judge has to decide on the basis of the facts whether or not the owner of the copyright consented. Consent can be implied explicitly as well as expressed, so there might be additional factual issues based on all of the circumstances. Then there is the issue

Table 9. Civil and Criminal Law Cases

	Civil Law	Criminal Law
parties	plaintiff versus defendant, e.g., Jones v. Smith, CCH v. Law Society of Upper Canada	the Crown versus a private party, e.g., R. (Regina) v. Jones
case initiated by	plaintiff	the Crown
source of law	various in different areas of liability; can be based on common-law principles or specific statute	specific statutory offences are enumerated in the Criminal Code and other acts
evidentiary burden	plaintiff generally has burden of proof on all elements of the claim (e.g., infringement); but burden is usually only at the level of preponderance of evidence; onus then shifts to defendant to establish defence (e.g., fair dealing)	Crown must bear heavier burden of proof (beyond reasonable doubt); in the case of criminal copyright liability, Crown must also negate fair dealing.
penalties in Copyright Act	sections 34 through 41	sections 42 and 43
legal costs borne by	plaintiff or defendant	Crown

of whether or not the user can defend the infringement—given that many technical instances of infringement do not amount to actionable infringement because of the availability of a defence such as fair dealing. Or perhaps the individual defendants are able to show that they did not have access to the work that they allegedly infringed and did not therefore actually "copy" the work. (It is possible for two people to create identical or highly similar works independently.) Various types of defence can be mounted depending on the specifics of the case. Assuming that there is actionable infringement, the issue then becomes a matter of what remedies are available to the aggrieved owner.

Section 27(2) lays out a set of five circumstances that constitute secondary infringement:

It is an infringement of copyright for any person to

(a) sell or rent out,

(b) distribute to such an extent as to affect prejudicially the owner of the copyright,

(c) by way of trade distribute, expose or offer for sale or rental, or exhibit in public,

(d) possess for the purpose of doing anything referred to in paragraphs (a) to (c), or

(e) import into Canada for the purpose of doing anything referred to in paragraphs (a) to (c),

a copy of a work, sound recording or fixation of a performer's performance or of a communication signal that the person knows or should have known infringes copyright or would infringe copyright if it had been made in Canada by the person who made it.

In other words, secondary infringement is the distribution of infringing works.

Significantly, most of the listed circumstances in this subsection deal with issues that arise in the course of trade: owners of copyright would most likely invoke this section as part of an effort to reduce the commercial circulation of pirated materials. The exception is subdivision (b), which does not require the infringer to be engaged in any sort of trade or business. That particular section may have an impact on a wider range of unauthorized users.

Another important point is that secondary infringement requires an element of knowledge: that is, infringers will not be found liable unless

Is it copyright infringement to link to somebody else's website?

To demonstrate copyright infringement, the copyright owner has to show that the infringer did something that only the owner can legally do, and that there was no permission. Linking to someone else's web page, even against their wishes and without their consent, simply does not implicate any of the copyright owner's rights as they are listed in section 3 of the Copyright Act: it is not reproduction, for example, or distribution, or authorization. It might violate someone's sense of Internet etiquette—but it is not copyright infringement.

they know (or should have known) that their actions would constitute infringement.[1] One would probably not be held liable for "accidental" secondary infringement.

Note that in the case of primary infringement, under section 27(1) there is no such knowledge requirement: liability attaches for general infringement on what is called a "strict liability" basis. In other words, ignorance is no excuse—although as we will see it can reduce damages to zero.

Assuming that a plaintiff can make out a successful case for infringement, what is that person entitled to collect from the defendant? According to section 34(1), "Where copyright has been infringed, the owner of the copyright is, subject to this Act, entitled to all remedies by way of injunction, damages, accounts, delivery up and otherwise that are or may be conferred by law for the infringement of a right."

An injunction is a court order to cease and desist from the infringing activity. (Under section 39.1, an injunction can be granted even before

---

I think my copyright is being infringed. What should I do?

You could:

- register your copyright if you haven't already;
- send a polite, factual, yet firm letter to the alleged infringer asking for them to cease; or
- seek legal counsel if you feel it is warranted.

I just got a letter from a lawyer stating that I am infringing his client's copyright. What should I do?

You could:

- comply with the demand;
- carefully compose a response letter asking for further clarification and support for the contention that there has been infringement;
- carefully compose a response letter explaining why you believe you are not infringing, or why your actions constitute fair dealing or some other defence; or
- turn it over to legal counsel if you feel it is warranted.

the case is heard if the court decides that the case is strong enough.) "Delivery up" means forfeiting the offending materials (see 38[1] and 38[2]). As for damages, section 35(1) provides clarification about their possible extent:

> Where a person infringes copyright, the person is liable to pay such damages to the owner of the copyright as the owner has suffered due to the infringement and, in addition to those damages, such part of the profits that the infringer has made from the infringement and that were not taken into account in calculating the damages as the court considers just.

In determining the extent of profits, the plaintiff is required to prove only receipts or revenues derived from the infringement—section 35(2)(a)—and the defendant is required to prove every element of cost that is being claimed—section 35(2)(b). In other words, profits are determined or estimated with regard to the infringing activity, not to the whole enterprise of either party.

In many situations, then, there would not be much risk of serious liability because the damage to the owner is minimal and the infringer has gained little or no profit. A reproduction of a photograph on a website, for example, would probably not trigger any liability from section 35. But two other provisions add bite to owners' rights. Section 38.1(1) provides that the copyright owner can elect to recover "statutory damages" instead of the actual damages set out in section 35. If a court awards statutory damages, it has the discretion to set them anywhere between $500 and $20,000, as the court considers just. In other words, just because there is no measurable (or only minimal) damage to the plaintiff, and no profit accruing to the defendant, there can still be an award of damages. In situations in which a person has infringed multiple works, such as a collection of recorded songs, the multiplier effect could lead to huge statutory damages.[2] As well, when the court decides that the conduct of the defendant was in bad faith or particularly egregious, it can also award "exemplary or punitive damages" according to section 38.1(7).

There is some good news here for the innocent infringer. Section 39(1) provides that "if the defendant proves that, at the date of the infringement, the defendant was not aware and had no reasonable ground for suspecting that copyright subsisted in the work or other subject-matter in question," no damages can be awarded. Section 39(2) states, however, that this opportunity for the defendant to avoid damages is not applicable if "at the date of the infringement, the copyright was duly registered under this Act." Section 38.1(2) applies specifically to cases involving statutory damages. It states that if defendants satisfy the court in such a case that they were not aware and had no reasonable grounds to believe that they had infringed copyright, the court may reduce the amount of the award to less than $500, but not less than $200. There is some guidance for the court in section 38.1(5), which directs the court to consider:

all relevant factors, including
(a) the good faith or bad faith of the defendant;
(b) the conduct of the parties before and during the proceedings; and
(c) the need to deter other infringements of the copyright in question.[3]

Of course, there is no way of knowing in advance if the court will accept a claim of lack of belief of infringement.

Criminal Infringement

Section 42(1) provides that anyone who knowingly does any of the following is guilty of a criminal offence:

(a) makes for sale or rental an infringing copy of a work or other subject-matter in which copyright subsists,
(b) sells or rents out, or by way of trade exposes or offers for sale or rental, an infringing copy of a work or other subject-matter in which copyright subsists,
(c) distributes infringing copies of a work or other subject-matter in which copyright subsists, either for the purpose of trade or to such an extent as to affect prejudicially the owner of the copyright,

Often, copyright holders threaten alleged infringers with the possibility of legal action in the hopes that a letter alone will produce withdrawal of the offending material. This can be a good strategy for an independent rights holder who doesn't have the time or money to hire a lawyer. But when such a letter comes from a corporate rights holder on law firm letterhead, it can intimidate individuals or small organizations, whether or not it actually stands for a plausible charge of infringement. Such letters often represent the law of the jungle more than the law of the land. The U.S. website Chilling Effects Clearinghouse (www.chillingeffects.org) has archived many such letters as a public service to others who might receive them.

In cases in which the alleged infringers have a plausible defence against infringement, or in which a lawsuit would produce more bad PR than it would be worth for the corporate rights holder, it often pays to stand firm against such letters.

In 2001 the AIDS Committee of Toronto (ACT) secured Ontario government funding for a large-scale social marketing campaign for AIDS prevention. Its organizers were excited about the opportunity to get their message out to gay men through the mass media, and working with the public relations company Naked Creative Consultancy they developed a series of billboards, TV ads, pamphlets, and print ads with the slogan "Welcome to Condom Country"—a takeoff on the well-known Marlboro cigarette advertisement. The ads were a huge success: they appealed to older men who knew the Marlboro imagery well, and they also, given that the Marlboro Man is ubiquitous internationally, had wide currency in multicultural Toronto. As John Maxwell, director of special projects for ACT, put it, "They were eye-catching; they were a little bit on the edge; they took an icon and turned it on its head." They also beat *Brokeback Mountain* by five years.

A couple of months after the launch of the campaign, the tobacco company Philip Morris approached ACT, threatening a lawsuit. But ACT stood its ground, and Philip Morris backed off. Too bad, in a way: we not only missed the drama of the world's tobacco giant suing a community AIDS prevention organization—but also could have had a case clarifying the status of parody in Canadian copyright.

Welcome to Condom Country.

HIV is on the rise in Toronto. Ride Safely.

actoronto.org 416.340.2437

(d) by way of trade exhibits in public an infringing copy of a work or other subject-matter in which copyright subsists, or

(e) imports for sale or rental into Canada any infringing copy of a work or other subject-matter in which copyright subsists.

Notice the similarity between criminal infringement and secondary infringement in terms of the emphasis on commercial practices. Also like secondary infringement, criminal infringement has a knowledge requirement. For criminal infringement, there has to be *actual* knowledge demonstrated, but for secondary civil infringement the knowledge requirement can be satisfied if defendants "should have known" they were infringing.

Section 42 provides the penalties for these offences: if convicted, the offender will be subject "(f) on summary conviction, to a fine not exceeding twenty-five thousand dollars or to imprisonment for a term not exceeding six months or to both, or (g) on conviction on indictment, to a fine not exceeding one million dollars or to imprisonment for a term not exceeding five years or to both."[4]

In the world of filmmaking and distribution, Hollywood argues that Canadian law is inadequate as a means of preventing piracy; but these penalties do seem to be fairly substantial.[5] In addition, section 43(1) defines the criminal offence of commercial public performance of musical and dramatic works, and lays out the penalties for such an action.

How active is criminal prosecution of copyright infringement in Canada? How active should it be? According to the RCMP:

Cases selected for investigation and prosecution should, as a matter of priority, constitute copyright piracy on a commercial scale. For purposes of this policy, "copyright piracy on a commercial scale" means commercial infringement by a manufacturer, wholesaler or importer. Infringement at the retail level is not an enforcement priority in its own right, although it may prove a useful means of gaining access to more serious offences of copyright piracy.[6]

Canada, along with many other countries, has come under criticism from the Office of the United States Trade Representative for a variety of copyright-related issues, including criminal enforcement.[7] The actual amount of commercial piracy being committed or facilitated in Canada is the subject of hot debate. In principle, we see no contradiction between taking a generous view of users' rights and enforcing commercial infringement: it is absolutely crucial to distinguish the legitimate exercise of users' rights from industrial-scale criminal copyright infringement—as far too little public discussion does.

At the same time, the criminal enforcement of copyright represents a public subsidy of private business interests—unlike civil litigation, it is paid for by taxpayers. Police, prosecutors, and courts have a raft of immediate public safety concerns that they need to focus on or address, and, clearly, decisions about Canada's priorities in the area of copyright protection need to be made in a broad policy context.

PART III: PRACTICE

General Resources

- John Lorinc, "Creators and Copyright in Canada," 2004.

- Laura Murray, "Protecting Ourselves to Death: Canada, Copyright, and the Internet," 2004.

8: Craft and Design

THE TERM "design" can be applied to many different practices—from graphic design to designs of mass-produced objects to (our focus here) the design of useful objects such as hats, cups, or chairs produced in small numbers by artisans.

Graphic design—for example, the design of book covers, signage, and advertisements—is basically commercial visual art, which copyright law treats under the rubric of visual art (see chapter 16). The design work that culminates in mass-produced objects is generally not automatically protected as intellectual property, but can be registered under the Industrial Design Act with the Canadian Intellectual Property Office and thus protected from copying for a term of ten years.[1]

The Canadian Copyright Act does provide specific treatment for some categories of design. Its section 64(1) defines design as "features of shape, configuration, pattern or ornament and any combination of those features that, in a finished article, appeal to and are judged solely by the eye." If the object has a "function other than merely serving as a substrate or carrier for artistic or literary matter," the act states, its design can be copyrighted *if no more than fifty such objects are made.* Hence a saddle, bowl, or dress is only covered by copyright if made in quantities of fewer than fifty-one. The Copyright Act thus implicitly defines industrial-scale production as production in quantities larger than this cut-off. Presumably the rationale is that there is a public interest in rapid innovation in industrial design, which can be facilitated by relatively weak intellectual property protection, whereas designs of useful objects outside the mass market (or prior to entering the mass market) ought to have some protection.

In all cases drawings or sketches of the designs are copyrighted as such: you might be able to imitate a mass-produced purse without permission, for example, but you can't copy its designer's drawings. The Copyright Act, under section 64(3), also includes exceptions to the fifty-object limit. For example, architectural works, patterned fabric, and graphics applied to the face of articles (such as images on T-shirts or mugs) retain copyright protection even if they are mass-produced.

Are the law's design protections of use to artisans? In practical terms, rarely. Industrial design registration is onerous and impractical for a truly innovative independent designer who has many different objects in production. Most artisans find it difficult if not impossible to make a

I design hats and make more than fifty of each kind. Is there anything I can do to protect myself from imitators?

You could obtain protection through the Industrial Design Act. The registration process is fairly simple (see the description at the Canadian Intellectual Property Office: www.cipo.ca). After an application is made and a fee is paid, the design goes through an examination process. If granted, the registration gives the owner exclusive rights for a period of ten years. The owner has the exclusive right to:

(a) make, import for the purpose of trade or business, or sell, rent, or offer or expose for sale or rent, any article in respect of which the design is registered and to which the design or a design not differing substantially therefrom has been applied; or

(b) do, in relation to a kit, anything specified in paragraph (a) that would constitute an infringement if done in relation to an article assembled from the kit.

living by keeping their quantities below fifty-one (a good candlestick or belt design, for example, will be replicated for many craft shows and retail outlets), so copyright is only helpful as their work approaches the "one of a kind" status. The legal distinction between a potter and a sculptor, or between a useful and a "useless" object, may seem to be rather arbitrary and unfair: a printmaker producing an edition of five hundred prints holds copyright in the work, but a maker of fifty-one identical art vases may not, simply because the vases can hold flowers. Furthermore, few artisans can afford to litigate the copying of their designs.

There is a widespread fear of "ripoffs" among artisans and designers. We are living in an era in which North American consumers can buy beautifully designed articles for their homes for very little money— articles produced in countries with lower labour costs than ours. The design of many of these inexpensive products is inspired or even copied, without authorization, from folkloric styles or the work of individual designers. In addition, trends in North American-produced crafts often derive from one artisan's "hit" design.

There is an emerging feeling in craft and design communities that "something needs to be done." But is copyright reform the appropriate tool to address these issues? Probably not, given that many artisans could not afford recourse to the law, whatever its shape. Furthermore, many

---

Jewellery-makers Wade Papin and Danielle Wilmore run Pyrrha Design Inc. in Vancouver. When a Saskatchewan accessories retailer ordered jewellery based on their designs to be made in Taiwan and started selling the products in Canada for a much lower price, Pyrrha Design took him to court. The legal question was whether jewellery was art or design: if design, it would not be protected by copyright, because Pyrrha produced the pieces of jewellery in quantities larger than fifty. Pyrrha's lawyer accordingly argued that the jewellery was useless, mere adornment: in other words, art.

It took five years and tens of thousands of dollars, but eventually, as the case slowly moved towards trial, the imitator agreed to settle. While Papin and Wilmore won satisfaction and compensation, the settlement meant that the case never went to court. It remains unclear whether jewellery, in Canadian law, constitutes art or design.

Source: Alexandra Gill, "It Glitters. It Sparkles. It's Art," *Globe and Mail*, April 5, 2006.

craftspeople are ambivalent about using the law because they envision their artistic practice in terms of sharing and giving, not market exchange. They know that they too base their work on established design vocabularies and traditions, used without permission. Given the cultural and economic situation, public shaming and constant innovation appear to be the most effective and appropriate responses to the pressures of the global design economy.[2]

Amateur crafters also face difficulties with copyright issues. The Internet has offered new possibilities for trading methods, patterns, ideas, and advice, and at the same time (not coincidentally, surely) the commodification of patterns for knitting, embroidery, or woodworking has increased. In the United States, "cease and desist" letters have been sent to those buying "pirated" patterns on eBay. Sewers and embroiderers are faced with aggressive copyright notices on patterns, telling them that they are not allowed to sell any work they make from the patterns. These are more often the actions of companies that own designs than the actions of independent designers. Insofar as they fail to distinguish between small-scale commercial use (such as church sales and school

> When you're trying to learn a technique, you learn to replicate something that you're seeing. All of the projects in school, that's what they are. But you're encouraged very early on to put your own stamp on it: we all know about not wanting to be copycats. You very quickly internalize this fear of being perceived as copying, even though copying is how we learn. It's very paradoxical.
>
> And the other thing is, we're all working with the same tools. We're all working with the same colour palette, we're all working with the same history of techniques, and we're all working three-dimensionally in the round: the material lends itself to certain things. So there are things, if you know glass, you can believe that people would come up with independently, because it's just what glass wants to do. Christmas balls are a very good example: everyone makes a blown globe of some sort, because glass just wants to be a bubble ... and that's the fundamental thing, the bubble. You can't claim that somebody's copying, because everybody's making a bubble from glass. You can't know who did it first.
>
> – Susan Belyea, glassmaker, interview with Laura Murray, Kingston, Ont.

fundraisers) and industrial-scale reproduction (making thousands of copies of a product for Wal-Mart), such companies make life difficult for crafters. But sometimes there is conflict between independent designers seeking to make a living from their work, and amateurs seeking to play and explore.[3] As art scholar Kirsty Robertson puts it:

> The debates over copyright within crafting communities are particularly thorny, jumping as they do from notions of a common shared history that should be open and welcoming to all, passing through the idea that as a gendered pastime crafting is regularly devalued—something its practitioners should work against—to more recent arguments that there are lucrative opportunities for professional crafters and designers that need to be protected through the copyrighting, patenting and trademarking of designs and processes.[4]

In practical terms, hobbyists probably have little to fear in terms of litigation. Even if a rights holder did object to the use of a design, there would be little hope for gain and a large chance of bad publicity in pur-

---

Is a sewing pattern covered by copyright?

- As an image, yes. You can't make a wallpaper pattern from it without first getting permission.
- As a process, no. When you make a dress from that pattern, you are essentially following its instructions; you are not copying the pattern itself. The Copyright Act, sections 64.1(1)(d), reminds us that copyright does not protect "any method or principle of manufacture or construction." By the same logic, we can all rejoice that making a cake is not an infringement of copyright in the recipe—even if the baker sells the cake.
- If the pattern bears a notice saying that you cannot use it to make products for sale, this may be considered a contract to which you agree by buying the pattern or using it. Whether this stricture is enforceable is not clear.

suing a lawsuit. When it falls to the individual to decide how to act in situations of dispute, the decision would probably be based as much on ethical considerations and community norms as on legal imperatives. For example, when the company Sew Fast/Sew Easy appropriated the name of a lively network of knitting circles by trademarking the phrase "Stitch and Bitch" and proceeded to pressure Internet servers to prevent others from using the name, an organized boycott emerged. The trademark, apparently, is legally but not politically valid.[5]

U.S. and Canadian law noticeably differ in the area of design.[6] The U.S. Copyright Act states, "The design of a useful article ... shall be considered a pictorial, graphic, or sculptural work only if, and only to the extent that, such design incorporates pictorial, graphic, or sculptural features that can be identified separately from, and are capable of existing independently of, the utilitarian aspects of the article."[7] This "separability requirement" has been understood to mean, for example, that clothing design is not covered by copyright. Canadian law has no such requirement; if a clothing designer in Canada makes, or authorizes the manufacture of, articles in numbers fewer than fifty-one, the work is copyrighted, whether or not the design is "separable" from the function of the article.[8]

Resources

- Canadian Intellectual Property Office, "A Guide to Industrial Designs," http://strategis.ic.gc.ca/sc_mrksv/cipo/id/idguide-e.pdf.
- Kal Raustiala, "Fashion Victims," *The New Republic Online*, March 15, 2005. A critique of U.S. efforts to give intellectual property protection to fashion design, http://www.tnr.com/doc.mhtml?i=w050314&s=raustiala03 1505.
- Pete Wells, "New Era of the Recipe Burglar," *Food & Wine*, November 2006. An account of celebrity chefs seeking intellectual property protection, http://foodandwine.com/articles/new-era-of-the-recipe-burglar.

9: Digital Rights Management

YOU TRY to copy a scene from a DVD into your movie editing software for a class presentation and find that you can't. You switch to Linux and lose access to your iTunes library. You see a photograph in a proprietary database, but you can't copy it—even though the copyright has expired and the work is in the public domain. You discover that a document that arrived two weeks ago has disappeared without a trace from your hard drive. You discover that a digital resource bought by your library a few years ago can no longer be accessed. You upload a CD and end up infecting your computer with a virus.

Welcome to the world of digital rights management, known, not always fondly, as DRM. DRM is a mechanism by which owners or vendors of digital intellectual goods can control access to and use of the materials they sell to consumers. Sometimes it is used to police copyright without having to go to court. Other times it is used to assert claims or regulate practices beyond the bounds of copyright. You often hear the acronyms TPM (technological protection measure) and RMI (rights management information) as well; we consider these to be subsets of the broader practice of DRM.

An economics of information approach can illuminate the effects of DRM. Intellectual or information goods, as we saw in chapter 1, are "public goods" in the sense that they have no built-in exclusion mechanisms; this is particularly true now that they can be embodied digitally. Legal and technological exclusion mechanisms make "public goods" into "private goods."

Economic theorists use the terms "intellectual goods" and "information goods" interchangeably. These "goods" include works and other materials covered by copyright; they also include data and information not covered by copyright, and works and other materials whose copyright has expired.

In recent years exclusion mechanisms have made digital technologies commercially and practically useful. Software encryption can ensure the security of your bank account and the privacy of your email. It allows online businesses to set passwords for subscription access, and it can guarantee the authenticity of electronically transmitted materials. But exclusion mechanisms improperly applied can be dangerous. Encryption systems are increasingly used as electronic gates, as new ways of fencing in or enclosing information spaces that in their analog form were open for common use. For example, a commercial enterprise might digitize old public domain books and make them available by subscription only.[1] Increasingly, corporate vendors of software, music, films, games, and texts are using DRM to limit uses and users of commercially publicly available materials.

Copyright law has several established safety valves that seek to ensure a reasonable balance between the rights of owners and the rights of users. Without users' rights, copyright would be an unmitigated monopoly, with all the economic and social disadvantages that monopolies pose. Digital locks, variously referred to as digital rights management systems, technological protections, or anti-circumvention devices, threaten to bypass the safety valves that have historically ameliorated the copyright monopoly.

But any technological device can be met with equally powerful countermeasures. Copy protection schemes can be defeated, just as locks on a safe can be opened with the right combination. This has led some rights holders to add a layer of protection for DRM systems through contracts (another exclusion mechanism), so that a customer who bypasses a DRM is also in breach of contract. There is also an increasing drive for Canadian legislation to follow the United States and make it unlawful to bypass digital locks, even in situations where it is perfectly lawful to get access to the contents of the material the lock is protecting.

DRM and Consumers

One way of understanding the effects or potential effects of DRM is to think of a DRM-free technology: the book. It used to be that copying a book required longhand transcription or retypesetting. Then we moved into the eras of photography, photocopying, and scanning. The copying of paper originals has become easier, but it is still expensive and time-consuming, and there is always a noticeable loss of quality. These constraints limit copyright infringement, which may make some rights owners look wistfully at the old technology of the book.

But we might also consider some of the qualities of books that are enabling for users—or, as we used to call them, readers. You can read books from beginning to end, in bits and pieces, or even backwards. You can read a book in secret or in public, in silence or out loud. You can quote from it. You can place bookmarks in a book, write in the margins, or even tear out the pages and tape them to the wall. You can lend a book to a friend. (Libraries, established by the mid-nineteenth century throughout North America, were designed to exploit this capacity.) You can also keep a book for a very long time. As long as you know the alphabet and the language and have taken care of the book, you can read it centuries after it was written. Finally, if you don't want a book any more, you can give it away or sell it.[2]

This quick summary reveals that we can do a number of things with purchased books that we may not be able to do with purchased digital files. There is nothing inherently limiting about digital technologies; in fact quite the contrary is true. But while digital media have the potential for expandability, unlimited usability, portability, sharing, and preservation, the prevalence of new forms of DRM brings new types of limitations.

For instance, if an electronic book, or "ebook," didn't have DRM imposed on it, you would be able to copy it, and your copy would be cheaper and better than most copies of paper books. But it does have DRM, and even if you know how to work around that limitation, another level of DRM might prevent you from doing anything with that copy. It doesn't matter what your goal is: your book might be an old one in the public domain, or you could be practising fair dealing, but the DRM would not discriminate.

> The Big Media conglomerates have realized that the traditional way of doing things—they sell you stuff and it's yours—isn't as good for them as—they sell you stuff and it's theirs. It's much better for them if they still own the stuff you buy from them.
>
> – defectivebydesign.org.

In any case, quite likely you never did hold all of the usual legal rights associated with ownership when you acquired the ebook. A careful look at the "terms of use" shows that you really only purchased a limited licence to do certain things with it. Under typical contracts for electronic media, you give up your rights to sell the material, or even lend it, and you give up the ability to change it into a different format or play it on a device other than the one preferred by the vendor. Customers of ebooks.com are made to acknowledge: "These limitations override (to the extent permitted by law) any right that I might have to use the Items under the copyright legislation in the country of use."[3] For the vendor, contractual provisions reserve rights that the Copyright Act does not— rights that historically belonged to *purchasers* of copyrighted materials. These reserved rights are part of what is known as "paracopyright." They are found in licences governing the use of computer programs and iTunes songs, for instance.[4]

While vendors' excuse for such restrictive practices is the need to prevent copyright infringement, they are actually unilaterally changing the nature of the market by limiting purchasers' uses of the goods and thus, if they're lucky, increasing their sales. (If you can't copy a CD to your iPod, for example, you might buy its contents again in a compatible format.) Vendors are developing "call home" mechanisms to track the

amount and nature of use and will increasingly base pricing or marketing strategies on the information gleaned in this way.

Economists refer to this practice as price discrimination: the idea is
that vendor and consumer both benefit from a price based on the amount
of use. But to enforce usage restrictions, along with other provisions in
the contract, "call home" mechanisms may be invading users' privacy.

Ironically, DRM is not proving to be effective against industrial-scale piracy.
The biggest "leak" in the exclusion mechanism for movies, for example, appears to be people with video cameras in cinemas, not people with advanced
de-encryption skills. What DRM *is* doing is frustrating law-abiding consumers'
use of material that they have legally acquired. Russell McOrmond, a well-
known Canadian digital rights activist, argues that the barriers that DRM places
on consumers pushes some of them to infringe more than they might do in its
absence:

> While I believe that DRM systems slow down the lawful use of content
> by law abiding citizens, I have seen no evidence of any DRM that has
> slowed down infringement. If anything, the inconvenience of using
> content on a DRM system provides its own incentive to circumvent the
> DRM. If circumventing the DRM is itself illegal, there is then no incentive
> to obey copyright or pay the copyright holder given the activity of ac-
> cessing the content on technology of our own choice is illegal. I strongly
> believe that DRM systems can only increase, not decrease, the rate of
> copyright infringement.

In other words, if consumers face hurdles to the reasonable use of materials
that they have legally acquired, they will feel no compunction about leaping
those hurdles, even if it becomes illegal to do so. McOrmond argues that DRM
reduces consumers' respect for copyright.

Source: Russell McOrmond, posting to CopyCamp, September 2006.

DRM and the Law

DRM is beginning to arouse debate and resistance as a consumer issue:
many people are feeling not just unfairly treated but also at risk. The

2005 Sony rootkit—which surreptitiously loaded software and exposed hard drives to a virus upon insertion of a copy-protected CD—became a notorious scandal.[5] But it is possible that fairer pricing, safer software, and more transparency in the terms of transactions may satisfy many people.

Problems resulting from the proliferation of DRM systems cannot be adequately addressed as a consumer issue. DRM has equally important consequences for freedom of speech, for the texture and dynamism of our social and cultural fabric, and for access to representations of the past. It does not allow the exercise of ethical, legal, or professional judgment. It routinely prevents people from utilizing material in customary and heretofore lawful ways. DRM systems and accompanying contractual limitations on use together clearly challenge the previously established copyright norm that—as Canada's Supreme Court put it in the *Théberge* case—"once an authorized copy of a work is sold to a member of the public, it is generally for the purchaser, not the author, to determine what happens to it." The Court, emphasizing society's long-term interests, warned against the "excessive control by holders of copyrights and other forms of intellectual property."[6]

In recent years the Canadian government has been under massive pressure from the U.S. government and lobbyists of large rights owners to make it illegal to circumvent DRM systems for any purpose whatsoever. In 1998 the United States passed its notorious Digital Millennium Copyright Act (DMCA), which offered special legal protection to digital rights management systems and technological protection measures.[7] Under the DMCA, it is unlawful to circumvent technological protections, even when the use made of the accessed material is not infringing. In addition to outlawing direct acts of circumvention of access controls, the DMCA also proscribes the provision of devices that could aid others in frustrating either access controls or copy protections.[8] These device prohibitions have proven to be the most troublesome aspect of the DMCA, because there is no general exemption for acts of circumvention and the making of circumvention tools for purposes that are otherwise justified and lawful—such as library or research purposes.

The DMCA has also come under severe criticism from researchers and innovators in software design and development because it has

What you can do to resist DRM systems.

As a consumer:

- Avoid buying products that feature DRM.
- Learn about DRM (see the resources listed at the end of this chapter).
- Encourage your workplaces and public institutions to take strong stands against DRM—a boycott by large purchasers can have a very real effect. (See chapter 13.)
- Use business models that don't depend upon DRM—for example, Creative Commons licensing used as a way of marketing licensed commercial uses. (See chapter 18.)
- Share information about how to circumvent DRM as it constrains users' rights.

As a citizen:

- Write (and even write again) to your MP and the ministers of Industry and Canadian Heritage, telling them of your concerns. Letters from ordinary Canadians do have political weight.
- Educate others.
- Practise users' rights: when they are limited by technology, complain to the vendor or tell your MP.

been construed to ban "reverse engineering" (looking at or taking apart source code for purposes of analysis), on which a great deal of research and development depends. It thus dampens innovators' ability to make new devices and software interoperable with existing ones. This may mean that consumers become locked into dependency on certain systems and are even more susceptible to the costs associated with planned obsolescence.[9] While some creators may see DRM as a promising development, they too would bear increased creative and financial costs under a Canadian DMCA.

Even though Canada has not passed DMCA-style provisions, it has already been influenced by the act: it is difficult to find software to circumvent encryption, and many Canadians wrongly believe such software to be illegal.

Resources

Canada

- Digital Copyright Canada website, http://digital-copyright.ca. Website run by Russell McOrmond, Open Source software developer.
- Michael Geist, "Anti-Circumvention Legislation and Competition Policy: Defining a Canadian Way?" Jeremy deBeer, "Constitutional Jurisdiction over Paracopyright Laws"; and Mark Perry, "Rights Management Information"—three articles in Geist, ed., *In the Public Interest*.
- Online Rights Canada website, http://www.onlinerights.ca. A grassroots advocacy organization.
- "30 days of DRM," by Michael Geist, September 2006, www.michaelgeist. ca/daysofdrm. Itemizes thirty public interest concerns about DRM, and thirty things you can do about it.

International

- British Library Manifesto on Copyright, September 2006, http://www. bl.uk/news/pdf/ipmanifesto.pdf. Focuses on the dangers of DRM and associated contracts for libraries, users' rights.
- Defective by Design,org.: A Campaign of the Free Software Organization website, defectivebydesign.org.
- Electronic Frontier Foundation, "Unintended Consequences: Seven Years Under the DMCA."

10: Education

THE EDUCATION sector is a major market for copyrighted products. Schools and post-secondary students buy hundreds of millions of dollars' worth of books, software, and other copyrighted material every year. For example, in 2005–06 the Queen's University Campus Bookstore sold $7.8 million in textbooks—almost $400 per student—which doesn't even include books bought beyond assigned texts or photocopied course packs licensed through Access Copyright. The average Canadian household spends only $280 on books per year. Given the scale of the educational market, publishers are anxious about any erosion of it. Leery of photocopying practices, and now equally anxious about the Internet distribution of teaching materials, they have advocated narrow understandings of fair dealing and expanded use of collective licensing.

While they might assert the users' rights articulated by the courts, school boards and post-secondary institutions are concerned about liability and statutory damages. They often pay hefty licence fees instead, imposing costs on taxpayers or students that are not always easy to justify, or they enact policies that restrict students' and teachers' activities.

Canadian law evidently does not provide sufficiently clear and flexible provisions for activities on our campuses and in our schools.

After all, educational institutions are not only markets: they are major incubators for future creativity and economic growth. Considering copyright's roots in the 1710 British act "for the encouragement of learning," we might expect copyright to make things easier for people working in learning environments. There are two avenues to improve this situation: legislation and internal policy and practice. Some of the proposals for legislative reform seem to confuse and constrain matters even further; others seem unlikely to gain a wide hearing. But we do not have to wait for Ottawa: with a growing awareness of the big picture of copyright, change can happen at the level of the institution and even at the level of the individual teacher and student.

Teachers and students often confuse three distinct mechanisms that allow them to make use of certain copyrighted materials without infringement. The first mechanism is the specific educational exceptions in the Copyright Act; the second is the licence that an educational institution signs with Access Copyright, granting certain photocopying rights in exchange for royalties. A third mechanism is fair dealing.

Who owns the copyright in student work?

The student. Any reproduction beyond the bounds of fair dealing must be done with her or his permission.

Who owns the copyright in teachers' work?

It depends. Elementary- and secondary-school teachers often do not own work done in the course of their employment: to determine the policy, they will have to check with the school board. In colleges too, copyright often rests with the institution. In universities, faculty research has conventionally been owned by the faculty, but other work such as correspondence courses may be treated differently; academic staff too should check the collective agreement or university policy. Contracts with funders also sometimes contain constraints and conditions. See chapter 5 for more on copyright and employment.

Educational Exceptions

The 1997 amendments to the Copyright Act (Phase II of copyright reform) contained new provisions applicable to certain educational institutions. Like the corresponding exceptions for libraries, the educational exceptions define a particular set of circumstances in which infringement will be excused; and the new rights (or newly explicit rights) are generally offset by counter-limitations, record-keeping requirements, or other constraints.

These sections of the act do not apply to all educational institutions: the act's definition of "educational institution" includes publicly administered schools, community colleges, and universities, as well as anyone acting under the authority of these institutions, but does not include private schools or training institutes unless they are formally registered as non-profit.[1]

The educational exceptions are highly restrictive (see Table 10). Given the limitations on place and audience,[2] a teacher cannot take a class to perform a school play at a nursing home or to listen to a recording in the park. It makes sense that schools pay royalties for large-scale publicized productions for which admission is charged, but not that smaller-scale or more impromptu community efforts be hampered. The requirement that copies of a work can only be made if no commercially available alternative exists places a heavy practical burden on teachers.[3] To comply they would have to plan certain activities well ahead of time to be able to search for, and possibly order, alternatives. Most teachers do not plan their classes or compose tests and exams months in advance. Similarly, the record-keeping requirements in section 29.9 reduce the flexibility and utility of the exceptions they pertain to. Significantly, the exceptions cover the playing of music in class, but not the showing of films. Copyright has historically treated works in all media equally, and given the variety of new technologies available such distinctions are especially confusing and constraining.[4]

Shortly after the new educational exceptions were added to the Copyright Act, David Vaver observed that they "do not always fully capture the wide range and diversity of modern educational practice. Their interpretation will therefore need a heavier-than-usual dose of common sense if they are to work effectively."[5] We hope that teachers are indeed exercising their common sense in the implementation of these exceptions, and seeing past them to fair dealing.

The Access Copyright Licence

Schools, school boards, and post-secondary institutions in Canada outside Quebec sign a licence with Access Copyright allowing certain photocopying.[6] There may be some variations among the licences, so you should ask to see your institution's licence to be sure of your specific circumstances. Broadly speaking, Part A of the Access Copyright licences allows multiple copies for classroom or administrative use of "up to 10% of a published work" or the following, whichever is greater:

- an entire chapter that is less than 20 per cent of the book's length
- an entire article or page from a periodical
- an entire story, poem, essay, etc. from a book or periodical containing other such pieces
- an entire artistic item from a book containing other such items
- an entire encyclopedia or dictionary item.[7]

I don't think all the material in my course pack is covered by copyright. Why am I paying copyright fees for it?

The bookstore personnel who put together these course packs at the request of an instructor usually simply count the pages and apply the Access Copyright charges. If instructors decide that a particular part of the readings does not require the payment of copyright royalties, they have to explain why to the bookstore. In some cases it could be straightforward. Maybe the work is a publication of the U.S. government in which no copyright subsists, or of the Canadian government, which is subject to a permissive reproduction licence. Sometimes the material is a copyrighted edition of a work in the public domain, in which case copyright subsists in the apparatus surrounding the public domain work. If that particular edition is not required, instructors might look to Project Gutenberg or other online public domain sources.

Table 10. Copyright and Education: Activities and Constraints

Activity permitted	Constraints	Copyright Act Section
to make a manual reproduction of a work onto a dry-erase board, flip chart, or other similar surface intended for displaying handwritten material	for the purposes of education or training, on the premises	29.4(1)(a)
to make a copy of a work for the purpose of projection using an overhead projector or similar device	for the purposes of education or training, on the premises; not applicable if the work is commercially available in a medium appropriate for the purpose	29.4(1)(b)
to reproduce, translate, or perform in public on the premises a work or other subject matter as required for a test or examination	on the premises; not applicable if the work is commercially available in a medium appropriate for the purpose	29.4(2)(a)
to communicate by telecommunication a work or other subject matter as required for a test or examination	same as above	29.4(2)(b)
to have a group consisting primarily of students perform a work publicly	for education or training purposes, on the premises, if the audience consists primarily of students, teachers, or persons who are directly responsible for setting the curriculum	29.5(a)
to play a sound recording	same as above	29.5(b)
to play a broadcast at the time of its communication to the public	same as above	29.5(c)

Table 10. (continued)

to make a single copy of a news program or a news commentary program, excluding documentaries, for the purposes of playing the copy for students	for education or training purposes; within a year of making the copy the institution must either destroy it or pay the applicable royalties	29.6(1)(a)
to play the copy of the news program referred to above in public within one year after the making of the copy	for education or training purposes, on the premises, to an audience consisting primarily of students	29.6(1)(b)
to make a single copy of a non-news program to decide whether to perform the copy for educational or training purposes.	recording can only be kept for 30 days before royalties are payable; records must be kept	29.7(1), 29.9
to play such a program	for education or training purposes, on the premises, to an audience consisting primarily of students, if the institution pays royalties; records must be kept	29.7(3), 29.9

The Access licences do *not* cover copying of government publications; print music; workbooks and other single-use materials; unpublished works; letters to the editor and advertisements; instruction manuals; newsletters; and works on the exclusion list or containing a notice preventing copying.

The Access licences only cover photocopying: they do not cover copying by means of recording devices, digital technology, or other means.[8] Nor do they cover copies used in association with political or commercial activities.

Part A of the licences allows copies to be made for educational or recreational purposes, but not for resale. The price for Part A is based on the number of full-time equivalent students (FTES). Post-secondary institutions now pay $3.38 per FTE. Elementary- and secondary-school licences are in a similar range, but Access Copyright has applied to the

Copyright Board to raise the rate to $12 per student per year.

Any copies made for sale, such as the compilation of course readings known as "course packs," fall under Section B of the licence; rights are paid for under a per-page scheme. University and college students pay 10 cents per print page (usually twice that per photocopied page) in addition to the cost of the copying itself.

Fair Dealing

CCH v. Law Society of Upper Canada (2004) explicitly held that users' rights are a part of Canadian copyright law. Since the case concerned library photocopying, the ruling specifically extended fair dealing concepts to libraries. Nonetheless, it is not a stretch to utilize some of the general principles set out in the *CCH* case to make strong arguments that the principles of fair dealing also extend to many of the activities covered by the educational exceptions and the Access licences, and others beyond. *CCH* makes it clear that fair dealing can be practised in libraries, by library patrons offsite, by library workers working on behalf of patrons, and even by lawyers and their employees in private (for-profit) practice. Why shouldn't the principle also extend to schools?[9] The Supreme Court stated:

> As an integral part of the scheme of copyright law, the s. 29 fair dealing exception is always available. Simply put, a library can always attempt to prove that its dealings with a copyrighted work are fair under s. 29 of the Copyright Act. It is only if a library were unable to make out the fair dealing exception under s. 29 that it would need to turn to s. 30.2 of the Copyright Act to prove that it qualified for the library exemption.[10]

It would follow from *CCH*, then, that an educational institution can rely on fair dealing in addition to the special educational exceptions.

That said, Canada's fair dealing provision has major limitations. Before you can get to the analysis of "fairness," you have to show that, strictly speaking, the use was made for the purpose of research, private study, criticism, review, or news reporting. Furthermore, it is not clear that multiple copies would meet the "character of the dealing" test that *CCH* proposes for determining the fairness of the use. *CCH* observes, "If multiple copies of works are being widely distributed, this will tend to be unfair."[11] That is why educational institutions rely on the Access Copyright licence.

Still, many of the uses for which Access is paid are classic cases of fair dealing. An image of an emu in a Grade 3 science project, a newspaper article circulated for critique, the fragments of a song transformed into a music project: these could all reasonably be construed as fair dealing. The price of the licence should reflect this principle much more than it does; and perhaps in the process of renewing their licences elementary and secondary schools will succeed in holding the price of the licences steady based on the strength of *CCH*. Furthermore, some activities not covered by the Access licence, such as the copying of advertisements and letters to the editor, or copying done for political purposes, may also constitute fair dealing.

Similarly, activities enabled but constrained by the exceptions may be more freely practised under the fair dealing umbrella. If a public performance of a work by a class of school children is not for profit and is done for educational purposes (how could it not be?), it will most likely meet the fair dealing criteria. It really shouldn't matter how many parents are in the audience or whether the performance is in a nearby church hall or community centre. A teacher should not be nervous about building class discussion around a clip from a documentary or a drama shown on TV, whether or not all the right forms are filled out. The activity probably meets the fair dealing criteria, and no royalty payment should be required.

Legislative Prospects

Most educators and students who pay attention to copyright agree that the educational community needs broader users' rights in line with the *CCH* decision. But there has been great debate about how this goal should be accomplished.

One approach is to tweak the existing exceptions, updating them here and there and adding in new ones as possible. That was the approach taken in 2005 by Bill C-60. The legislation included a number of specific provisions intended to amend—or we might say complicate—the collection of exceptions. One provision, for example, tried to account for distance education activities, also referred to as "technology enhanced learning."[12] The reliance on specific exceptions has also generally been the approach taken by the associations that represent the educational institutions (or rather the administrators of the educational institutions) such as the Council of Ministers of Education, Canada (CMEC) and the Association of Universities and Colleges of Canada (AUCC). Their position is not surprising, because educational administrators are notoriously risk-adverse and prefer situations that are fairly cut and dried and do not rely on interpretation by students and teachers.

One provision that was not part of Bill C-60, to the disappointment of CMEC and AUCC, was an exception that would have explicitly permitted use of the Internet in educational settings. This idea of such an exception arose in 2004 when the House of Commons Standing Committee on Canadian Heritage recommended that the government "put in place a regime of extended collective licensing to ensure that educational institutions' use of information and communications technologies to deliver copyright protected works can be more efficiently licensed."[13] The proposal generated quite a bit of controversy. Along with libraries and museums, schools and universities themselves generate a massive volume of high-quality, freely available online educational material. This and other material they may use has been placed online with no expectation of payment, even though copyright does subsist in it.

A central issue here is the nature of the Internet. Publishers and evidently some members of Parliament see the Internet as fundamentally a commercial realm, from which a few public spaces can be carved out, like conservation areas or parks. But many others see publicly available material as the essence and norm of the Internet. By this logic, those who want to limit access to or use of Internet material are certainly free to do so with passwords and low resolution images, but other material is governed by "implied consent" for non-commercial use.

In response to the extended licensing proposal, CMEC and AUCC have proposed that a special exception be added to the Copyright Act to ensure that educational use of publicly available sites on the Internet is not infringing. They continue to make this proposal a priority in their discussions with policy-makers.[14]

The "educational exception" idea has met with great opposition from publishers and Access Copyright, who both want to exploit the emerging possibility for a digital educational market. We find the idea of licensing educational Internet use egregious. However, our position is that specific exceptions will always be inadequate to the practice of teaching and learning, especially given the rapidly shifting nature of technology. We are concerned that such an exception may be taken to imply that fair uses not covered by exceptions *are* infringing.

In the end, along with many other copyright scholars and the Canadian Federation of Students, we contend that educational needs would more properly be addressed through a broadened version of fair dealing (see chapter 19). Such a move would advantage both artists and educational enterprises, neither of whom are well served by the current categorical approach to fair dealing. The *CCH* tests for fairness would, of course, continue to apply.

Resources

- Canadian Federation of Students, "Copyright for the Public Interest," 2006.
- Copyright Management Centre website, http://www.copyright.iupui.edu. For information on copyright issues in U.S. education.
- Howard Knopf, "Excess Caution," 2006. A convincing critique of "Copyright Matters!" an educational resource provided by CMEC.
- The Learning Commons website, http://www.learningcommons.co.za. This South African site is a rare example of a multidimensional and balanced educational resource on copyright.

11: Film & Video

WHILE THE Copyright Act contains few provisions specific to film and video, copyright pressures are especially pronounced in this field of artistic endeavour. The independent documentary or non-commercial filmmaker is a "canary in the coalmine" for freedom of expression in Canada. If copyright is not working for these people—and it is not—we are all affected because independent films and videos provide an important stream of commentary on our world. Furthermore, the recent proliferation of outlets for amateur filmmakers (YouTube being the most famous at the moment) increases the number of creators affected by copyright.[1]

One pressing problem for filmmakers is that urban spaces are overflowing with trademarked or copyrighted material—any shot is likely to contain a corporate logo or a fragment of recorded music. Even inside shoots are risky: clothing, background posters, and TV constantly present proprietary images to the camera. If you are working on a large project, the prospect for "product placement" fees can work to your advantage, even though you might be expected to give up some artistic control. But if you are working with a small audience in mind, or trying to maintain artistic independence, companies might try to collect money from *you* for these glimpses of proprietary images.

Meanwhile, prices for clips from television or commercial cinema are extremely expensive, well beyond the means of many beginning or independent filmmakers—and yet they are the main access to the raw material and popular culture of the past hundred years. As filmmaker Walter Forsberg says, "I wasn't around before 1980, so if I'm going to show those times, I have to use somebody else's footage."[2]

What should a filmmaker do? Well, first the good news.

Many of the constraints on film come from trademark law, not copyright law. There is little basis in trademark law for demands from trademark owners for royalties from filmmakers for including images of a trademark logo. The courts have demonstrated repeatedly that unless there is a strong likelihood of consumer confusion, reproducing or mimicing a trademark does not constitute trademark infringement. In other words, a finding of trademark infringement requires some use of the mark in a related line of trade. In two recent Canadian Supreme Court cases, a fast-food restaurant chain, Barbie's, and a clothing store, Boutique Cliquot, were allowed to keep their names because they were not selling the same thing as the original trademark owner.[3] These decisions suggest that under trademark law, if you're not selling hamburgers, you can reproduce the "Big M"—and if you're not selling leatherwear or sweatshirts, you can reproduce the Roots logo.

But commercial logos are not only trademarks: they are also artistic works in which copyright subsists. Still, there are several reasons why reproducing copyrighted artwork without permission might not constitute infringement. For one thing, there is always the threshold requirement of substantiality (chapter 4). Many fleeting bits of music and other copyrighted material constitute non-substantial reproduction and thus would not even implicate section 3 rights.

Also, your use may fall under the rubric of criticism or news reporting: if you think it does, try out the other five parts of the fair dealing test from the *CCH v. Law Society of Upper Canada* case (see chapter 6). The appropriation of clips and images from commercial culture is part of a widespread practice in video and media art—work shown primarily in galleries rather than in theatres or in the media. Much of this work is critical of various aspects of popular culture—and hence possibly is "criticism" within the terms of the *CCH* case.[4] The *CCH* decision offers a further

line of defence for this type of work in its recognition of the importance
of norms of particular "trades and industries." Other documentaries reveal
hidden facts that the public has a right to know, and hence clearly constitute reporting. Dramas might not fit the fair dealing categories so easily,
but it is certainly not out of the question that they could.

In addition to the substantiality test and fair dealing, two specific exceptions in the act may help: the "incidental use" and "buildings and
public art" exceptions. Section 30.7 states:

> It is not an infringement of copyright to incidentally and not de-
> liberately
>   (a) include a work or other subject-matter in another work or
> other subject-matter; or
>   (b) do any act in relation to a work or other subject-matter that
> is incidentally and not deliberately included in another work or
> other subject-matter.

This exception has never been tested in court, and proving "incidental"
inclusion in an edited film might be quite difficult. Still, it would seem
to have been devised just for the serendipitous documentary situation in
which the mental-hospital patient breaks out into song, or the firefight-
ers are sitting around watching *The Sound of Music*.

Section 32.2(1) states:

> It is not an infringement of copyright ...
>   (b) for any person to reproduce, in a painting, drawing, engrav-
> ing, photograph or cinematographic work
>   (i) an architectural work, provided the copy is not in the nature
> of an architectural drawing or plan, or
>   (ii) a sculpture or work of artistic craftsmanship or a cast or
> model of a sculpture or work of artistic craftsmanship, that is per-
> manently situated in a public place or building.

This provision should allow filmmakers to ignore permission demands
from owners of buildings and public art—unless permission is needed to
get access to private property.

One day in 2005 an employee of CKY, the Winnipeg CTV network affiliate, called the filmmakers of a collective called L'Atelier National du Manitoba and offered them three carloads of videotapes that the station was about to throw away. The product of this gold mine was a film about the demise of the Winnipeg Jets NHL franchise. *Death by Popcorn* attracted attention in Winnipeg hockey and art circles, but it didn't become nationally famous until CTV decided to go after its makers for copyright infringement. The *Globe and Mail*, CBC, and *Winnipeg Free Press* pounced on the story, and public outcry emerged in letters to the editor and blogs.

L'Atelier member Matthew Rankin recollects:

> And then out of the blue we get an e-mail from the general manager of CKY, and he was like oh jeez, I didn't know that this was such a big deal, I think we can meet and talk about this. So we went and talked to him, and it was really bizarre because he was very friendly and he bought us lunch. And he apologized. He said I'm sorry that I sent the operations manager after you. This is my responsibility, we were just worried about the liability if the NHL came after us … Just disregard that letter, you don't have to sign or anything. You can show this movie at film festivals, that's no problem, because that's definitely not a commercial type vehicle, and I hope we can be friends. You should come and pitch us documentary ideas, and this kind of thing. It was the most amazing thing because literally the last time I was at CKY they really treated us like we were the scum of the earth, and now their general manager is begging for forgiveness. I really feel that it can be kind of an inspiring story to people who run into this kind of problem. I can't help but feel very cynical about it in a way, because if they didn't get a bunch of bad press then I would have had to sign something saying that I broke the law. And I could've been sued, and all of this. So a little bad press went a long way with them and they ended up dropping the thing.

Source: Matthew Rankin, Winnipeg, interview with Kirsty Robertson.

Outside of the statutory provisions an evolving and subtle general practice in the industry also comes into play. Fear of public embarrassment can sometimes restrain would-be copyright bullies. Some recent well-known films have not sought clearances and have not triggered

In 2000 I did a personal documentary called *Sea in the Blood*, and I wanted to use a line of text from Joni Mitchell, which goes "The wind is in from Africa/ last night, I couldn't sleep." There was not to be any music used, just the line of text you'd see on screen, and I decided because [the video] would be aired that I would try and clear copyright on it. And first of all it took a *long* time to find out who held the rights for it, even within Sony, like who actually was responsible for assigning permission. And that was with the help of a friend of mine, a feature film producer who put me on to lawyers who were very helpful. And then they decided that they wanted $2,000 U.S., which would have been a huge portion of the budget for this line of text that takes about two seconds to go across the screen. The total budget of my video was just over $14,000. So we went back and forth, back and forth, back and forth and eventually I think they charged $200 U.S.—that was just for a particular territory, and over a very limited period of time. So in the end I got a much better deal.

But it struck me how copyright really is meant to work from corporation to corporation. To do independent work, well, for one we don't have producers, generally, and two, the dividends are so small for the copyright holding companies like Sony, that they don't really want to deal with us. So it's easier for them to say no, you don't have permission than to go through this elaborate process, which then will give them something like $200 in the end.

– Richard Fung, video artist and faculty, Ontario College of Art and Design, Toronto, interview with Kirsty Robertson.

lawsuits: *Super Size Me*, the documentary film about a man who lived entirely on McDonald's food for a month, is a prominent example.

Filmmakers might decide to go ahead and make a film without clearances, but here is the bad news. If they ever want to get their work on TV or into wide distribution, they have to get by the "Errors and Omissions" insurance lawyers. Documentary filmmaker Kevin McMahon explains the experience this way:

Anything we sell to a broadcaster has to be insured. They demand E & O insurance to protect them in case they're sued. The way it works is that our lawyer will go through a production and they'll flag it: they'll say this, this, this, and this are a problem. Change 'em.

If you decide to stand your ground, then the ultimate decision is made by a lawyer working for the insurance company. And so I might want something to be in, and even a commissioning editor at a broadcasting company might want something to be in, but both of us are overruled by, first, the corporate policy of the broadcaster that you must have this insurance, and finally by a lawyer in the employ of an insurance company.[5]

Countless filmmakers say the same thing: it is E & O insurers who make the law. In this environment, filmmakers have to design their films and schedules to minimize permissions (which may amount to a misrepresentation of the commercialized world), and they have to budget time and money for the permissions that do remain. Often in the end they can only afford permissions for limited territories or time periods, which dooms their work to obsolescence. In what the Documentary Organization of Canada (DOC) calls a growing "clearance culture," even student film festivals are now asking for copyright clearance at the time of initial application.[6]

As in so many of the other realms we are discussing, we can't expect corporate culture to change its set of practices anytime soon. But Canada's generous investment of public funds in the film and TV industries does offer some opportunities. Public institutions such as the National Film Board and CBC could and should be doing more to make their material accessible and affordable to filmmakers—and indeed to all Canadians who have paid for the creation of that material in the first place. As things now stand, publicly funded broadcasters or distributors are demanding money from filmmakers who are working off grants from public agencies, and each stage of this cycle wastes both time and money. With the whole industry being publicly subsidized, it makes little sense to be shifting money from one pocket to the other. At the very least public broadcasters should enact and publicize a sliding permissions scale; they could even look into the Creative Commons licence as a way of distinguishing between commercial and non-commercial use (see chapter 18).

The NFB, CBC, TVO, and other state-funded media organizations could also reconsider their insurance arrangements. Along with granting agencies, they could take a firm public interest stand on fair dealing and users' rights—promoting, for example, the explicit inclusion of documentary films within the "news reporting" category of fair dealing. They could place more of their archives online—following an experiment set in place by the BBC in 2003 and expanding on the NFB's posting of fifty animated shorts on its website.[7]

> Fifty short films are great, but instead of calling it a collection, let's call it a start. The power and beauty of the Internet aren't found in carefully curated exhibits. Rather, they lie in giving people access to information in its breadth and depth.
>
> If you want us to engage with the history of Canadian animation, don't show us just one piece from an animator such as Evelyn Lambart, a pioneering Canadian I discovered through the NFB site. Let us explore the archive of her work, and to explore the links between her work and that of her peers and successors. Indeed, *Mr. Frog Went A-Courting*, the Lambart film that the NFB calls her masterpiece, is mentioned on the site, but not screened.
>
> Instead, I found it on YouTube. Let's bring her home.
>
> – Ivor Tossell, "Much Is Missing from NFB Freebie," *Globe and Mail*, July 21, 2006

Of course, such projects have large technological and legal overheads for institutions strapped for money—but if those bodies started sharing their wealth, they would only increase the number of allies they have in the country.[8] Or imagine the converse: if CTV or Global were to beat the CBC to the punch on open access to television news archives, the very idea of public broadcasting would be undermined.

Resources

- Keith Aoki, Jennifer Jenkins, and James Boyle, *Bound by Law? Tales from the Public Domain*, March 2006. An informative and entertaining comic book treatment of copyright issues in U.S. documentary films.
- Center for Social Media, American University, Washington, D.C., website, http://www.centerforsocialmedia.org/. A rich source of information about documentary filmmaking, new media, and citizen participation. Would be a great model for a Canadian initiative.
- Howard Knopf, "The Copyright Clearance Culture and Canadian Documentaries: A White Paper on Behalf of the Documentary Organisation of Canada," Nov. 22, 2006, http://www.docorg.ca.

12: Journalism

JOURNALISTS FACE copyright issues coming from two directions: they need to assert their own rights in a media marketplace increasingly dominated by large corporations; and they need to have strong fair dealing rights so they can tell the stories they uncover. The public interest is served when freelance journalists can support themselves well enough to develop their expertise and skills over a lifetime. But it is also served when the citizenry has broad access to the news record: news is a powerful democratic tool and is the embodiment of shared history. The Copyright Act and the courts are quite sensitive to the various rights and interests at play in this profession, but concentration of media ownership poses serious challenges to a productive balance of interests.

Who Owns What?

Who owns copyright in a given newspaper column or magazine story? Not surprisingly, the answer is, it depends. If there is a contract between writer and publisher, that's where you'll find your answer. However, there are clear default rules for staff writers and freelancers. Section 13(3) of the Copyright Act applies to staff writers along with bank workers, civil servants, and all employees: it provides that, without any agreement to the contrary, the employer is the first owner of work done in the course of employment. Employees cannot benefit from or control reuse of material they have created in the course of employment.[1] Staff journalists do have one special right compared to other employees: "in the absence of any agreement to the contrary," they have the "right to restrain publication" beyond newspaper or magazine form. It is not clear what this right is worth, but it might be something that staff journalists should try not to sign away.[2]

Freelancers are not employees, and hence they are the first owners of their work.[3] They are governed by the general rule on copyright assignments in section 13.4, which states: "The owner of the copyright ... may assign the right, either wholly or partially, and either generally or subject to limitations relating to territory, medium or sector of the market or other limitations ... and either for the whole term of the copyright or for any other part thereof." The journalistic convention, until recent years, was for freelancers to license "first North American rights" to the first buyer: that is, you might be paid one dollar per word in exchange for first publication rights in a New Brunswick newspaper. You could then go on to sell reprint rights in British Columbia, translation rights in Germany, and broadcast rights in Japan. However, with the rise of media conglomerates and digital technologies, freelancers have lost many opportunities to redeploy their work. While new possibilities exist for syndication or selling digital rights, freelancers are increasingly facing strong-arming. For example, a notorious Canwest/Global contract transfers all rights "throughout the universe, in perpetuity," and the individual who refuses to sign such a contract risks losing the job to someone who will.[4]

According to a study by the Professional Writers Association of Canada (PWAC), the average freelance writer lost 26 per cent in purchasing power in the decade from 1995 to 2005.[5] This problem is not directly caused by copyright, nor can it be resolved by copyright alone. But it is still (or all the more) important for freelancers to know that they have more rights than media outlets often let on. The increasingly

> Many young journalists leave the profession. One of them says: "Every year the rates get a little worse, and every year the real features give up a little more space to packaged stuff. Suffering for art's sake is one thing, but suffering for charts about $5,000 barbecues? Life's too short."
>
> Source: Posting to Canadian Magazines discussion, by anonymous journalist, May 29, 2006.

standard publisher demand for an exclusive grant of all rights represents a unilateral *change* to traditional industry practice. It is backed by bargaining power, not by anything in the Copyright Act.

At the same time as a large media corporation might be demanding all rights from its "content providers," it is licensing fewer and fewer rights to consumers. Thus someone who pays for access to the *Toronto Star*'s "Pages of the Past" archive, which goes back to 1892, must agree to ignore that a great deal of the material to be found there is in the public domain: "Distribution, transmission, or republication of any material from The Toronto Star—Pages of the Past is strictly prohibited without the prior written permission of Toronto Star Newspapers Limited."[6] The British Library noted in 2006 that "twenty eight out of thirty licences [for electronic resources] offered to the British Library and selected randomly were found to be more restrictive than rights that currently exist within copyright law."[7] Large media corporations are amassing more and more rights by fiat at the expense of writers and readers alike.

Despite or because of this situation, PWAC maintains, "There is no such thing as a non-negotiable contract, so negotiate."[8] The Association's main overall advice is to make sure that all licensed rights are enumerated in writing and separately paid for. Following this advice means that all rights not explicitly mentioned in a contract are reserved to the writer. Thus, "selling a story" to *Canadian Gardening* might actually mean licensing a one-time print publication, website display for a set time span, and resale to commercial archival databases on specified terms. The writer could then go on to sell other rights, such as translation or secondary publication, to other publishers. This distinction between an exclusive right and a non-exclusive right is important: it is to an author's advantage to enter into non-exclusive arrangements, or to make very sure indeed that the price for an exclusive right is high enough to make it worthwhile. If the magazine wants exclusive web publication rights, for example, it

Robertson v. Thomson (2006)

The situation:

In 1995 Heather Robertson wrote two articles for *The Globe and Mail*. Subsequently, the *Globe* included them without her permission in three electronic databases, and Robertson sued for copyright infringement. The *Globe* argued that it had copyright in the newspaper as a compilation, and thus had the right to this reproduction.

The result:

In 2006, in a 5-4 decision, the Supreme Court dismissed the *Globe*'s claim:

> We ... agree with the Publishers that their right to reproduce a substantial part of the newspaper includes the right to reproduce the newspaper without advertisements, graphs and charts, or in a different layout and using different fonts. But it does not follow that the articles of the newspaper can be decontextualized to the point that they are no longer presented in a manner that maintains their intimate connection with the rest of that newspaper.... These products are more akin to databases of individual articles rather than reproductions of the *Globe*. Thus, in our view, the originality of the freelance articles is reproduced; the originality of the newspapers is not.

The Court said that the *Globe* could reproduce aggregated pages of its newspaper if the emphasis were on the compilation as a whole; but unauthorized reproduction of articles by freelancers in a search engine enabling more fine-grained and independent searching by individual article would be infringement.

should pay more than if it is allowing the writer to license web publication rights to others as well. Similarly, prices for permanent rights transfers and for temporary licences might differ considerably. "You get what you pay for" should be the freelancer's motto.

The *Robertson v. Thomson* case of 2006 confirmed that a publisher holds only those rights that are explicitly itemized in the contract. Absent such a specification, all remaining rights are reserved to the freelancer. Philosophically, however, the issue is much more complex, relating to

Allen v. Toronto Star (1997)

The situation:

In 1985 Liberal Party Member of Parliament Sheila Copps made the cover of *Saturday Night* magazine, dressed in black leather and sitting astride a Harley. In 1990 the *Toronto Star* ran an article discussing Copps's change of image as she ran for leadership of the Liberal Party—illustrating this article with a reproduction of the *Saturday Night* cover, contrasted with a more recent photograph of Copps dressed and posed more sedately. *Saturday Night* did not object to the unauthorized reproduction of its cover, but Jim Allen, the photographer whose work was featured on the cover, sued the *Star* for copyright infringement.

The result:

Allen won at trial, but the *Star* appealed. The higher court noted that Allen did not own the copyright on the cover in question, which is what the *Star* had reproduced—even though he still owned copyright in his photograph. Furthermore, it held that the *Star*'s use was fair dealing for purposes of news reporting. "In our view," the court stated, "the test of fair dealing is essentially purposive. It is not simply a mechanical test of measurement of the extent of copying involved." In this case, even an entire magazine cover was held to be fair dealing, given "the nature and purpose of the use": it was central to the topic of the story, and it did not give the *Star* an "unfair commercial or competitive advantage over Allen or *Saturday Night*."

the nuanced layering of rights. The *Globe and Mail* exercised considerable skill and judgment in its editorial, selection, and arrangement functions, and does indeed hold copyright in the newspaper as a whole. In a dissenting opinion, Madam Justice Rosalie Abella argued that as new media allow new structuring of content, the newspaper's copyright should not be eroded: "The conversion of a work from one medium to another will necessarily involve changes in the work's visual appearance, but these visual manifestations do not change the content of the right." The puzzle is that arguments on both sides in this case were based on a reasonable expectation of extending current practice in a digital environment: the freelancers wanted to be paid for electronic articles, and the newspapers wanted to utilize new modes of archiving and searching.

Furthermore, the dissent in this case made it clear that a third interest is at play in the battle between publishers and freelancers: the public interest. As Abella put it, "The public interest is particularly significant in the context of archived newspapers. These materials are a primary resource for teachers, students, writers, reporters, and researchers. It is this interest that hangs in the balance between the competing rights of the two groups of creators in this case, the authors and the publishers."[9] Given that the larger publishing enterprises have been for some years pushing their contributors into contracts that permit archiving, this problem may be largely retrospective, but that does not make it less grave: the *Robertson* decision may mean that large swaths of Canadian journalism from the 1940s through the 1990s will be inaccessible to all but specialist researchers just at a time when digital technologies could give the pieces broader exposure.[10]

Users' Rights

Negotiating over ownership and owners' rights appears to be the most prominent copyright issue facing journalism today. But as an institution journalism has long been equally dependent on the unauthorized reproduction of facts, ideas, and even substantial portions of copyrighted material. Some of this recycling simply falls outside of copyright law—story ideas, for example, spin from one media outlet to another in breathless flurries, and then die out. But other practices present exceptions to an owners' rights logic. By tradition of the trade, media outlets often lift substantial portions of copyrighted material from each other or from the entertainment industry: movie stills, images from websites, and magazine covers, for example. That they don't ask for permission in these situations is not an oversight. Many of these excerpts essentially serve as free advertising for their source: Janet Jackson almost nude on the cover of a magazine is not only free salacious content for the staid *Globe and Mail*, but also promotion for both Jackson's album and the magazine.[11] But more serious democratic principles are also at stake. When the *Vancouver Sun* covers an incident in an election campaign, it does not ask permission to quote candidates or members of the public, or to reproduce the text of a ten-year-old letter showing a candidate up to be a liar. If the CBC then picks up the *Sun's*

Glenn Gould Estate v. Stoddart (1998)

The situation:

In 1956 reporter Jock Carroll interviewed and photographed pianist Glenn Gould for an article for *Weekend* magazine. In 1995, after Gould's death, Carroll published a book with Stoddart featuring a wider sampling of photographs and interview materials from those sessions. The Gould Estate sued.

The result:

The Appeal Court found that Carroll owned the copyright in the photographs, and also in the interviews—since Gould's unscripted words did not meet the fixation requirement of copyright, and since there was no evidence of any special contractual arrangements between Gould and Carroll. Carroll was the sole author of these materials, and as such held sole right to publish them. "Once Gould consented, without restriction, to be the subject matter of a journalistic piece," the court held, "he cannot assert any proprietary interest in the final product nor can he complain about any further reproduction of the photographs nor limit the author of the journalistic piece from writing further about him."

The implications:

Nowadays the subject of a major interview project would probably demand a contract, and things would be clearer. But the Gould case states that absent a contract, unscripted words are not copyrightable, whereas their transcription is. This result is good for journalists with drawers full of old interview notes, but it shows a legal bias in favour of the written word that is more than a little problematic.

Copyright law does, however, protect more considered spoken words: a storyteller could almost certainly argue successfully in court that his or her words constituted a "performer's performance," protected under section 26. Similarly, the Gould Estate would probably win in court if anybody circulated CDs of an unauthorized recording of a Gould concert or practice session. Finally, an interview subject whose words were used in unexpected ways might have recourse beyond copyright via privacy or implied contract arguments.

"scoop," it does not ask permission to reprint or pay for the *Sun*'s labours, although by convention it cites the source.

The principle here is that it is the media's job to reveal the truth to their listeners or readers, and to do this they need to be fast and unhampered. Certain journalistic customs have arisen to permit and regulate the necessary borrowing and citing. But what is the law that speaks to these customs and practices? At an exalted level, journalists making unauthorized reproductions may look to the Charter of Rights and Freedoms for protection of their right to freedom of expression. One cannot, after all, express oneself freely on matters of politics and power, or demonstrate a fact, without displaying the basis of one's concern or authority. So an appeal to the Charter could be part of a defence against infringement arising in the media. (While *Michelin v. CAW* [1997], the only Charter case dealing directly with copyright infringement so far in Canada, does not represent a promising indication of the success of such a strategy, it is of questionable validity given the finding of *CCH v. Law Society of Upper Canada*.)[12]

The largest and most practical window for unauthorized journalistic use lies in the Copyright Act. If the uses in question are substantial enough to constitute infringement under section 3.1 (and they may not be), they may still be fair dealing according to section 29 if the source is mentioned: "news reporting" is the fifth acceptable purpose for fair dealing. Case law suggests that journalists should not be hesitant to practise fair dealing. In *CCH* the Supreme Court endorsed the practice of considering the custom or practice in a particular trade or industry as one of the fair dealing criteria. If the borrowing in question follows normal newsroom practice, then, it would most likely fall within the provision of fair dealing (depending on the other circumstances of its use). *Allen v. Toronto Star* indicates that journalistic fair dealing includes very substantial uses, if they are necessary to the reporting end.

Resources

- Professional Writers of Canada website, www.pwac.ca. Contains an excellent blog and many practical resources.
- Writers' Union of Canada website, http://www.writersunion.ca.

13: Libraries & Museums

IN A democratic society, libraries, archives, and museums serve as store-houses of cultural heritage and history, as engines of public education (especially continuing or lifelong learning), and as promoters of public discourse on a range of issues. They collect; they select; they preserve; they catalogue; they reveal; they circulate. They often perform such functions with works whose copyright they do not own.

Reproduction, communication, performance, and exhibition rights are exclusively granted to copyright owners by the Copyright Act. By some interpretations of copyright principles, much of what libraries, archives, and museums do might be infringing. It is not incidental, new, or surprising, then, that a tension exists between copyright law and the fundamental mandate of libraries, archives, and museums, known collectively in the Copyright Act as "LAMs."[1] With the possibilities that digital technologies offer for copyright owners to control their products past the point of sale, on the one hand, and for LAMs to offer wider access to their collections, on the other, the tensions are increasing. Although the normal functions of these institutions are compatible with copyright law, overly expansionist legal reform or interpretation of the present law could inhibit them from doing what they do best: providing public access to a range of cultural and intellectual goods.

Libraries and Copyright Advocacy

Canadian librarians, working through their various library associations and in their individual libraries, have a history of advocacy work on copyright policy issues. Indeed, until recently they were one of the only voices defending users' rights to Parliament. After the Phase I amendments in 1988, the library community was particularly concerned: the gist of these amendments was to strengthen owners' rights, particularly through the new powers given to copyright collectives. Provisions that would have provided more balance were deferred, and at the time fair dealing was thought to be a limited defence that might not cover various well-established practices of librarians and library patrons. Over the next several years, mindful of the apparent weakness of fair dealing, librarians pushed for specific exceptions that would protect established library practices such as copying for preservation purposes, interlibrary loans, and self-serve photocopying for patrons.[2]

When copyright legislation was introduced in 1996, in Bill C-32, library associations initially applauded it as a move in the direction of copyright balance.[3] But publishers objected to the provisions of the bill that granted specific exceptions for libraries, and within a few months the Standing Committee on Canadian Heritage added major limitations on the exceptions. Library organizations withdrew their support, but the bill passed.[4] In the end, as enacted, it was a messy compromise measure. Regulations developed around the new provisions were dismissive of librarians' professional judgment and immensely burdensome on their time.[5] David Vaver predicted, "The 1997 Act will require robust interpretation if the structure it sets up is to work smoothly," and his words proved quite prescient. The 1997 amendments were not robustly interpreted, and libraries slid into a period of resignation and acquiescence in which users' rights were given short shrift and the demands of the collectives were routinely obeyed without much in the way of organized resistance.[6]

The 2004 Supreme Court case *CCH v. Law Society of Upper Canada* represented a major victory for libraries, clarifying that:

a) fair dealing applies to libraries and their patrons regardless of the more specific and restrictive LAM provisions added in 1997 (and now contained in sections 30.1 through 30.5 of the *Copyright Act*);

b) fair dealing is a much broader category than had previously been thought;

In the Queen's University medical library a stark sign is posted above the photocopy machine: "If you think fine print doesn't matter, try photocopying this poster without reading it."

Beneath half a page of blank space the fine print appears, under the logo of Access, the Canadian Copyright Licensing Agency. Libraries arrange a licence with Access so that their patrons can perform certain limited photocopying; Access distributes the funds to publishers and authors. As this poster and others like it explain, the licence covers (for example) the copying of an entire newspaper article, but only 10 per cent of a book; it does not cover copying letters to the editor of a newspaper or advertisements; it does not permit the sale of the copies made; and "it does not extend to copies made for use in association with political activities." The poster acknowledges the existence of fair dealing, but notes, "It is not clear what is meant by 'fair dealing' in our laws." In other words, be afraid, be very afraid.

Why do libraries put these posters up, when they could be educating patrons about the Supreme Court's rather different take on the subject? Because they have to: their licences with Access require it. The licence goes even further:

> If or when the Institution distributes or disseminates to Library Workers, Professors, Students and all other persons authorized or represented by the Institution information that refers to *Access Copyright* by its corporate name "The Canadian Copyright Licensing Agency" or its trade-mark "Access Copyright" or "*Access Copyright*," or both, for the purpose of providing information on the making or ordering of Copies under this Agreement, the Institution shall give to *Access Copyright*

c) librarians acting on behalf of patrons may "stand in their shoes" for purposes of helping them use their fair dealing rights; and

d) the provision of freestanding photocopiers in a library does not constitute an infringing "authorization" under Section 3 of the *Act*.

These rulings provide a solid underpinning for a more proactive approach to library advocacy on copyright issues—and early signs of a new boldness came in 2006, when the Canadian Library Association passed a

notice pursuant to this clause in advance of such distribution, which notice shall enclose a copy of such material, to enable *Access Copyright* to have a reasonable opportunity to comment on the material if it so chooses. If *Access Copyright* fails to notify the Institution of any objection that it may have with respect to the material within 10 days of receipt of such notice, *Access Copyright* shall be deemed to have agreed to the form and content of the material and the use of the material for the purposes specified in clause 9 of this Agreement.

Like the puzzling clause in the Access licence denying coverage to copying for political purposes, this provision does not sit easily with the freedom of expression central to academic practice. But does it really mean that libraries' hands are tied if they want to interpret copyright law to their patrons without consulting Access Copyright? In fact, the licence does not say that permission from Access is *required*; nor would it appear to limit discussion of the terms of the Access licence within a broader realm of copyright information that a library or institution might provide, or discussion of licensing issues without mention of the name of the agency formerly known as Cancopy.

And by the way, despite the threatening tone and design of this poster, we see no reason why people can't reproduce it for fair dealing purposes: criticism, review, research, private study, or news reporting.

Sources: See the University of British Columbia's post-secondary licence, an instance of a general form, Provision 10-1, 10, http://www.library.ubc.ca/home/about/welcome/cancopy.html; Murray, "Protecting Ourselves to Death." For several examples of misleading copyright notices in libraries, see Wallace McLean, "The National Lieberry?" Jan. 20, 2007; and "Copyright Chill, Just West of the Hill," Nov. 11, 2005, http://www.copyrightwatch.ca.

resolution condemning Access Copyright's "Captain Copyright" web-site, declaring that it "poses a threat to our shared information commons by providing biased copyright information to the Canadian public, particularly children and schoolteachers." After a temporary suspension of the site, Access Copyright ultimately withdrew the campaign permanently.[7]

Libraries, Technology, and the Copyright Act

At the intersection of law and new technologies, three specific issues confront librarians: pricing and contract terms, interlibrary loans, and self-service photocopying.

Pricing and Contract Terms

The broad diffusion of the Internet, including the widespread use of resources such as Google and Wikipedia, may seem to have undermined the importance of libraries. Many people now find more information at home, at their fingertips, and the information industry has, not surprisingly, responded to the revenue implications of these emerging markets. But not all people enjoy the benefits of networks and digitization. The affluent can afford the latest computers, private Internet services, training, entertainment packages, and subscriptions to digital databases, journals, and other media, while the less affluent remain dependent on the public library for access to these services.

To meet the increased demand for online resources, libraries increasingly serve as "portals" for licensed digital materials rather than as the traditional "repositories" of purchased material. This shift makes them vulnerable not only to price increases by the vendors of these services, but also to licensing terms that circumscribe users' rights. Librarians now have to study—and recognize the importance of—the specific terms of licensing agreements, and do this quickly and well.[8] For example, if a licence that allows subscribers to view but not copy the material can be had for half the price of a licence that allows copying, during a time when libraries are sorely pressed for funds a library would be tempted to agree to such an arrangement.

Another issue involves the question of preservation and continued access: many electronic resources are now marketed on what amounts to
a rental basis. If a library terminates its subscription, patrons will lose
access to all of the materials previously provided unless the subscription
terms permit permanent archiving. A digital encyclopedia or magazine
is not sitting bound on the shelf, and can evaporate in an instant.

For university libraries, price inflation in subscriptions to scholarly
journals, known as the "serials crisis," has become a major problem.[9] The
high prices of these journals are especially galling given that university
faculty provide, select, and edit their content for free—and in some cases
even pay "page fees" for publication. As for the commercial academic
journal publishers, scholars Judith Panitch and Sarah Michalak say they
"find themselves in the enviable position of selling research which they
neither produced nor paid for to a high-demand market. They maintain
an additional advantage because each journal title is a unique commodity, characterized by its specific focus and also by its prestige."[10]

To deal with this situation, libraries are using consortial purchasing—where a number of libraries band together to get a better price.
Some librarians and their associations are also strong advocates for open
access publications—in which libraries, educational institutions, or other
non-profit entities host journals that are made available at no charge to
the end user.[11]

Interlibrary Loans

One tool that libraries have long used to make dollars stretch further and
enhance their patrons' ability to perform research is the interlibrary loan
(ILL): a patron of one library can arrange through that library to borrow
material from another library—perhaps in another city or even country.[12] Digital technologies can make ILL much easier: instead of sending
the physical book, a library can fax or email a digitized version of the
pertinent material.

Questions have arisen about whether this practice constitutes copyright infringement. While librarians and patrons see ILL as a way of
equalizing access to information resources across different communities,
the vendors and rightsholders see it as a threat to their income streams.

The section of the Copyright Act concerning ILL (Section 30.2, added by the 1997 amendments) places many limits on the ability of librarians to provide full ILL services to patrons. Section 30.2(2)(b) and 30.2(3) state, for example, that no article from a periodical less than one year old can be copied for the purposes of ILL, nor can any "work of fiction or poetry or a dramatic or musical work." Section 30.2(4)(a) states that such a copy can be made only if "the person for whom the copy will be made has satisfied the library, archive or museum that the person will not use the copy for a purpose other than research or private study." Digital copies are not permitted under section 30.2(5). And so on: the section is a mess of limitations and detail that few librarians and far fewer library patrons understand.[13]

After the 1997 amendments came into force, it was generally believed that any interlibrary loans needed to comply with the special limitations contained in section 30.2 and the associated regulations. But *CCH v. Law Society of Upper Canada* (2004) asserted that libraries can also use the umbrella of fair dealing, stating: "It is only if a library were unable to make out the fair dealing exception under s. 29 that it would need to turn to s. 30.2 of the Copyright Act to prove that it qualified for the library exemption."[14] The ILL provisions of Bill C-60 (the Copyright Reform bill introduced and abandoned in 2005) tinkered with section 30.2 in various ways in an attempt to make it more useful to librarians.[15] The confusion and constraints of the existing exceptions and the pertinent Bill C-60 provisions suggest that ILL should be treated as another one of many situations that can arise under a general fair dealing provision.

Self-Service Photocopying

In *CCH*, the publishers took the position that by making free-standing photocopiers available to its patrons, the defendant library was "authorizing" acts of infringement of its copyrighted materials. (See chapter 4, where we saw that one of the sticks on the owners' bundles of copyright rights contained in section 3 of the act is the right to authorize exercise of the other exclusive rights, in this case the reproduction right.) The Great Library of the Law Society of Upper Canada did not have a licence with Access Copyright, but it posted this notice above its self-service copy machines:

> The copyright law of Canada governs the making of photocopies or other reproductions of copyright material. Certain copying may be an infringement of the copyright law. This library is not responsible for infringing copies made by the users of these machines.[16]

The court ruled that the library was not liable for infringement because "a person does not authorize copyright infringement by authorizing the mere use of equipment (such as photocopiers) that could be used to infringe copyright."[17] This is a statement that librarians should be aware of as they consider what types of notices to post around their photocopy machines.

In 2005 the Frontier School Division in Manitoba came up with an idea for a new Education Centre in remote Norway House. They would obtain and display reproductions of some Paul Kane paintings of Norway House and its inhabitants done in the 1840s, bringing them home, in a sense, to the descendants of Kane's subjects. The paintings in question are owned by the Stark Museum of Orange, Texas. Given that Kane died in 1871, the paintings' copyright ended in 1921. The Stark Museum donated digital reproductions of its Kane paintings for the project, and they are now on display in the new school. But then the Frontier School Division folks got to thinking that an explanatory plaque about the artist was in order. When they contacted the National Gallery of Canada in Ottawa for a reproduction of a photograph of Kane taken in 1850, they were quoted a price of $150, which, the Gallery explained, included a permissions fee of $80. Raymond Shirritt-Beaumont of the Frontier School Division pointed out to the Gallery that copyright in the photograph had expired at least one hundred years earlier and that therefore no permission ought to be charged.

It took many volleys of letters to have the $80 waived—and the Frontier School Division continues to maintain that the remaining $70 is an unreasonably high fee for a copy of an existing digital file of a public domain work. Meanwhile, the schoolchildren of Norway House are deprived of seeing an image of the man who painted their ancestors.

Source: Raymond Shirritt-Beaumont, personal correspondence, June-December 2005.

Libraries, Museums, and Users' Rights

Libraries deserve credit for serving the needs of their patrons and defending users' rights in the shift to digital holdings. It is exciting to see that libraries and museums are increasingly using the Internet to make more of their collections available to a far-flung Canadian public: projects such as the Virtual Museum of Canada and Alouette Canada may well develop into important national resources.[18] However, in an environment of constrained funding, it is always tempting for these institutions to use copyright law to generate income. In many of these efforts, they may be weakening their image as public resources worthy of generous public funding. In some cases, they are actually stretching their claims beyond the rights that copyright law offers them.

What copyright information do museums provide to online users?

The Virtual Museum of Canada website offers this nonsensical statement: "Individuals are not permitted to use the images for their own use." Which only makes one wonder, why does the website exist? The National Gallery declares, "Under copyright law, all reproductions of works of art, except when intended for private consultation only, must be licensed by the National Gallery of Canada." What about the public domain? The website for Alouette Canada, a developing network for the free distribution of cultural materials, trumpets its goal of making such materials available for free educational use, and yet certain editorial cartoons available on the site are labelled "copyright Simon Fraser University." The terms of use are unclear: notice of a Creative Commons licence would seem to be more appropriate than notice of copyright.

To be fair, it is difficult for such institutions to stay on top of developments in law and technology—never mind to keep websites updated. But it is important for them to get things right—for the public's good, and their own good.

Sources: http://www.virtualmuseum.ca/English/About/faq.html; http://www.gallery.ca/english/default_64.htm; http://www.alouettecanada.ca/images/brochure-e.pdf. For a cartoon on the site copyrighted to Simon Fraser University, see, for example, http://www.lib.sfu.ca/cgi-bin/edocs/Cartoons?CartoonID=3.

The legal rationale for the library reproduction fees may be the idea that the photograph of a public domain image itself is a work in which copyright subsists—but such a claim is fishy law and fishy policy.[19] Too many institutions are setting up barriers to the use of public domain images. In her book *Permissions: A Survival Guide*, Susan Bielstein puts a humorous twist on an unacceptable situation: "Chasing images is time-consuming and expensive. So if you can live without images, do it. Put that money toward orthodontia or a down payment on a house."[20]

For Canada's libraries, archives, and museums it would be wise to heed a warning provided by consultant Diane Zorich:

> Museums need to consider the ethical and moral dilemmas they create if they impose such restrictions as a matter of policy, for they would not wish to face similar restrictions imposed on them by others.... Whether such restrictions are worth the price is an ethical question that museums must ask themselves when they consider access issues in their IP policies.[21]

Resources

- Canadian Library Association, Copyright Information Centre, web-site, http://www.cla.ca/resources/copyright.htm; and a position paper, "Protecting the Public Interest," January 2006, http://www.cla.ca/resources/protecting_the_public_interest.pdf.
- "Intellectual Property: A Balance (The British Library Manifesto)," September 2006, http://www.bl.uk/news/pdf/ipmanifesto.pdf. A visionary yet brief document.
- International Federation of Library Associations and Institutions (IFLA) Copyright Committee, http://www.ifla.org/III/clm/copyr.htm#Introduction. Vast information on international copyright advocacy and issues.

14: Music

MUSIC HAS been the focus of most of the media hysteria and consumer
discontent about copyright. It's a battle of studies and statistics: one week
the recording industry seems to have facts on its side indicating that the
world of recorded music as we know it is ending, and the next week it
doesn't.[1] The recording industry demands protection from the Internet;
consumers demand protection from the music industry; and musicians—
well, perhaps they don't have much hope that anybody will look out for
them. Setting aside the question of who's right and who's wrong, there
is clearly a massive disconnect, when it comes to music, between socio-
cultural norms and emerging artistic forms on the one hand, and the law
(or rather what people think the law ought to be) on the other. Music is
a hotbed of the copyright legitimacy crisis.

We cannot attempt to cover all of the ins and outs of the situation in
one chapter, but we will try to shed light on the extraordinarily complex
system of rights ownership and management that emerged in the music
industry and copyright law over the course of the twentieth century—a
system that is being challenged by the rise of digital technologies.

Twentieth-Century Music Rights

You are holding a CD in your hand. You even successfully extricated it from the cellophane and stickers and jewel box. Congratulations! You bought it; you own it. You can play it for your friends, give it away, re-sell it, copy it for personal use, or hang it on a tree to scare crows.

But while you own the thing, and have some "user's rights" in the music embedded in it, other people and companies hold rights in other aspects of the CD: the underlying musical composition, the performance of that music, the recording itself, and the cover art and liner notes are all materials in which copyright may subsist.

Let's consider the composition first. The original composer may own the rights embodied in the sequence of notes, rhythms, and chords. A lyricist or an arranger might also have been involved. These creators of the underlying music may have made an agreement with a publisher, which now owns their rights—and may have required a waiver of moral rights—but pays them royalties.

Then there's the performer or performers. Rights in the performance exist separate and apart from the rights in the original work. The performer may have signed with a label—a company that promotes and manufactures records—so it's not always easy to know who exactly holds these rights.

Another "neighbouring" right rests in the sound recording (or pho-nogram). The maker of the master recording—the person who arranged for it to be done—owns the copyright in that master.[2] For commercial music, this "maker" would usually be the record label. If the CD is a remastered reissue (an old jazz recording digitally cleaned up and enhanced, for example), additional rights may be held by whoever orga-nized that undertaking.

The possibility exists that some of these rights holders may be dead. Recordings have a copyright term of a flat fifty years from fixation, as do performances, but compositions have the usual term of life of the au-thor plus fifty years. If a composer/lyricist/arranger died fewer than fifty years ago, an estate will represent that person and reap whatever revenues come along. But if the composer/lyricist/arranger died more than fifty years ago, the work will have become part of the public domain, where ownership rights are extinguished.

As complex as this may sound, it is the simplified version. Fortunately, however, most of us don't need to know all the details, largely because copyright collectives mediate most use and reuse of music.

Thus, for example, the Society of Composers, Authors, and Music Publishers of Canada (SOCAN) acts as an intermediary between its members and radio stations, who pay it for the right to broadcast, or "perform," a "repertoire" of recordings. Radio stations also have licences with the Neighbouring Rights Copyright Collective (NRCC), which represents performers and sound recording makers. If a radio station wants to reproduce music for storage or convenience, it also gets a "mechanical rights" licence with the Canadian Musical Reproduction Rights Agency (CMRRA), which represents music publishers. Music in coffee shops, skating rinks, airplanes, dance clubs, and answering services is similarly licensed.[3] While some areas of confusion might exist for business owners—for example, if they play a radio in their store out of one set of speakers they don't need a licence, but more elaborate setups will more likely attract SOCAN's attention—the average consumer doesn't usually have to worry, other than to ask whether the licence fees are appropriate and getting to the right people.

But let's look at things from the perspective of the composer. Let's say you have written a song. Apart from various users' rights exceptions, you hold the sole right to reproduction, performance, and broadcast of any substantial part of that song—and you hold the moral rights as well. You might seek a publisher's help in publicizing the song and negotiating terms with performers or labels: in this case, they collect payments from collectives and pass on royalties to you. Through SOCAN, you can be paid when people perform your song or play a recording of it in public, according to a formula based on broadcast surveys. If your music is more likely to be played in a concert hall than on the radio, your rights will be the basis for your negotiation for performance or commission fees. If you want to encourage non-commercial use, you could arrange for a Creative Commons licence specifying the terms on which you want that to happen (for more on Creative Commons, see chapter 18).

If you are a performer, things are a little different. You have the right to fix your performance—which is to say, if somebody tapes your live show and puts it on the Internet without your permission, that's infringement. Once you have given permission for your performance to be fixed, you have no say in its redeployment, but if you join an affiliate of NRCC you will be paid royalties when your recording is played in public.[4] In the law as it now stands, performers have no moral rights—that is, no recourse to protect the integrity of their work or to demand attribution.[5] The copyright term in performances—fifty years from its fixation—is shorter than the term for authored works, where the fifty-year period begins only after the author's death.

If you perform material whose rights are owned by others, these rights have to be cleared. In most performance situations, rights clearance is arranged by the promoter or the venue, not the musicians. For example, a cover band in a bar works under that bar's performance rights licence with SOCAN, which represents the songwriter. If you want to record a cover, you have to clear the "mechanical rights," which is the industry's term for reproduction rights. This is done on a case by case basis. It's not expensive: if the song is in the repertoire of CMRRA, and is less than five minutes long, the current rate is $38.50 for five hundred CDs.[6] If you can't find your composer through CMRRA or SODRAC (Society for Reproduction Rights of Authors, Composers, and Publishers in Canada), you can make arrangements independently. If the composer has been dead more than fifty years, you owe nothing: the material is in the public domain.

Now let's say you want to *sample* a song—you want a second or two or three out of it. If you know about the copyright substantiality requirement (chapter 4), you might think you don't need clearance. After all, if the source song is five minutes long, and you use three seconds, you've used 1 per cent of the song, which doesn't seem substantial. But the "substantiality" test isn't just about quantity. If you've taken the signature riff of that song, your use is substantial. More importantly—because often samplers transform sounds well beyond recognizability—the industry practice that evolved in the wake of the 1991 Gilbert O'Sullivan/Biz Markie case in the United States is that rights have to be cleared for any amount or type of use.[7] The logic here is that if it's worth sampling, it must be worth collecting on. Thus, if you expect to distribute your recording at all widely, and/or if you have any personal assets, unlicensed sampling is legally risky.

In September 2006 an artist went into some record stores in the United Kingdom and bought five hundred CDs. After replacing each CD and its paper insert with a parody of the original, he returned the substitute CDs, newly shrink-wrapped in cellophane with bar codes intact, to the store shelves. Matthew Rankin, a film-maker and appropriation artist himself, indicates what the story means to him:

> Have you heard about that British artist Banksy? He bought a Paris Hilton album and then he re-created his own Paris Hilton album ... the cover is the same but he changed the music ... it's a different CD. And on the inside flaps he's created all of these strange Paris Hilton collages and in one of them she's coming out of a limo and there's all these homeless people gathered around oil barrel fire behind her and things like this. It's illegal on hundreds of different levels because he actually went back to the record shops and put them on the shelves, and he kept the original bar codes so they would actually ring up as Paris Hilton albums when you bought them. He put out five hundred copies of these, and yeah, it's breaking so many laws. But to me it's such a good use. The fact of the matter is that Paris Hilton is everywhere: she's on all the newsstands, all the news racks, on the TV, on the radio. Her music might be playing in an elevator somewhere. As a private citizen you are encountering Paris Hilton in the public space con-stantly. Paris Hilton didn't sign any release form, or get any permission from me to be part of my life. I mean technically my life, that's private property to some degree. My consciousness, that belongs to me, and Paris Hilton is in it and she didn't have my permission. And so to suggest that these images and these sounds that bombard my public experience daily, don't belong to me in any way ... to me that is just insane.

Interestingly, neither Hilton's label nor the record stores involved took action over Banksy's prank. An HMV spokesman said: "I guess you can give an individual such as Banksy a little bit of leeway for his own particular brand of artistic engagement. Often people might have a view on something but feel they can't always express it, but it's down to the likes of Banksy to say often what people think about things. And it might be that there will be some people who agree with his views on the Paris Hilton album." This was indeed a tactful response, considering the public outrage that might have erupted if HMV had tried to take legal action.

Sources: Matthew Rankin, Winnipeg, interview with Kirsty Robertson; "Paris Hilton Targeted in CD Prank," BBC website, Sept. 3, 2006.

If a person taking a sample is sued for copyright infringement the fair dealing defence is not likely to be useful, because the sampler would have to demonstrate that the use was for purposes of "criticism" (on parody, see also chapter 16). The sampler could try to gesture to *CCH v. Law Society of Upper Canada*, arguing that in the particular "trade or industry"—let's say, DJ-ing—this is what everybody does; but the label would say that if the sampler was distributing a recording, he or she is working in *their* industry, which expects rights clearance. In the United States the high-profile DJ Drama was arrested in January 2007 for copyright infringement, even though the music industry had generally been ignoring and sometimes bankrolling DJ-produced mixtapes.[8]

Canada has not yet seen such crackdowns, but it may be that practitioners of a major twenty-first century art form will be forced underground. A fair and affordable licensing scheme for sampling has been proposed, but it would be culturally anathema to hip-hop culture and would arouse enormous resistance. An open-ended approach to fair dealing would probably be more appropriate to this evolving practice among musicians and DJs.

Twenty-First-Century Music Rights

The structure of rights management in the Canadian music industry gets even more complicated when we take the Internet and digital music into consideration. The Internet has allowed more people access to more recorded music than ever before. The record store at your local mall might carry Mariah Carey and Madonna, but you can get access to their songs for free on your computer, which can also lead you even further, to formerly inaccessible field recordings, basement sessions, bootlegs, and remixes. Finding and sharing music online can lead to a sense of euphoria—with even more fun to be had sampling and mashing up the music.

These activities do not go unnoticed by the consumer electronics industry, which often bases its advertising campaigns on these types of uses—following Apple's 2001 campaign exhorting people to "Rip. Mix. Burn." Indeed, whole genres of creative activities are opening up because of the possibilities unleashed with new digital technologies. It is fair to say that the old distinctions between creators, producers, and consumers are imploding. Reproduction, recording, editing, and distribution have become cheap and easy enough that the middlemen roles of record labels seem less necessary than they once were.

This is good news for many music lovers and some music creators, but it's bad news for the music industry, or at least for the bigger labels that want to cling to the old ways of doing business. That, of course, is where copyright comes into the picture. By increasing the sophistication of copying controls, lobbying for laws to layer on top of them, taking people to court, and otherwise intimidating consumers as best it can, the music industry has been trying to shut down or claim for itself the

Is downloading legal in Canada?

Section 80(1) of the Copyright Act indicates that the downloading (or other copying) of a song for a person's private use does not constitute infringement—if certain specific conditions are met.

To take advantage of this special exception, the copying has to be made to "an audio recording medium," and it has to be for the purpose of the private use of the person who actually makes the copy. That is, you cannot use this exception to make a copy for someone else. The exception is also not available if the copy is going to be sold, rented out, distributed, or communicated to the public by telecommunication or performance. Any distribution will take the copying out of the exception, even if it is not done for the purposes of trade or sales.

The question that remains somewhat unclear in Canadian law is whether putting a file in a shared directory ("uploading") constitutes authorization to reproduce it—if so, that act would be infringement on a right reserved to the owner of the copyright in the file.

In the Federal Court case *BMG Canada v. Doe*, Justice von Finckenstein suggested that merely making a file available on a shared server did not infringe the owner's reproduction, distribution, or authorization rights. But this statement was not central to the case, which otherwise decided that record labels could not compel Internet service providers to identify subscribers suspected of copyright infringement. The Federal Court of Appeal affirmed this ruling, but said that the lower court should not have commented on the copyright issue.

new capabilities of digital technologies. In Canada the music business has been lobbying heavily to stop downloading, which is ironic considering that the industry provided the impetus for the mechanism that makes downloading legal: the private copying levy by which Canadians pay a premium on blank media on the presumption that they will use them to copy music.

While the recording industry purports to speak on their behalf, most musicians have little time or money for lobbying—nor are they eager to bite the hand that sometimes feeds them. Many artists are resentful about downloading, but many of them also see the Internet as a way of asserting both professional and political independence from the large trade

> The last record deal I had was the last time I'd ever relinquish the ownership of master recordings, which is the worst thing an artist can do. But you never realize that because you're desperate for the money, so you sign it away for an advance that may or may not be significant, you know (laughs). I have several recordings I don't own the masters for, and the labels that did own the masters have been bought and rebought and bought again, and who would even know where those things are?
>
> Now, you could go to any artist and most will say this: you're out there busting your ass, driving around in a van like a maniac, making no money, and your label rep shows up at the gig and takes you to some interviews. Those guys work hard, for sure, but they get to go home afterwards while you're climbing back in the van, and unlike most artists, they also get paid a middle-class wage.
>
> With our last thing, we just sold it online. So if you were in Kelowna, or you were in Labrador, and you wanted a copy, it was there. The Internet's been great for that kind of stuff. And as far as pirating goes, this is a conversation that's going on primarily among the representatives of huge, wealthy, global corporations. That's what's happening: it's the rich freaking out about their future riches, and it's got almost nothing to do with most artists. You can paraphrase James Michener: the music business has been up to now a place where an artist can make a fortune but not a living. The Internet is changing that equation. Maybe fewer artists will make a fortune, but more will make a living.
>
> —Andrew Cash, musician, Toronto, interview with Laura Murray.

groups. Steven Page of the Barenaked Ladies, along with other prominent Canadian musicians, has established the Canadian Music Creators Coalition, which speaks out against suing consumers and locking up digital content and calls instead for more direct funding of artists.

"Record companies and music publishers are not our enemies," the CMCC says on its website. "But let's be clear: lobbyists for major labels are looking out for their shareholders, and seldom speak for Canadian artists. Legislative proposals that would facilitate lawsuits against our fans or increase the labels' control over the enjoyment of music are made *not in our names*, but on behalf of the labels' foreign parent companies."[9]

Practical alternatives to the big label model are clearly needed. Musicians may want to be independent from the big labels, but the "everybody for themselves" model of selling CDs through personal websites is ineffective and inefficient for most. Collective licensing is one solution under discussion. Instead of trying to shut down the circulation of music on the Internet, its proponents say, let's charge Internet Service Providers (which is to say, their subscribers) a fee, and share the revenues in the same way that existing collective societies do. Collective licensing of P2P (or peer to peer) would legalize a practice that is already prominent, and would presumably avoid the irritating or dangerous digital locks that record companies could otherwise be inclined to impose on purchased materials.

That said, past experience might lead many Canadians to doubt the appropriateness of a levy solution to Internet music issues. On the creator side, a levy system could present as many problems of fairness or accuracy when it comes to survey techniques or allotment mechanisms as there are today with the big label system. For consumers, the pitfalls are multiple (see the discussion of the levy on blank media in chapter 5). On the decentralized Internet, even more than previously licensed media, we have the added problem that a large amount of the music circulating is either already in the public domain, "orphaned" (we can't name or locate the rights holders), never intended to be commercial, or already paid for by individual contract (iTunes, for example). Levies would probably be inflated without due recognition of these conditions. Finally, there is something inherently distasteful to many in the idea of switching the default conception of the Internet from an open-ended information commons to an enclosed and metered market. (For a similar debate, see chapter 10.)

Canada's cautious approach to responding to the "music piracy crisis" has been productive. Not a week goes by without a new solution or angle being discussed. We know the current system doesn't work, but we need to take our time to see what its replacement might be.

Resources

Canada

- Department of Canadian Heritage, "Music Is My Business," www.music. gc.ca. This site uses flash animation and a glossary to explain where the money goes, how the collectives work, and other mysteries of the music business. Highly recommended.
- Jeremy F. DeBeer, "The Role of Levies in Canada's Digital Music Market," 2005. A clear overview of the Canadian situation, and a critique of the levy model.
- Paul E. Sanderson, *Musicians and the Law in Canada*, 2000. Now a bit out of date, but it lays out information specific to Canada.
- Shelley Stein-Sacks, "The Canadian Independent Music Industry: An Examination of Distribution and Access," 2006. Another accessible resource.
- Websites of SOCAN, CMRRA, NRCC, SODRAC: all of the music collectives offer their version of music copyright basics.

United States

- Columbia Law School Music Plagiarism Project website, http://ccnmtl. columbia.edu/projects/law/library/entrance.html. A fabulous collection of recordings, cases, and commentary on U.S. music copyright.
- William W. Fisher, *Promises to Keep: Technology, Law, and the Future of Entertainment*, 2004.
- David Kusek and Gerd Leonhard, *The Future of Music: Manifesto for the Digital Music Revolution*, 2005.
- www.samplinglaw.com. A good source of information on U.S. cases and controversies.

Our Wedding

15: Photography

LIKE WRITERS or filmmakers, photographers make their art, and sometimes their living, from representing the products of nature and of human activity. Sometimes we think of photography as a document of "how things really are." But photographs are also the product of selectivity and greater or lesser degrees of creativity. Indeed, we can see the work of photography as a range of practices that fall between two poles. At one pole are mounted cameras monitoring security or highway speed with little or no human intervention. Nearer the other are the artistic photographers carefully crafting the environment of photo shoots and modifying images with darkroom or digital wizardry. Somewhere in between these poles of "high objectivity" and "high creativity" we find the wedding photographer, or the photojournalist capturing the stunning moment that will perhaps define a generation. And somewhere else in between, we have the everyday cellphone photographers in nightclubs, at protests, at birthday parties, and on the subway.

With such a range of practices, practitioners, and things and people being photographed, it is not surprising that copyright law pertaining to photography is confusing and controversial.

The Copyright Act Present and Future

According to section 2 of the Copyright Act, the category of "artistic work" includes photographs. In defining "photograph," section 2 includes "photo-lithographs and any work expressed by any process analogous to photography." Sections 10(1), 10(2), and 13(2), which also concern photography, recognize that not all photographs have negatives. The act, then, is written in such a way that it accommodates both the oldest and the newest photographic techniques.

While the act defines photographs as original works in which copyright subsists, in some respects it treats them differently than other artistic works (see Table 11).

Over the past few years, there has been a strong impetus to "harmonize" the treatment of photographers with that of other creators. It has been argued that when the Copyright Act deems the owner of the first plate or negative to be its author, it carries with it ideas from the early years of photography, when photographers were thought to be mere technicians rather than artists. Eliminating section 10 would eradicate this anomalous treatment. The main practical effect of doing so, however, would be a copyright term extension for corporation-produced photographs (photographs owned by photographers already have a term of life plus fifty years), and a convincing policy justification for this has not been provided.

Harmonization must be undertaken with extreme caution. Until recently, all photographs had a copyright term of fifty years from the date they were taken. In 1999, on the rationale of making things fair for photographers, the act was changed so that photographs owned by "natural persons" had their term tied to the death of the author, like other works. While this change has been to the good for professional photographers— or rather, for their heirs—it has posed difficulties for archives and their users. When we are dealing with historical photographs, photographers are particularly difficult to identify—compared, say, to the authors of letters or books: the date, venue, and subjects of old photographs are hard enough to determine, and the finger on the shutter even more elusive. It was much easier to make use of archival photographs when the term was a simple fifty years from the taking of the photograph.

Proceeding any further in harmonizing authorship and copyright term

Table 11. Copyright in Photographs

	Photography	Other Works
authorship	first owner of plates or negatives is deemed the author—whether or not that person took the photo; could be a corporation. Section 10(2)	the creator is the author
copyright term	end of year in which author died + 50 years if author a natural person OR end of year in which negative or photograph was made + 50 years if not. Section 10(1)	end of year in which author died + 50 years
first ownership in commissioned work	"the person by whom the plate or other original was ordered shall be the first owner of the copyright." Section 13(2)	author is the first owner of commissioned work

of photographs with other works must be done in tandem with changes to the Copyright Act's treatment of untraceable copyright owners. Instead of the current system, whereby one must clear use of works with untraceable owners with the Copyright Board (see chapter 5), Canada needs a system in which liability for infringement is removed by a reasonable attempt to locate the copyright owner.[1] Otherwise, the reluctance of publishers, photo shops, and archives to permit the reproduction of old photographs—already a major problem—will be increased, and an essential part of Canadians' family and cultural heritage will be hidden from view.

Downloading images off my website? That would be great ... it would be the best thing that could happen to my career. But in terms of selling limited edition prints, that's a different animal. I have to have really tight control over that if I want to survive as an artist. I'm not just going to give the negative or the master digital file to someone over in Finland who doesn't want to pay for it. But on my website, they can copy my low resolution images and use those pictures as they see fit.

—Colwyn Griffith, photographer, Ottawa, interview with Kirsty Robertson.

The default ownership rules for copyright in commissioned photographs have also prompted debate. Freelance and studio photographers have argued that it is unfair that they are treated differently than, say, freelance journalists. This is also a multidimensional issue. Section 13(2), according to which "in the absence of any agreement to the contrary, the person by whom the plate or other original was ordered shall be the first owner of the copyright," covers distinct circumstances. On one hand, it applies to wedding and baby photographs. It means that, absent a contractual override of this provision, consumers can reproduce commissioned photographs and/or keep them private if they so wish. Since consumers are usually the least informed about the law, it seems reasonable that the default rules fall in their favour. On the other hand, 13(2) is also the default for freelance photographers working with large corporate clients, and although its ownership provision may be and often is altered by contract, it can weaken photographers' bargaining position. In 2005 the Liberals' short-lived Bill C-60 tried to address this problem by eliminating 13(2) and adding an exception to the act allowing those who have commissioned photographs for personal purposes to use or reproduce those photos without infringement.[2]

Undoubtedly, any changes made to the Act with regard to photography will have complex effects. Business and industry, educational institutions and libraries, the media, professional and amateur photographers, and consumers all have stakes in the law in this area, and all of these parties must have their interests recognized. But there is no need to panic when it comes to the role, and effect, of new technologies. The Internet provides challenges to professional photographers (their work, for instance, may be at greater risk of unauthorized use), but it also provides a powerful tool for career promotion. Through the use of watermarks, low-resolution images, and other technical means, professional photographers are quickly learning how to gain exposure while isolating some use of their work as profit-producing.

Practical and Legal Issues on the Job

Legal issues also arise at an earlier stage in the creation of photographs, because the raw material often includes private property, intellectual property, and people claiming rights of privacy or celebrity. Not infrequently, people try to stop photographers from taking, developing, or distributing pictures. They may assert more rights than the Copyright Act or other law accords them, but often a photographer will not have the resources or patience to get to court and confirm those rights. The issues in this area are wide-ranging, but a few in particular often pose problems.

A photographer commissioned by the Quebec tourist board to take photographs with famous Quebec landmarks as backdrops eventually abandoned his attempts to feature the 1969 Jean-Paul Riopelle sculpture *La Joute* near Montreal's Palais de Congrès. After the Riopelle estate claimed the right to authorize such a photograph, the photographer, wanting to avoid a large fee or a lawsuit, walked away.[3] That response is understandable, but let's test the estate's claim against the Copyright Act. A court might begin by asking: Does a photograph of the sculpture constitute reproduction of the sculpture? Surely not according to common sense: only a three-dimensional casting could do that. The convention in legal interpretation may well be that photographs constitute reproduction, although in a sense that is a misunderstanding of photography, which is an act of representation. On another tack, perhaps the photograph could be said to "exhibit" the work, but that would seem to stretch that right beyond reason; besides, the sculpture is too old to benefit from this recently added right of section 3(1)(g). There may be other angles, but the first hurdle for the Riopelle estate would be to demonstrate that the photograph actually infringed one of its section 3 rights. Even if the court found this to be so, the estate would surely have a harder time arguing around the exception in section 32.2(1)(b), which seems specifically designed to permit this kind of photography. The

It is not an infringement of copyright ... for any person to reproduce, in a painting, drawing, engraving, photograph or cinematographic work

(i) an architectural work, provided the copy is not in the nature of an architectural drawing or plan, or

(ii) a sculpture or work of artistic craftsmanship or a cast or model of a sculpture or work of artistic craftsmanship, that is permanently situated in a public place or building.

—Copyright Act, 32.2(1).

La Joute, Montreal.

only strategy remaining for the estate might be to claim infringement of moral rights, though it is doubtful it could convince a judge that use in a tourism poster damaged Riopelle's reputation or honour: it might be different if the photograph were destined to serve as PR for a sex shop or an insurance company. In sum: the Riopelle estate's claims are unsupported in law.

Another specific exception in the law occurs in section 30.7, which permits the appearance "incidentally and not deliberately" of copyrighted material. This is of great importance to news photographers, though it would presumably stand up less well for photographers whose work involves more overt crafting.

Some constraints on photographers' work may be mistaken for copyright issues but belong to other realms of law. Like filmmakers, photographers often face demands for payment from property owners at the locations at which they want to shoot. These are not copyright fees per se, but rather access fees, and owners of private property have

the right to assert them. Some publicly owned historic sites also charge
for the taking of commercial photographs on site. While some "cost recovery" might be justified for big-budget fashion shoots and the like, a
sliding scale would be appropriate in these situations because many professional photographers earn fairly modest sums for their work.

Similarly, public archives often charge high fees to people who want
to photograph images or objects in their collections. Other times they
ban photography outright. Such policies may be based on preservation
or decorum concerns, or on the terms of contracts with donors, but they
are just as likely based on the desire to protect revenue sources. Surely
the public's right to enjoy the fruits of their taxes should include the
right to document and reimagine those places and experiences. This is
not strictly a copyright issue, but the principles are continuous with the
principles of users' rights.

Photographers may be told by trademark holders that they may not
photograph trademarked signs, logos, or images. The law does not support such a prohibition. Unlike copyright law, trademark law does not
prevent reproduction of the trademark. It only prevents reproduction
that may cause consumer confusion over the product that the trademark
is associated with, as two recent Supreme Court cases have confirmed
(see chapter 11).[4] Only in rare cases does photography produce such a
confusion.

Finally, human subjects are increasingly presenting legal issues for
photographers. Even though the subject of a photograph holds no part
of its copyright, that person may have a say in its redeployment on such
grounds as privacy or implied contract. When Montreal photographer
Gilbert Duclos published a photograph of a teenage girl sitting on a
doorstep, she sued, and when the case went to the Supreme Court of
Canada, Duclos lost.[5] He was devastated. As he puts it:

> The whole story of street photography is based on images taken on
> the street without permission. The most beautiful photos are taken
> on the street just like that. When you ask permission, it's no longer
> natural. I feel that if the photo is degrading, then I can understand
> people objecting, but if it's somebody walking on the street eating

an ice cream on a hot day or something, then it's not defamatory, there's nothing wrong with it.[6]

Again, this is not a copyright issue, and technically the Supreme Court's ruling only applies in Quebec, but questions of public interest arise once again. If we are out in public, can we really expect an isolation bubble between us and any observers who might happen to be there? Can we try to extract money from those who record our public presence? As Duclos suggests, the law should clearly distinguish between defamation and documentation.

Resources

- Alex Cameron, "Lights, Camera, … Harmonize: Photography Issues in Copyright Reform," 2005.
- Canadian Association of Photographers and Illustrators in Communications (CAPIC) website, www.capic.org. Resources on contracts and legislation.

16: Visual Arts

THE VISUAL arts in Canada have a tradition of collective action and advocacy, and within the art community copyright has generated a number of controversies. Exhibition rights, moral rights, and appropriation and parody have been at the centre of discussion and action.

The Exhibition Right

One peculiarity of the "art world" is that many visual artists reach their most desired audiences and markets not through the reproduction of their work (as do writers and many musicians), but through the exhibition of original or limited edition work. Since legislative changes in 1988 visual artists have had the exclusive right to exhibit their work (or authorize its exhibition); since the Status of the Artist Act came into force in 1992,[1] they have been able to collectively negotiate standard rates for exhibition in Canada.

When individual artists sell a work, either to a collector or a gallery, they are understood to be selling only the rights in that physical object, unless a contract explicitly states that they are also transferring or licensing reproduction, exhibition, or moral rights. The exhibition right, set out in section 3(1)(g) of the Copyright Act, grants the artist the sole right "to present at a public exhibition, for a purpose other than sale or hire, an artistic work created after June 7, 1988, other than a map, chart or plan." Exhibition is a different sort of right than most of the others in the Copyright Act in that it does not involve reproduction, but we can make sense of it by understanding the display of a work of art as a sort of performance: just as writers and composers have a right to benefit from performances of their works, visual artists have an analogous right.

> Our argument essentially is that [galleries] have to adjust their priorities. They can't go to their staff and say, take half a wage to do the work you're doing. And the argument we're putting forward to them that they don't really like, is that we're peers and that we're an equal participant in that economy. Without us they wouldn't have their exhibitions, just as without a curator they wouldn't have somebody to organize the exhibitions. So we deserve to be paid on a level that's eventually on par with the senior people working in the system. You know, what curators get paid, and directors get paid, etc.... And the whole idea is that exhibitions enhance your sales, or enhance your academic career, or enhance your ability to get grants, and all that's true. But it still doesn't account for the fact that we're participating in an economy and we contribute to it.
>
> –Karl Beveridge, artist, CARFAC negotiator with the National Gallery, Toronto, interview with Kirsty Robertson.

The exhibition right can frustrate the public education mandate of galleries and museums: it may mean, for example, that they cannot put thumbnails of works in their collection on a public website without permission. Canadian Artists' Representation/Le front des artistes canadiens (CARFAC), an organization that represents many artists on these issues, argues that the galleries simply need to budget to pay for the right. The galleries cite benefits to artists of such exposure, and new opportunities to license use of their work—and they say furthermore that they can't afford to pay the fees expected by CARFAC. The two parties seem to be stuck in something of a stalemate.

Moral Rights

Since 1988 some visual artists have had a slightly special status when it comes to moral rights. Whereas writers or filmmakers have to show damage to their honour or reputation to win a case of moral rights infringement, section 28.1(2) states, "In the case of a painting, sculpture or engraving, the prejudice referred to in subsection (1) shall be deemed to have occurred as a result of *any* distortion, mutilation or other modification of the work."[2] The Act stipulates: "(a) a change in the location of a work, the physical means by which a work is exposed or the physical structure containing a work, or (b) steps taken in good faith to restore or preserve the work shall not, by that act alone, constitute a distortion, mutilation, or other modification of the work."

Even before this section was added to the act, the 1982 case of *Snow v. Eaton Centre* in the Ontario High Court of Justice showed that courts were likely to recognize moral rights in unique visual works of art (see chapter 4). The Supreme Court set a higher bar for moral rights infringement in *Théberge v. La Galerie d'Art du Petit Champlain* (2002), which concerned the reuse of reproductions of paintings: the Court was not convinced by Claude Théberge's claims that his reputation had been damaged by the actions of the gallery in question, given that he had already authorized them to make thousands of posters of his work.

Appropriation and Parody

In the *Théberge* case, the artist had signed a contract with a gallery for the reproduction of his paintings on posters, postcards, and other stationery products. When he found that the gallery was selling his images on a canvas backing—to which they had been transferred from a poster by a new chemical process—he applied for an injunction and seizure of the offending objects. Ultimately, the Supreme Court found that there was no infringement in this case, because there was no reproduction.

> An expansive reading of the economic rights whereby substitution of one backing for another constitutes a new "reproduction" that infringes the copyright holder's rights ... tilts the balance too far

in favour of the copyright holder and insufficiently recognizes the proprietary rights of the appellants in the physical posters which they purchased.[3]

Many artists find this case disturbing. The gallery made a new thing, which it sold for a higher price, presumably skimming off the extra profit; the court's idea that this did not constitute reproduction may seem mere sophistry. However, there was indeed no reproduction: the original poster paper was blank after the image had been transferred to the canvas. An analogous situation occurs when an artist uses pages from a book as the basis for a collage or an installation. If there is no reproduction, there is no infringement. It is a fundamental principle of the law. If the *Théberge* case had been decided the other way, practices such as collage or found-object art might have been in jeopardy. Artists might well see some merit in the court's statement that "once an authorized copy of a work is sold to a member of the public, it is generally for the purchaser, not the author, to determine what happens to it."[4]

Collage, a major genre of the twentieth century, is a pre-digital form: whereas a Robert Rauschenberg might glue together material bits and pieces (as he has said, "I think a painting is more like the real world if it's made out of the real world"), an artist in the twenty-first century is likely to make collage out of reproductions: printouts of material found online, or manipulated digital files. It is often said that copyright law should be technologically neutral. Has a formerly permitted practice become legally ambiguous? If so, artists have cause to be concerned because they will be vulnerable to legal action over previously acceptable practices.

Ironically, this new vulnerability to infringement lawsuits has emerged just as appropriation art has exploded in quantity and reputation. This problem is as present in the case of commercial work—big-label hip hop—as it is with fine arts. As more and more of us live in highly human-made environments, those are the worlds we seek to represent or see represented. As the Coalition of Art Professionals states: "Aspects of [popular culture] are often reproduced as part of the work of art, but in such a way that the subject is transformed…. The new works that are produced comment on the world in which we live and reflect the nature of creativity itself."[5] Journalist Roberta Smith eloquently elaborates the social benefits of appropriation art:

> Our surroundings are so thoroughly saturated with images and logos, both still and moving, that forbidding artists to use them in their work is like barring 19th-century landscape painters from depicting trees on their canvases. Pop culture is our landscape. It is at times wonderful. Most of us would not want to live without it. But it is also insidious and aggressive. The stuff is all around us, and society benefits from multiple means of staving it off. We are entitled to have artists, as well as political cartoonists, composers and writers, portray, parody and dissect it.[6]

But what does Canadian law permit by way of appropriation art? Unfortunately, the answer is not quite clear. Reuse of works created by others is less likely to result in liability if:

- it does not involve copying the material;
- the copied material is in the public domain;
- the copying is not "substantial"; or
- the material is copied for one of the fair dealing purposes stipulated in section 29, and meets the other *CCH v. Law Society of Upper Canada* tests for fairness.

On the question of substantiality, no mathematical formula exists for making a determination (see chapter 3). Substantiality depends on the nature of the material and the nature of the use. Still, certain genres, particularly songs and poems, have accrued their own particular "substantiality" practices—and the "law on the street" here lies not in statute or cases but in what rights holders can get away with, which forms an industry norm or standard after a while.

Let's say that as the artist of a work that makes use of the copyrighted material of others, you do think your use is "substantial." You still might not need to seek permission because your use might be fair dealing—*if* it can be called research, private study, criticism, or review, and in the latter two cases *if* you mention the source. So then we have to ask, how might the courts define these terms? Private study would probably permit most basement remixes or children's collages from magazines—but if you wanted to release them for others to hear or see, you would have no protection. Research and review don't seem terribly relevant to most artistic practice—or at least its end products. But what about criticism? How would the courts define it? What kinds of artistic practices would be called "criticism"?

Michelin v. CAW clearly disqualified parody from the category of criticism—probably to the surprise of most parodists. The *Michelin* case raises serious questions about the viability of parody in Canada. However, in *CCH v. Law Society of Upper Canada* (2004) the Supreme Court demolished the fundamentals of the *Michelin* logic. "Fair dealing," the highest Court declared, "must not be interpreted restrictively" because it is a way of recognizing users' rights in the copyright balance. This higher court ruling would probably permit parody to count as criticism. Oddly enough, then, Canadian artists might have less chance of

Michelin v. CAW (1997)

The situation:
Canadian Auto Workers, running a unionization drive at Nova Scotia Michelin plants in 1994, made posters featuring a robust Michelin Man and two scrawny workers. Michelin sued for trademark and copyright infringement. CAW argued that their use was fair dealing, and/or constituted protected expression under the Charter of Rights and Freedoms.

The result:
Justice Teitelbaum decided that the reproduction of the "beaming marshmallow-like rotund figure composed of tires" was not a violation of trademark: CAW wasn't advertising a product that could be confused with Michelin's. However, he did find the use to be copyright infringement. "It is immaterial if the defendants have employed some labour and some originality if there is nonetheless reproduction of a substantial part of the original," he said, adding that the use was not fair dealing because parody "should not be read in as a form of criticism to constitute a new exception." He also noted that CAW did not mention the source of the figure, as required by section 29.

infringing works they detest than works they love—if the use features attribution as the act requires. Attribution runs counter to the game of parody, but then again the act merely requires "mention" of the source; fine print may suffice.

Still, fitting into one of the five categories is only the first of six tests for fair dealing (see chapter 6). Assessing the risk level of the work in question means proceeding through the other tests. Then too, even if your use is fair dealing, you might still be vulnerable on charges of defamation, an entirely different area of law.

A final point on parody: it is important to distinguish Canadian from U.S. law on this question, because the laws are different. The United States has a stronger tradition of assessing parody as "fair use." The idea is that a parody must reproduce enough of its target to "conjure it up."

In *Campbell v. Acuff-Rose Music* (1994), the U.S. Supreme Court stated that parody's "art lies in the tension between a known original and its parodic twin." That case concerned 2 Live Crew's rap version of Roy Orbison's "Oh Pretty Woman." The court was convinced in the end that the 2 Live Crew version was a parody and did not require clearance. Interestingly, the successful legal strategy was a bit of a stretch from an artistic point of view: many who heard the song probably didn't know the Orbison original, so it could not have served as a parody for them—nor was it clear that 2 Live Crew had parody in mind. Similarly, when Alice Randall rewrote *Gone with the Wind* from the slaves' point of view and called it *The Wind Done Gone*, she might have thought of it as a critique or "writing back," but her lawyers called it a parody. They were able to get a preliminary injunction lifted in 2001.[7]

If these two U.S. cases embrace a broad definition of parody, we find a different approach in *Rogers v. Koons* (1992). In that case, a New York district court ruled that Jeff Koons's sculptures based on Art Rogers's photographs constituted infringement. The judge said that the sculptures constituted satire of social attitudes rather than parody targeting Rogers's work—in other words, the court decided that Rogers's work specifically was not required for Koons to make his point.[8] A similar reasoning would probably obtain in Canada: as *CCH* puts it, "If there is a non-copyrighted equivalent of the work that could have been used instead of the copyrighted work, this should be considered by the court."[9]

A defence of unauthorized parody in either Canada or the United States has to show the necessity of using that *particular* source. Furthermore, the Koons case reminds us that the addition of "parody" to the list of five permitted fair dealing purposes does not necessarily catch the range of artistic practices represented in today's art world; adding a "such as" clause to the fair dealing section of Canadian law would do more to keep judges out of the business of theorizing parody and satire and make for a more flexible, if not more precise, law.

Resources

Canada
- Appropriation Art website, http://www.appropriationart.ca.
- Jane Bailey, "Deflating the Michelin Man: Protecting Users' Rights in the Canadian Copyright Reform Process," 2005.
- Canadian Artists' Representation (CARFAC) website, http://www.carfac.ca.

United States and United Kingdom
- Illegal Art website, http://www.illegal-art.org. A gallery of appropriation art, with many legal resources, mostly U.S.
- Image Rights website, http://www.law.harvard.edu/faculty/martin/art_law/image_rights.htm. An excellent site by a Harvard law professor and librarian on U.S. visual arts law.
- Simon Stokes, "Some Reflections on Art and Copyright," 2004.

17: Websites

IN THE era of personal websites, blogs, and other forms of Internet communication, the old distinctions between publisher and consumer, content provider and user, are quickly breaking down. The author of material on the Internet may also be its publisher, and its reader may soon become a co-author because of some interactive feature that encourages instant transformation. One effect of this situation is that people who know nothing about copyright law, people who have never thought of themselves as publishers or owners of copyrighted works, are routinely in a position to produce, reproduce, transform, and distribute works. These works will then be used by others who will repeat this process of transformation.

The general point to remember is that copyright law treats material on the Internet the same way as it treats any other material: if the material meets the requirements for copyright (see chapter 3), it is automatically copyrighted. Reproduction of substantial portions of works on the Internet in which copyright subsists requires consent from the owner. By making materials available on the Internet, owners are not foregoing their copyright interests, nor are they authorizing anyone to go out and reprint and distribute the work on a commercial scale.

But users' rights also obtain on the Internet: the standard exceptions and limitations (such as fair dealing) can justify some types of use of the work. If an owner of copyrighted material uploads it to a server from which members of the public can gain access to it without further limitation, that uploading is a form of consent for a range of non-commercial uses. Even if the web page in question does not say the magic words— "the owner of the copyright in this work hereby gives you consent to make reasonable use of the material including downloading it, printing it out, distributing it to others, and using the copy and paste function to extract portions of it for reuse"—that sentiment, we believe, is reasonably implied. After all, that is how people use the Internet. Users can reasonably expect refusal of consent for such uses to be explicitly stated or, more likely, demonstrated through encryption, passwording, or the application of some other technological measure to limit or restrict what they can do with the file. Only a few years ago it would have been difficult for the non-technically minded to apply such technological protections; today it is simple and routine. For example, when you save a PDF file in Adobe Acrobat, you can disable users from using the copy function.

A specific section of the Copyright Act allows you to copy music available online—or anywhere—for your own personal use. Section 80 of the act provides that it is not infringement to make private copies of any musical material if you don't redistribute it—a privilege we pay for through levies on CDs and blank cassettes.

Consent and Terms of Use

Websites that state specific terms of use show a wide range of approaches. Wikipedia offers its articles under a GNU Free Documentation License—a quick summary of which is that you can reproduce articles in Wikipedia with acknowledgement as long as you offer your work under the same free licence.[1] Other sites have different restrictions. For example, the *Globe and Mail*:

grants you a limited non-exclusive, non-transferable license to use and display on your computer or other electronic access device, the Content and Services for your own personal, private and non-commercial use only, provided that you do not modify the Content and that you maintain all copyright and other proprietary notices. Except as provided herein, you agree not to reproduce, make derivative works of, retransmit, distribute, sell, publish, communicate, broadcast or otherwise make available any of the Content obtained through a BGPI Site or any of the Services, including without limitation, by caching, framing or similar means, without the prior written consent of the respective copyright owner of such Content.[2]

This statement renders itself rather absurd given the routine caching functions of any personal computer, not to mention the print button offered on globeandmail.com itself. And then there is fair dealing: although copyright exists on the Internet, so too do users' rights. If a website's use policy tells you that you can't quote from it, or print it out for a scrapbook or research file, remember your users' rights.

If you are creating original content that you are uploading to a website, you too can customize copyright law to some extent and clarify what use of the material you consider appropriate. You can do this in your own words—by entering a line such as "Non-commercial use of material on this site freely licensed" or "All rights reserved. Copyright 2006 Joe Dragoneater." For many purposes, the Creative Commons licensing system is useful: it offers an array of choices in licensing terms, such as permission for non-commercial use only, or permission for reproduction as long as no changes are made to the original.[3] If users want to make a non-permitted use, they can contact you and negotiate, which means that Creative Commons licences can even be suitable for people who seek commercial outlets for their work. Visual artists and photographers have another way of making work available while limiting lost income: they can put work online in low resolution—suitable for browsing but not for reproduction. If you want to limit access to your material even further, you can require registration and a password to enter your site.

When it comes to reusing copyrighted works owned by others directly on your own website (whatever the source of those works), the "implied consent" argument is not strong. Redistributing a movie, or

In the Public Interest: The Future of Canadian Copyright Law, a collection of essays edited by Michael Geist—while it was published by a commercial publisher and is available for sale in the regular book market—is also available online under the terms of a Creative Commons licence.

To obtain it online, you take the following steps.

- Go to the publishers' web page for the book at http://www.irwinlaw.com/books.aspx?bookid=120.
- Select any one of the essays from the Table of Contents.
- Scroll down until you see a box labelled "Creative Commons Legal Code Attribution-NonCommercial-NoDerivs 2.0 Canada." While the text seems to be full of legal jargon, if you read it section by section it is understandable, and a more streamlined version can be found at http://creativecommons.org/licenses/by-nc-nd/2-0/ca. If you indicate your agreement to the terms, you are being granted a "a worldwide, royalty-free, non-exclusive, perpetual (for the duration of the applicable copyright) licence" to exercise certain enumerated rights.
- At the end of this text, there is another small box labelled "I agree to the terms and conditions listed above."
- If you check that box, you can then download the PDF of the article. Notice that the PDF file is the exact reproduction of the page in the book as published, with the page numbering intact. You are also able to use features such as save, copy and paste, print, and forward with respect to the article.

Clearly, the editor and the authors of articles in this collection *want you to use their work*. They want you to read it; they want you to share it with others; they want you to cite the articles in your own transformative work; and they probably want you to ask your librarian to purchase the hard copy of the book. Creative Commons can facilitate all of these actions.

a substantial part thereof, would be an actionable copyright infringement. Putting an image from somebody else's website on yours without permission would probably be infringement—unless you can show it to be fair dealing for the purpose of criticism, review, or news reporting. Reproducing a piece of writing (or a substantial portion of the work in question) from a website for your newsletter or zine without permission

Can I use cartoons from the Internet in my powerpoint presentations?

It would depend on the facts and context. Such a use might be fair dealing, but probably only if it genuinely engages in criticism or review of the given cartoons, and if you can justify that you had to use those *particular* cartoons. If you are making your presentation in an educational institution, section 29.4(1) of the Copyright Act allows projection of copyrighted materials. But "educational institution" is defined in the act as a non-profit government-recognized institution, which does not cover sales conferences, some private schools, or public lectures. You might decide to go ahead based on the rationale that it is practically impossible to determine the author or copyright owner of some much-circulated but unlabelled images on the Internet—and it is hard to imagine that the Copyright Board would want to bother with licensing one-time ephemeral use on behalf of such unlocatable owners. You might suppose that the potential for liability is negligible (probably true if your presentation is ephemeral), or that the creators wouldn't mind in any event (might or might not be true). You might argue that it's an established practice in your industry or sector—meaning that the practice is generally accepted in like situations, in which case you are getting close to an implied consent argument.

would also be infringement. The usual infringement guidelines (chapter 7) apply on the Internet as everywhere else: you have to review, for example, the consent situation, the substantiality of the reproduction, and possible defences to infringement.

Internet Linking

In practical terms, the Internet offers one alternative to reproduction not available so easily in other media: linking. Linking to someone else's website is a perfectly legitimate practice. Using hypertext links is the essence of the World Wide Web, and it seems strange that anyone would object to having external links coming to their site. Yet owners of websites do raise such objections, and as a result linking practices can raise certain other legal problems.

Linking practices range through three different types: direct linking, deep-linking, and framing.

Direct linking is the simplest form of using a hypertext link. It's hard to imagine anyone complaining about getting an external link sent over from another site. After all, it's getting to be all about eyeballs, and the more eyeballs the better. But some websites do not want the "wrong kind of people," and they try to discourage external links that are created without their permission. For example, the Exxon/Mobil website advises, "You may not link to this site without prior written permission from ExxonMobil." The web page for the New York Stock Exchange says, "NYSE prohibits caching, unauthorized hypertext links to the website and the framing of any Content available through its site."[4] These kinds of restrictions, though, are blatantly unreasonable, and if you come across statements like these you should not give them much concern from a copyright point of view.

For its part, Access Copyright has generated quite a bit of criticism for its anti-linking policy. In 2006 this copyright collective received negative attention in the press and in blog circles because of "Captain Copyright"—the cartoon character, directed towards children, that carried an anti-copying message. Critics argued that the message was inaccurate and biased. As law professor Michael Geist reported in the *Toronto Star*:

> Captain Copyright critics were also troubled by the terms and conditions on the site that seemingly sought to shield the superhero from criticism. The site features a linking policy that stipulates that "permission to link is explicitly withheld from any web site the contents of which may, in the opinion of the Access Copyright, be damaging or cause harm to the reputation of, Access Copyright."[5]

Geist argued that "permission is not needed to link on the Internet and it cannot be denied in legal terms and conditions," and "when Access Copyright chose to freely display its content on the World Wide Web, it surrendered the right to restrict who might link to the site or comment on it." He concluded that the principle against restricting access "should resonate particularly strongly with Access Copyright, given that it is a copyright collective whose members rely upon freedom of speech for their livelihoods."[6]

The practice of deep linking presents slightly different issues. According to Wikipedia, "Deep linking ... is the act of placing on a Web page a hyperlink that points to a specific page or image within another website, as opposed to that website's main or home page."[7] Linking to an internal page in a website is much like going to a card catalogue at a library, finding the book on the shelf, and looking through its index for the material you are seeking: you don't have to start reading at page 1 to find what you want.

Deep linking has been the subject of controversy because some website owners want visitors to enter through the front door, and only through the front door. They do not want other sites to send visitors into the interior of their site without passing through the portal of the home page. This may be because there is advertising on the home page, because they want readers to follow a certain order of presentation, or because they just want to maintain more control over the situation. As a copyright issue, demands to refrain from deep linking should not carry much weight. In any event, a web page designer should be able to redirect users back to the appropriate web page if someone tries to enter through a restricted page.[8]

Framing is a very different practice than linking or deep linking because you are actually bringing the external web page into a portion of your presentation, as a framed screen. Depending on how you set the frames up, the boundary between the external materials and your own may or may not be entirely clear. From a copyright point of view it is hard to argue that there is any direct infringement because you are not really reproducing the external site on your own page. But it could appear that way to the end-user. Be careful that you are not setting your frames up in a way that misrepresents exactly what content is yours. While copyright issues are remote in this regard, other legal theories such as misrepresentation or passing off could be relevant.

These restrictions on different types of linking have generated litigation in other countries, but so far we know of no cases in Canada.

PART IV: POLICY

General Resources

- David Bollier, *Silent Theft: The Private Plunder of Our Common Wealth*, 2002.

- Rosemary J. Coombe, *The Cultural Life of Intellectual Properties: Authorship, Appropriation, and the Law*, 1998.

- Michael Geist, ed., *In the Public Interest: The Future of Canadian Copyright Law*, 2005.

18: Copyright's Counterparts

COPYRIGHT IS the market's central mechanism for fostering the production and circulation of culture and human expression; along with patent, it is a major tool for promoting innovation. We find it ingenious. Despite our critiques of copyright in its particular current state, and despite our observations about the legitimacy crisis it now faces, we are not among those who predict or demand its end.

But copyright does have its drawbacks. It doesn't always seem to perform well when it comes to policy objectives such as freedom of expression, broad participation, and preservation. As a monopoly mechanism, however tempered, copyright tends to limit access and constrain use. As a market mechanism, copyright privileges market value over other ways of assigning value. It thus incentivizes some kinds of creativity and dissemination, but not others. We need, then, to be aware of alternative mechanisms where they exist.

Copyright is simply not the only tool we have. There are at least four alternative mechanisms we can consider: Aboriginal cultural property protocols, "copyleft," citation economies, and public funding. Each of these systems is in some ways or in some contexts capable of promoting policy objectives usually associated with copyright. They are not pie in the sky: they are thriving now, and indeed two or three of them are much older than copyright. These systems—we call them economies of knowledge—challenge some of copyright's fundamental principles, but they are not incompatible with some forms of copyright legislation. In fact, copyright will really only work in concert with such counterparts—which is why we are choosing to spend some time with them before we proceed to specific policy recommendations.

Aboriginal Cultural Property

Although the recent increase in copyright controversy is often ascribed to the birth of the Internet and digital technologies, older technologies such as story-telling and traditional medicine also pose a challenge to the intellectual property system. Over the past couple of decades, indigenous people around the world have begun to co-ordinate their efforts to resist appropriation of their cultural knowledge and to assert other modes of governing its circulation.[1] They have been pushing their case at the local, national, and international levels.

Some of the motivation is economic: Aboriginal cultural knowledge has commodity value and may be one basis for sorely needed economic development in First Nations communities. Inuit art co-operatives may be one model here—even though most of the money in the global Inuit art market does not flow north. But Aboriginal traditional knowledge (TK) has other sorts of value as well, value that motivates many of those advocating its special treatment. It has been developed collectively by generations of people building up community, sacred, ecological, and political value along the way. Aboriginal groups have difficulty effectively protecting these kinds of value through the copyright and patent systems, because these systems place TK in the public domain, where it may be harvested by outsiders for financial gain or artistic glory. (Because it is old, unfixed, and has no single author, TK is an awkward fit within the conventional scope of copyright.) In Canada as in other countries, Aboriginal groups and individuals are working out ways of articulating their own laws and practices governing the circulation of cultural objects and images to those outside their communities.

> Within our customary law only a clan member can wear or use anything
> carrying the clan crest. The clan, not an individual member, can give
> others the right to use the clan crest. The right to use the crest is gener-
> ously given out, but only when requested in a good way, only for a good
> purpose and only for the narrow purpose requested. For example, we
> might allow an artist to use the crest in a carving, but would not sell the
> crest symbol to adorn a Coke bottle.
>
> —Christle Wiebe, Carcross/Tagish, "Customary Law and Cultural
> and Intellectual Properties," 2005.

In the light of copyright law, some Aboriginal statements on copy-right are reminiscent of the spirit of moral rights: they warn against reproducing or altering works in such a way as to produce damage to honour or reputation. But the honour or reputation of concern here is not the author's, but rather that of the clan, culture, or nation. And indeed, many indigenous people emphasize that the "author" of a specific expression is a tradition-bearer, not an originator. It is this person's responsibility to transmit what has been entrusted to her or him to the right people in the right way and at the right time. Depending on the particular tradition, the (re)creator may not be free to reinterpret the material in a new way, to disseminate it to strangers, or to sell it.[2] Thus while alienability is foundational to Western ideas of property and intellectual property—you know you own something if you're allowed to sell it—Aboriginal ownership, as many explain it, is based on ideas of custodianship, community, and responsibility.[3]

Tensions often exist between Aboriginal and non-Aboriginal approaches. For example, non-Native poet and scholar Robert Bringhurst has long been devoted to celebrating and publicizing Haida culture. Between 1999 and 2001 he published three books of retranslations of hundred-year-old transcriptions of Haida material. Bringhurst was eager to induct Haida storykeepers Ghandl and Skaii as poets into the "polylingual canon of North American literary history," and one of the books brought him a nomination for the Governor General's Literary Award.[4] But some critics considered his work appropriation. As Jusquan wrote in the magazine *Redwire*:

These Haida stories have been mysteriously defined as "Canadian" by those who write book reviews and teach Canadian literature courses, as well as those Canadians and others who are buying those books…. The richness and complexities of Haida history and spiritual beliefs are now nicely understandable and transparent for Canadians and other non-Haidas, and oh isn't it all so quaint and glorious. Now there is an assumed ownership of our stories, not only by Bringhurst but by those who read his books, and there was no payment. And by payment I mean in recognition of the significance of those stories, or in the recognition of the living Haida today and what those stories signify and mean to the on-going struggles of our culture.[5]

To some readers, Jusquan's anger may seem extreme. But consider the abundant totem pole key rings and raven T-shirts at the Vancouver airport, or the (astounding) choice of a Gumby version of the Inuit inukshuk as a logo for the 2010 Vancouver Olympics. The irony with the Olympic logo is that the Olympic Committee has gone so far as to arrange for special legislation to fortify its rights in this appropriated image. Canada does help itself to Aboriginal culture on a regular basis.

Although Aboriginal protocols are specific to their various nations, they also have wider importance. They are, after all, part of Canada's colonial past and present. In nineteenth-century Canada, white settlers were given land just for showing up and cutting the trees down on government-"owned" tracts appropriated from indigenous people; in twenty-first century Canada, white settlers can stake claims on First Nations cultural

There are hundreds of indigenous nations in the Americas, and every one of those nations has customary laws that regulate how their knowledge is used and accessed. These legal regimes are at least between five thousand and twenty thousand years old. The great irony about the status quo today is that Western intellectual property rights are only two or three hundred years old at the most!

And there's the other irony, that is being told that indigenous legal regimes are not legitimate and that we have to adhere to this so-called universal system, which came from a very small part of the world called Europe. The intellectual property rights system was imposed on indigenous knowledge systems without the consent of indigenous nations, and the conflict is a conflict of legal regimes. It's a legal power play; it's an unjustly and immorally applied conflict between laws and sets of laws.

—Greg Young-Ing, Chair, Indigenous Peoples' Caucus, Creators' Rights Alliance, Vancouver, interview with Laura Murray.

materials that Western law claims for all Canadians. It's an uncomfortable parallel, and it ought to be addressed. Some creators are concerned about limitations on freedom of expression that might result if increased authority is accorded to First Nations cultural protocols. But the copyright system works by imposing exclusion mechanisms on instances of culture; while these mechanisms constrain the actions of users of this material, we accept them if on balance their effect is judged to be productive. This should be the principle by which we explore the place of First Nations cultural property within or alongside Canadian IP law.

Beyond the political imperative, Aboriginal ideas about cultural property function as a powerful critique of certain elements of copyright thinking: they illuminate a range of different cultural practices and contexts. For example, copyright does acknowledge collective creation in provisions for joint authorship, corporate ownership, anonymous publication, and the resource of the public domain, but at its heart is the fiction that the individual creator can make something alone. Some critics would say that Aboriginal protocols go too far in the other direction by downplaying the creative initiative of individuals in favour of a collective, inherited foundation, but at the very least this emphasis is a potent corrective.

Copyleft

Copyleft, a term associated with free software, is used loosely to refer to a wide range of collaborative and recirculation practices in digital media. More specifically, Wikipedia (a copyleft phenomenon *par excellence*) defines it as "the practice of using copyright law to remove restrictions on distributing copies and modified versions of a work for others and requiring that the same freedoms be preserved in modified versions."[6] In other words, copyleft uses copyright against itself: it takes the rights the Copyright Act grants to authors, and deploys them differently.

Copyleft began with the open source software movement (FLOSS), and in particular the General Public License (GPL) through which it operates. Programmers working under the GPL retain the right to be recognized for their contributions, but do not hold exclusive economic rights, and cannot block reuse of the work. In provisions that have come to be known as "share-share-alike," subsequent generations of innovators must adhere to the same type of licence.[7] A later programmer needs no permission to use, improve, or customize the program, but cannot commercialize it: he or she must "pass it on." This is indeed a very different protocol from copyright. Despite a lack of the profit incentive that economists assert as a necessary incentive for creativity, and despite institutional and market pressures to limit the spread of free software, the system has clearly thrived.[8]

In 2001 the GPL model was adapted for a wide range of other creative practices through the Creative Commons licence, launched by Lawrence Lessig and others at Stanford University. Canadian versions of the licences appeared in 2003. In essence Creative Commons licences allow a creator to choose which rights from the copyright bundle to reserve, and which to waive. Or, as the Creative Commons website puts it, "We use private rights to create public goods."[9] Rights holders have a choice of a range of different licences. All require attribution, but some permit non-commercial use only, or require that the work not be changed. If a creator stipulates that the derivative work be licensed on the same terms as its source—offering a "share-alike" licence—he or she is fostering a "copyleft" economy of circulation by perpetuating the terms of sharing. One of the important and sometimes unappreciated features of these licences is that creators who choose them do not have to forego financial reward: users who want to work with material in ways not permitted by the licence negotiate with the rights owner to do so, just as they would in mainstream copyright. Thus a song might be available for free non-commercial sampling, but Avril Lavigne will pay for the rights if she puts it on her next album.

> Today, as the Internet and the digitally networked environment present us with a new set of regulatory choices, it is important to set our eyes on the right prize. That prize is not the Great Shopping Mall in Cyberspace. That prize is the Great Agora—the unmediated conversation of the many with the many.
>
> –Yochai Benkler, "From Consumers to Users," 565.

Over only a few years, Creative Commons licences have been taken up not only by individuals but also by prominent educational projects—the Public Library of Science (PLOS) and MIT's Open Courseware program are prominent examples. Open access academic journals use similar sorts of licences to make research available for free while protecting authenticity and integrity. Specific licences have become a way of marking a certain vision of the Internet, in which access to information goods, their transformation into something new, and their redistribution to another creator-in-waiting is experienced as an ongoing process.

While in its strong streak of libertarianism, much "copyleft" or "free culture" thinking contrasts with the Aboriginal viewpoint (copylefters celebrate appropriation, while Aboriginal people often speak against it), the two approaches have points in common insofar as they are both based on an idea of responsibility for shared culture. They both strive, for example, to serve community goals, to use cultural engagement to build community, and to recognize in custom a kind of law. They both ask us to think twice about how we use other people's creations, rather than simply waiting for the one and only law to tell us what to do.

Citation Economies

There is a widespread tendency in today's media and water cooler chatter to conflate copyright infringement and plagiarism. True, they both constitute inappropriate borrowing of the work of others. But they are significantly different infractions, and they take place in two distinct economies of knowledge: copyright and citation. The fundamental expectation in the copyright system—notwithstanding users' rights—is permission, but the fundamental expectation in a citation system is attribution. Hence copyright infringement is use without permission (again, with all the caveats mentioned in chapters 4 and 6), and it's a matter of law, whereas plagiarism is use without attribution, and it's a matter of community or professional practice.[10]

Beyond the practical headaches caused by this confusion, we see it as a disturbing indicator of society's lack of awareness of the workings and vitality of citation economies. Citation tends to be associated with academic scholarship—and we'll get to that realm shortly. But listen closely: people can't even talk about the weather without quoting each other. To mark the authority or tone or social value of these quotations, ordinary conversation often requires citations as well. "Who told you that?" your friend asks—she wants a footnote. Or "Where'd you get that lick?"—musicians want to trace their lineage as they reinvent it. In their everyday lives people seem to "get" the idea that, as language theorist Mikhail Bakhtin put it so well, "the word in language is half someone else's. It becomes 'one's own' only when the speaker populates it with his own intention, his own accent, when he appropriates the word."[11]

In a citation economy such as conversation or improvisational music or the blogosphere, you don't need to get permission—you just need to acknowledge your sources. The General Public License of the Open Software movement and the "share-share-alike" Creative Commons licence are thus specific formalizations of citational practice. What these systems may lack in terms of financial incentives (though they often do indirectly provide those), they make up for in other ways.

Citation economies work for a number of different reasons. While some people speak of citation economies as "gift" economies, this useful analogy should not be taken as a licence to view them through a

Hallmark haze. Citation economies build on individuals' desire for recognition and communication. We quote others to call them to account, to bolster our authority, or to add zest to our communication, and we deeply hope that others will do the same with our contributions. Policing happens not through law but through social expectations—plagiarism is seen as an insult to the group's honour and legitimacy. The vast majority of human communication and knowledge production emerges out of such environments.

Why do citation economies work?

- no friction of time, money, effort, rejection risk in seeking permission
- less vulnerable to censorship than copyright
- effective at tracing origins, relationship of ideas
- effective at moving information and expression fast and far
- effective at innovation
- appeal to altruism
- appeal to egotism
- build community
- allow social differentiation, status markers
- lead to opportunities for remuneration.

Academic research, along with its junior siblings in schoolroom citation practices, is the most formal and established of the widespread citation economies. In the "web of science,"[12] each person's writing is understood as a contribution to a network of dialogue and expertise. Since currency in this citation system is reputation, barrier-free access and circulation are essential. Today this citation economy is under considerable pressure. Universities give away publicly funded knowledge to for-profit journals and buy it back, if they can, at high prices. In agreements with private funders, or in an effort to generate income, they constrain access to research data or resources that were formerly broadly available. Out of fear of liability, they pay licensing fees for uses that are customarily and often legally acceptable.

These constraints are not only happening at the post-secondary level. School boards are being fed the mantra that it is their responsibility to educate children about copyright.[13] Doing so would be, in our view, irresponsible—at least in elementary schools. If children get the message too young that they must ask before they can use anything around them, they will become obedient consumers before they have the chance to become fearless learners or budding creators. Let's get our priorities straight. People create because they want to—and they do this long before, and often long after, they are motivated by money. After we are sure that students have a sense of engagement with their cultural and intellectual heritage, and a sense of participation in its development, *then* we can tell them about copyright. Copyright has a place in cultural development, and it's a secondary one.

We recognize that it's not easy to make a living off being quoted; as artist John B. Boyle said, "This is Canada: you can die of exposure."[14] We are by no means suggesting that the copyright system be replaced by citation modes—or "copyleft" or Aboriginal models, for that matter. Our argument is simply that crowding these systems out will impoverish us all—culturally and indeed, ultimately, financially. As Brewster Kneen, David Bollier, and other activists say, we need to build the commons.[15] Letting copyright govern our educational environments and places of creative experimentation might seem efficient, modern, and lucrative, but there is a powerful analogy to be made here with the hidden environmental costs of capitalism: we can pave over messy and apparently useless swamps, but sooner or later we may learn that the costs of so doing are far larger than the benefits.

Public Funding

Another counterpart to copyright can be found in public support for education, science, research, broadcasting, and the arts. Government funding has been an essential motor of cultural and intellectual production in Canada. But what is government funding? If we speak instead of taxpayer, public, or citizen funding, we might better evoke the responsibility that funded institutions and creators have to the public. Nowadays copyright and other IP mechanisms are being held up as a new great hope for funding education, research, and the arts. This is a kind of offloading. Along with the trend towards user fees, this approach produces unconscionable access barriers. Along with increasing dependence on private-sector funding, it shifts the products and results of this sector to the detriment of Canadians. Although IP has a role in cultural and economic growth, it can't do the job alone.

The nation's well-being and future success require proper levels of funding for educational institutions and public libraries. These institutions are the bedrock for an informed citizenry; they provide future creators with the intellectual tools needed to go about their work; they nurture the audience and indeed the market for creative work. Their universal accessibility is a public good of the highest order. But accessibility is not only about funding levels: it is about attitude. Schools and libraries could do much more to multiply the effectiveness of the funding they do get by sharing the fruits of their labours as widely as digital technologies now permit.

You have high-end big name visual and media artists, who might make video art tapes with editions of three: they choose to increase their capital through having very small editions of work, because they're usually in a more conventional system—say they have a dealer in Soho, or they're showing at the Whitney, and they're selling their tapes on the open art market. But then you also have other artists who go the Creative Commons route and have their stuff on YouTube and have their own websites. And it's freely downloadable. I think these two spheres should be able to co-exist: people should have the choice, as artists, about how they want to market their work, and how they want their work to be purchased, or enjoyed, or experienced.

[Debate over copyright reform] has all just been so negative ... so doom and gloom. Why aren't we talking about what an opportunity [legislation] could provide to restructure the country? But nobody is really engaging that question. If the debate is a paradigm, it's the user groups versus artist creators, and there have been a lot of people digging in their heels on both sides of the issue. If we had less of that, we could look at a really novel opportunity, in our legislative history, to have something interesting happen. Something truly "creative."

–James Missen, Ontario Region Board Member, Independent Media Arts Alliance, Ottawa, interview with Kirsty Robertson.

Generous support for public broadcasting, performing arts organizations, and museums and galleries is also essential. In this regard we can clearly see the costs of "cost recovery" strategies: when the CBC charges a documentary filmmaker $187 for one second of footage, or a museum bedecks its website with misleading copyright warnings, they are preventing Canadians from benefiting from resources they have already paid for.[16] In their dealings with government, these institutions continually pronounce their indispensability—but they would see better results if they focused on a new or renewed commitment to serving the public and valuing the contributions of creators. As John Holden declares, "If a sustainable base for culture is to be secured then cultural professionals need to think of 'advocacy' not just in terms of generating 'evidence' for their funders, but as establishing broad support with the public."[17]

A good place to start on public relations is to make digital archives and collections available free for non-commercial use—and on a sliding scale for revenue-generating use. Free and sliding-scale admission prices fit this philosophy well too. Of course, these sorts of policies and projects cost a great deal of money—but we believe they are the only way of reversing the slide in government funding. In a strange but compelling paradox, arts, research, and broadcasting leaders could demonstrate their indispensability more dramatically than ever before by giving away the shop—emulating Google, MIT, and other leaders in the open access movement. They could also improve their image with government and private funders by showing generosity to creators, and working to change the adversarial relationship that often seems to exist between management and "content-providers."

Direct funding to creators and researchers is also an essential part of Canada's intellectual and cultural economy. At least in theory, granting councils don't pay out for what is popular, but for what juries of peers think is important, beautiful, or provocative. In this way they support currents of ideas and art that may not generate immediate income, but that will make people see new things or scratch their heads. Other mechanisms such as the Public Lending Right and targeted tax policy do or could provide direct support to creators as well.[18] Such mechanisms have value in themselves and also in the economic spinoffs they produce as creators and audiences alike develop and diversify. There are accessibility issues in this area as well: publicly funded work ought to be widely available. Academic researchers can publish in open access journals or resources and thus reach beyond the walls of their discipline or institution. Artists can at least make thumbnail images of their work available for free so that people can know of their existence.

To emphasize a responsibility to the public is not to say that all publicly funded art or research ought to be widely popular, widely understandable, or widely approved. Some art is offensive or altogether perplexing, and much research is hedged in by biochemical or sociological jargon. So be it. The principle is that such work must be available without undue constraints to those members of the public who want to engage with it. In a world dominated by market ideology, "cheap" is a derogatory term, and "free" may sound like garbage or trickery. But as many corporations and collectives are discovering, giving things away can be an enriching

Resources

Aboriginal Cultural Property
- Aboriginal and Torres Strait Islander Arts Board, Indigenous Protocol Guides. Detailed recommendations for working with indigenous cultural materials, http://www.ozco.gov.au/arts_resources/publications/cultures_indigenous_protocol_guides.
- "Project for the Protection and Repatriation of First Nation Cultural Heritage in Canada." A project led by Professor Catherine Bell, University of Alberta. Site includes specific case study reports and other materials, http://www.law.ualberta.ca/research/aboriginalculturalheritage.
- "Traditions: National Gatherings on Indigenous Knowledge," Department of Canadian Heritage, 2005, http://www.traditions.gc.ca/index_e.cfm.

Copyleft
- Creative Commons Canada: http:www/creativecommons.ca.
- Electronic Frontier Foundation: http://www.eff.org/IP.
- Lawrence Lessig, *Free Culture: How Big Media Uses Technology and the Law to Lock Down Culture and Control Creativity*, 2004.
- Peter Suber, "Open Access Overview," http://www.earlham.edu/~peters/fos/overview.htm.

strategy.[19] There are costs and arrangements to be worked out: creators of materials in public collections may need to be paid extra for the digital use of their work, and in some cases such as certain Aboriginal work, limitations on access may be necessary. Fees for commercial reuse will be necessary and in some cases might be increased. But with a mixed and flexible approach, the educational, research, and cultural sectors will be better positioned to fulfil their democratic mandates.

Citation Economies

- C. Fisk, "Credit Where It's Due: Attribution Rights without Intellectual Property Rights," 2006.
- Lisa Maruca, "The Plagiarism Panic: Digital Policing in the New Intellectual Property Regime," 2004.
- Onthecommons.org website: "Dedicated to building a new commons movement. It explores the varieties of commons in our midst; the many ways that commons can be managed fairly and sustainably; and the exciting new kinds of commons-based activism and research that are now occurring."
- Laurie Stearns, "Copy Wrong: Plagiarism, Process, Property, and the Law," 1999.

Public Funding

- Culturescope.ca website: "the interactive hub of the Canadian Cultural Observatory." A resource on Canadian cultural policy.
- John Holden, "Cultural Value and the Crisis of Legitimacy: Why Culture Needs a Democratic Mandate," 2006. A lucid and compelling argument for articulating public benefit in cultural funding.

19: Copyright's Future

SINCE 2001, when the departments of Industry and Canadian Heritage began working towards a new round of copyright legislation, we have seen several different ministers and indeed governments come and go. We have also seen many different reports on various copyright issues. So far Bill C-60 is the only legislation to emerge. That bill did attempt to chart a Canadian policy direction somewhat distinct from U.S. legislation, and it avoided the excesses of the Canadian Heritage Committee's unbalanced Bulte Report, but its provisions were unworkably complex and the bill lacked any broad policy vision.[1] The Liberals also did not seem to listen to the important recent Supreme Court cases. All in all, there are few to mourn C-60, but it may serve as an important touchstone for future discussion.

More legislation is sure to follow on this well-travelled but tricky terrain. The minority Conservative government came to power in early 2006 with the opportunity of developing a more innovation-friendly copyright strategy, but instead seemed to bend to corporate and diplomatic demands for a protection-driven approach—which means that the time is ripe for citizen engagement in this area. Canada does not just need copyright reform: it needs effective copyright reform appropriate to its particular cultural and economic needs.

The New Policy Environment

Whatever happens next in terms of proposed legislation, it is sure to provoke lively discussion. This is the first change to notice from ten or even five years ago: copyright has become an important issue for more and more people. Copyright was once thought of as a technical specialty area of the law, of interest to a few practitioners and law professors, but it is now understood as a broad-based domain of cultural practices and constraints. People increasingly recognize that copyright affects, or could affect, their daily lives.

The Internet has caused a great deal of the concern—people want to know that they can continue to make use of what they see as an exciting new resource, or that they can protect their copyright in what they see as a jungle. The Internet has also provided a platform for education and discussion. In 2002 Canada had only one blog critiquing the dangers posed by U.S.-style copyright reform; by 2007, there were several.[2] Many other blogs and websites also frequently weigh in on these issues. Newspapers and news broadcasts often feature copyright stories, and Michael Geist's *Toronto Star* column appears regularly. These virtual communities have real effects. In 2006 they played a significant role in the election defeat of Sarmite Bulte, the parliamentary secretary for Canadian Heritage. When critics suggested that a recording-industry-sponsored benefit supporting her campaign was part of a continuing effort to buy her support for a certain vision of copyright reform, she referred to those critics as "user rights zealots," confirming suspicions of bias.[3] There has also been a huge increase in "creator-made" policy interventions, voicing a range of opinions about the copyright needs of creators as distinct from corporate owners.[4]

A second shift in the policy environment is that the traditional lines between creators and users of intellectual goods are breaking down. Dualities—performer/audience, broadcaster/viewer, sender/receiver, producer/consumer—are losing their relevance as discrete categories. As intellectual goods become increasingly severable from their traditional containers, these traditional polarities fail to keep up with the speed, ease, and intensity of new information transfer processes. The same person is at once a consumer of existing intellectual goods and a creator and owner of new ones. This does not mean that we no longer need mechanisms to pay creators: many forms of creativity require individuals to spend hours upon days upon weeks labouring for their craft, and as a society we have to find ways of supporting that. But many people believe that their new-found ability to interact with culture instead of merely watching it is also something to be protected, and indeed enabled, by public policy.

(1) Everyone has the right freely to participate in the cultural life of the community, to enjoy the arts and to share in scientific advancement and its benefits.

(2) Everyone has the right to the protection of the moral and material interests resulting from any scientific, literary or artistic production of which he is the author.

–Article 27, United Nations Universal Declaration of Human Rights, 1948.

Yet another change in the policy environment—and this one hits the pocketbook of some of the most powerful industries in North America— is the erosion of old business models in cultural and information goods. Consumers have increased expectations for speed, variety, interoperability, and interactivity, and they are not waiting around for publishers and labels to catch up. On the creator side, the ability to reach an audience is less constrained by production costs, communication barriers, and a need for complex technical expertise. While a decent income may still be elusive, musicians, writers, and artists are increasingly able to self-publish and distribute their works without having to rely on the traditional intermediaries. Even areas associated with higher production costs, such as filmmaking, are showing at least the beginnings of new distribution mechanisms, which are poised to eclipse those that have been in place for almost a hundred years. Sites such as YouTube are in some ways primitive and amateurish, but this type of distribution mechanism seems likely to take on more importance as storage and memory increases, as compression techniques improve, and as digital photography skills become more ubiquitous.

These tendencies (increased public engagement, breakdown of traditional stakeholder categories, and shifts in business models) integrate cultural/social, technological, and economic factors into a new mix. As a result, attempts to legislate further restrictions on the productive and transformative uses of intellectual resources are bound to generate new forms of resistance and engagement.

In this highly contested, indeed volatile, climate, the success of any new legislation will depend not only on its content, but also on process: it is appropriate and productive for the government to engage in wide and open consultation, avoiding previous patterns of bias and "insider" connections, and looking to the grassroots as well as to traditional advisers from large organizations and institutions. The discussions should include young Canadians as well as old, and should make sure to recognize the differences in interests that exist between creator and non-creator copyright holders.

Given that many Canadians now encounter copyright law in their daily lives, clarity in legislative drafting ought also to be a top priority. A new copyright bill should as much as possible be devoid of messy legalistic jargon.[5] This is not a matter of writing style: it is about the nature of the law. Rather than rattling on for pages in endless detail, legislation is most effective when it sets out general principles that can be readily applied. This approach also makes for a law that will prove able to adapt to changing technologies, artistic practices, business models, and consumer expectations. We are not asking for vague laws that will throw more decision-making power to the courts. We are arguing for sensible, clear guidelines that can help reasonable people arrange their copyright practices.

Policy Proposals

Fair Dealing

Canada's fair dealing provisions should be open-ended: an enumerated and limited list of categories should not be the gateway to a defence of fair dealing. Instead, decisions should be based on factual tests, such as those outlined in *CCH v. Law Society of Upper Canada* (see chapter 6).

A minimalist approach to reconciling the fair dealing provision in the act with the results of the *CCH* case might be as simple as revising sections 29, 29.1, and 29.2 along the following lines:

29. (1) Fair dealing for purposes such as research, private study, criticism, review or news reporting does not infringe copyright.[6]

(2) In determining whether the use made in any particular case is fair dealing, the factors to be considered shall include—

(a) the purpose of the dealing,

(b) the character of the dealing,

(c) the amount of the dealing,

(d) the nature of the work or other subject matter,

(e) available alternatives to the dealing,

(f) the effect of the dealing on the work or other subject matter,

(g) the extent to which attribution was made where reasonable in the circumstances.[7]

Augmenting the list of categories might be part of a clarification of fair dealing. But adding categories alone would be unlikely to create law flexible enough to address the range of appropriate and fair uses—and it might also prove to be divisive. There is no point in setting up the artists who need broader parody rights, the musicians who need broader sampling rights, the teachers who need broader classroom display rights, the librarians who need broader access rights for their patrons, the computer scientists who need clearer rights to engage in reverse engineering and to promote interoperability—the list could go on—to be played off against each other in the final stages of the legislative process.[8]

Anti-Circumvention

Any provisions concerning the circumvention of technological protection measures should be explicitly limited to direct acts of infringement and should be paired with consumer protection limitations.

Canada is under considerable pressure to adopt anti-circumvention rules to conform with the requirements of the WIPO copyright treaties. We are not convinced that it is either necessary or desirable for Canada to implement these WIPO treaties. There is strong evidence that anti-circumvention rules, especially in their strong form as enacted in the United States, would be contrary to Canadian interests, and proponents have failed to explain the downside of Canada not fully entering into these treaties.

If Parliament is intent on enacting such implementing provisions, it should proceed in a way that minimally satisfies the requirements of the treaty. The law should be explicit that engaging in circumvention of DRM is not proscribed where it is being carried out for lawful purposes. There should be no prohibitions of circumvention devices like the ones contained in the U.S. Digital Millennium Copyright Act: there are lawful reasons to circumvent DRM, and people need to have access to devices for doing so. As the Supreme Court has ruled, users' rights are an integral part of copyright, and practices such as library preservation, digital backups, reverse engineering, and quotation ought not to be prevented by DRM. We also suggest that any anti-circumvention provision be accompanied by language that places reasonable limits and constraints on the ability of rights holders to interpose DRM without the consent of the consumer. Corporate rights holders often claim that digital rights management needs protection from consumers, but we believe that consumers need protection from DRM.

Other Issues

While fair dealing and DRM are the major areas for immediate legislative reform, a range of other provisions would be productive elements in new legislation.

- **Abolition or limitation of Crown copyright**. Crown copyright constrains public use of government-generated materials, which taxpayers have already paid for once, and causes confusion. There is no convincing justification for it.

- **Modification of statutory damage provisions**. Statutory damages need to be restricted if not eliminated because they subject users to disproportionate risks and end up creating a chilling effect on the full exercise of users' rights. A good faith belief that an act constitutes fair dealing should not subject a user of copyrighted materials to the risk of excessive damage awards.

- **Limitations on the waiver of moral rights**. Creators are routinely deprived of their moral rights by contracts that they have little power to change. Moral rights should be neither assignable nor waiveable. But like economic rights, they should be subject to fair dealing rights in order to protect transformative downstream uses such as parody.

- **Droit de suite**. Artists sometimes sell their work for very little money and watch from the sidelines as it becomes worth millions of dollars. A "droit de suite" would give living artists a small share of subsequent sales of their work—putting them in a position akin to other creators whose royalties are tied to the market success of their work.

- **New procedures for unlocatable copyright owners**. The current Copyright Board system is onerous, unpredictable, and particularly unsuited to Internet materials. When a copyright owner cannot be located by a reasonable search, the work in question should be available for free use. If the copyright owner should later appear, a schedule should dictate a reasonable recompense.

- **Sanctions for misuse of copyright**. Frivolous claims and demands chill legitimate unauthorized uses of copyright material—and even public domain material. The law might offer an avenue to discourage or penalize such behaviour.

- **Protection of Internet service providers from liability**. Internet service providers cannot control or monitor the activity on their servers. In the U.S. "notice and takedown" regime, they are only exempt from liability if they take down material upon receipt of an allegation that it is infringing. This is an unfair and inappropriate demand upon their time and role, and it puts in the hands of copyright owners decisions that should rest with judges. We prefer a "notice and notice" system whereby ISPs communicate allegations to their subscribers, who are alone responsible for responding.

In addition, Canada should hold the line on copyright term. There is no justification for extending it past its current period of life of the author plus another fifty years.

The precise drafting of some of these proposals will certainly require more thought; some of them will provoke outright debate. And the list is not complete: a truly open and inclusive consultation process will bring forward additional ideas from Canadian creators and users—people like yourselves. The law gets its life from these interventions. Copyright, like other law, is too important to be left to lawyers, politicians, and lobbyists.

Resources

- Canadian Association of Law Libraries Copyright Information page, http://www.callacbd.ca/articles.php?frmArticleID=55&staticId=1.

- Canadian Internet Policy and Public Interest Clinic (CIPPIC) website, University of Ottawa, www.cippic.ca. Information on emerging policy issues in copyright, privacy, and other areas.

- Michael Geist website, www.michaelgeist.ca. A blog and archive of the writings of Canada's pre-eminent copyright policy commentator.

Notes

For further details about the sources listed in these notes, please refer to the "Bibliography" and "Legal Cases Cited."

Introduction

1. Lorinc, "Creators and Copyright in Canada," 15.
2. *Théberge v. Galerie d'Art du Petit Champlain Inc.*, para. 32.
3. Ibid., para. 31.

1. Copyright's Rationales

1. Milton, "Areopagitica" (1644); the full text is available at http://www.uoregon.edu/~rbear/areopagitica.html. The anonymous author is quoted in Rose, *Authors and Owners*, 55. Rose notes the possibility that the author of this pamphlet was in fact a bookseller—and therefore using the "authors' rights" rhetoric to bolster the booksellers' interests.
2. William Fisher divides copyright justifications into four categories: utilitarianism, labour theory, personality theory, and social planning theory. We have combined labour theory and personality theory together as "natural law" theories; what Fisher calls "social planning theory" is reflected in part in the third section of this chapter on information as "public good." Fisher, "Theories of Intellectual Property," 168–99.
3. Locke, *Second Treatise of Government*, ch. 5.

4. Locke, *Second Treatise of Government*, ch. 5, sect. 27.
5. Ibid., sect. 31.
6. See Hughes, "Locke's 1694 Memorandum (and More Incomplete Copyright Historiographies)."
7. Reports of Sir Edward Coke 107, 77, English Reports 638.
8. 1 English Reports 837 (House of Lords), 17 *Cobbett's Parliamentary History* 1078 (1813). For a further analysis of the case see Rose, "Author as Proprietor."
9. A similar result was reached in the United States in the 1834 case of *Wheaton v. Peters* (33 US 591), where the Supreme Court rejected the argument of common law copyright in favour of a strict reading of the statute. For discussion of this important case, see Patterson, *Copyright in Historical Perspective*, ch. 10; and McGill, "Matter of the Text."
10. Civil law systems date back to Roman law, and are based on codes that set out the specific provisions of law. These codes are then applied and interpreted by judges when disputes arise. In contrast to code-based legal systems, the English common law is based on custom and practice as reflected in judicial precedent. For an accessible explanation of Canada's history of combining both "civil law" and "common law" systems, see http://www.canadiana.org/citm/specifique/lois_e.html.
11. Bentham, *Introduction to the Principles of Morals and Legislation*, ch. I, article VII.
12. Section 91 of the Canadian Constitution merely lists copyright as an enumerated power of the federal government, with no rationale or guidance provided. See also Murray, "Protecting Ourselves to Death"; and also *Théberge v. Galerie d'Art du Petit Champlain Inc.*, para. 32.
13. Austin, *Province of Jurisprudence Determined*, 9.
14. The most famous proponent of the realist philosophy was Oliver Wendell Holmes: see Holmes, "Path of the Law." For an accessible discussion of related issues, see Macdonald, *Lessons of Everyday Law*.
15. Richardson, "Stupidity of the Cost-Benefit Standard," 136.
16. Examples are advance knowledge of weather conditions that will send the price of a crop's futures soaring, or inside financial data indicating that a company will have to restate its books to show a large loss. There are whole bodies of law protecting trade secrets and confidential information, and prohibiting certain uses of insider corporate information.

2. Copyright's Histories

1. For the text of the Statute of Anne, see Avalon Project, Yale University.
2. On the history of the print trade and incipient copyright in this period, see Rose, *Authors and Owners*, especially chs. 2, 3; Feather, "From Rights in Copies to Copyright," 191–209; and Loewenstein, *Author's Due*.
3. Loewenstein, *Author's Due*, 214.
4. Daniel Defoe, "Essay on the Regulation of the Press" (1704), quoted in

Loewenstein, *Author's Due*, 215.

5. Rose, *Authors and Owners*, 43. It is worth noting how the rhetoric of the Stationers' Company bears a similarity with that of the modern recording industry. In both cases changes in technology, the economy, and cultural practices challenge the settled order or, as we would say today, existing business models. See, for example, Hatch, "Toward a Principled Approach to Copyright Legislation at the Turn of the Millennium."

6. Patterson, *Copyright in Historical Perspective*, 148.

7. In a memorable phrase, the counsel for the appellant in *Donaldson v. Becket* (1774) said that booksellers "had not, till lately, ever concerned themselves about authors … nor would they probably have, of late years, introduced the authors as parties in their claims to the common law right of exclusively multiplying copies, had not they found it necessary to give a colourable face to their monopoly." Quoted in Loewenstein, *Author's Due*, 14.

8. For differing accounts of *Donaldson v. Becket*, see Rose, *Authors and Owners*, ch. 6, and Loewenstein, *Author's Due*, ch. 1.

9. Under this authority, Congress has enacted various laws including the Copyright Act, the Patent Act, and the Semi-Conductor and Chip Protection Act of 1984 (codified respectively at 17 USC sections 101, *et. seq.*; 35 USC sections 1, *et. seq.*; and 17 USC sections 901–14).

10. For examples of courts' invocation of this principle, see *Sony Corp. of America v. Universal City Studios, Inc.*; *Feist Publications v. Rural Telephone Service.*

11. For a discussion of the relationship between censorship and copyright law, see, for example, Cohen, "Constitutional Issues Involving Use of the Internet: Intellectual Property and Censorship of the Internet"; and Netanel, "Copyright and a Democratic Civil Society."

12. "Nothing in this act shall be construed to extend to prohibit the importation or vending, reprinting, or publishing within the United States, of any map, chart, book or books, written, printed, or published by any person not a citizen of the United States, in foreign parts or places without the jurisdiction of the United States." Copyright Act of 1790, stat. 124, section 5; http://ww.copyright.gov/history/1790act.pdf.

13. McGill, *American Literature and the Culture of Reprinting*, 1.

14. Justice Oliver Wendell Holmes, quoted in Hesse, "Rise of Intellectual Property," 42. For more on *Bleistein v. Donaldson*, see Zimmerman, "Story of Bleistein v. Donaldson Lithographic Company," 77–108.

15. Hesse, "Rise of Intellectual Property," 42. For extensive commentary on the shift to expansionism in U.S. copyright law, see Vaidhyanathan, *Copyrights and Copywrongs*; Boyle, *Shamans, Software, and Spleens*; and Lessig, *Free Culture*.

16. Hesse, "Rise of Intellectual Property," 42.

17. For information on the early history of French copyright, see Hesse, *Publishing and Cultural Politics in Revolutionary Paris*; and Ginsburg, "Tale of Two Copyrights."

18. Davies, *Copyright and the Public Interest*, 152.

19. Copyright Act (France, 1957) quoted in Davies, *Copyright and the Public Interest*, 153.

20. As a matter of federal jurisdiction, copyright law is identical across Canada. However, francophone and anglophone judges come from different jurisprudential or intellectual traditions. For a suggestive discussion of the murky relationship between "copyright" and *"droit d'auteur"* in Canada, see Tawfik, "Copyright as Droit d'Auteur," 59–81.

21. WIPO (www.wipo.org) is a United Nations agency that administers international intellectual property agreements such as the Berne Convention. It is separate and apart from the WTO, which causes a considerable amount of confusion and concern that the proliferation of treaties is causing unnecessary overlap and complexity.

22. Parker, *Beginnings of the Book Trade in Canada*, 109; this is the main source for the account offered here. See also Nadel, "Copyright, Empire and the Politics of Print," which acutely emphasizes the imperial dynamics of the situation.

23. Parker, *Beginnings of the Book Trade in Canada*, 130. Eventually publishers in Britain began to realize that they simply could not sell to Canadians at British prices. In the 1850s the Commissioners of National Education in Ireland even gave away their copyrights on textbooks to British North American booksellers in an effort to address concerns about the bad influence of U.S. materials.

24. Parker, *Beginnings of the Book Trade in Canada*, 168-69, 173.

25. John Lovell quoted in Parker, *Beginnings of the Book Trade in Canada*, 174.

26. Parker, *Beginnings of the Book Trade in Canada*, 193.

27. The act was amended in 1931, 1935, 1936, 1938, 1971, 1988, 1993, 1995, 1996, and 1997. John Kennedy, chairman and CEO of the International Federation of the Phonographic Industry (IFPI), is only one promulgator of the tedious mantra: "It's astonishing that a sophisticated nation like Canada has dragged its feet for so long while the rest of the world has adapted its copyright laws to the digital age." CRIA press release, 2 March 2, 2006, http://www.cria.ca/news/020306a_n.php. From that assumption, all sorts of errors rise like urban myths. CTV, in a story on a recording industry lobby day on Parliament Hill, reported, "The musicians, who included Blue Rodeo's Jim Cuddy and rocker Tom Cochrane, say the Copyright Act, which was drafted in 1908, is ill-equipped to address the issues of the 21st century." Musicians Call for an Update on Copyright Law," Nov. 24, 2004, http://www.ctv.ca/servlet/ArticleNews/story/CTVNews/1101331178030_15?hub=Canada.

28. Different branches of government have produced or commissioned reports on various aspects of copyright reform, including:
    - Isley Commission, 1957 (officially the Royal Commission on Patents, Copyright, Trademarks and Industrial Design);
    - Report on Intellectual and Industrial Property, 1971 (Economic Council of Canada);

- Keynes and Burnett Report, 1977 ("Copyright in Canada—Proposals for Revision of the Law");
- Copyright Revision Studies, 1980–83 (fourteen separate studies on different aspects of copyright reform with emphasis on economic issues);
- "From Gutenberg to Telidon: A White Paper on Copyright: Proposals for the Revision of the Canadian Copyright Act," 1984;
- A Charter of Rights for Creators, 1985;
- Final Report, Copyright Sub-committee of the Working Group on Canadian Content and Culture: Information Highway Advisory Council (Industry Canada, 1995);
- "Connection, Community, Content: The Challenge of the Information Highway," Final Report of the Information Highway Advisory Council, 1995 (Industry Canada);
- Consultation Paper on Digital Copyright Issues, 2001 (Industry Canada and Canadian Heritage), http://strategis.ic.gc.ca/epic/site/crp-prda.nsf/en/h_rp01102e.html;
- Supporting Culture and Innovation: Report on the Provisions and Operation of the Copyright Act, 2002 (often referred to as the Section 92 Report), http://strategis.ic.gc.ca/epic/internet/incrp-prda.nsf/en/rp00863e.html;
- Status Report on Copyright Reform submitted to the Standing Committee on Canadian Heritage by the Minister of Canadian Heritage and the Minister of Industry, 24 March 2004, http://strategis.ic.gc.ca/epic/internet/incrp-prda.nsf/en/rp01134e.html;
- Standing Committee on Canadian Heritage, Interim Report on Copyright Reform, May 2004 (often referred to as the Bulte Report), www.parl.gc.ca/InfocomDoc/Documents/37/3/parlbus/commbus/house/reports/herirp01/herirp01-e.pdf;
- Government Statement on Copyright Reform, March 2005 (Industry Canada and Canadian Heritage): http://strategis.ic.gc.prda.nsf/en/rp01142e.html.

29. An Act to amend the Copyright Act, S.C. 1988, c. 15; An Act to amend the Copyright Act, S.C. 1997, c. 24, www.parl.gc.ca/bills/government/C-32/C-32_4/C-32TOCE.html.

30. North American Free Trade Implementation Act (1993, c. 44), http://laws.justice.gc.ca/en/N-23.8/index.html; World Trade Organization Agreement Implementation Act of 1994. S.C. 1994, c. 47.

31. For the U.S. government, see the United States Trade Representatives' 2006 Special 301 Report, http://www.ustr.gov/Document_Library/Reports_Publications/2006/2006_Special_301_Review/Section_Index.html; for Canadian Heritage, see Murray, "Copyright Talk," 15–40; for CRIA, see Graham Henderson (President, Canadian Recording Industry Association), "Protect Artists: Reform Canada's Copyright Laws," National Post, May 11, 2006.

32. Berne Convention for the Protection of Literary and Artistic Works, Sept. 9, 1886 (1971 Paris Revision), 1161 U.N.T.S 30, http://www.wipo.int/treaties/en/ip/berne/trtdocs_wo001.html.

33. Agreement on Trade Related Aspects of Intellectual Property (TRIPS), Annex IC, "Establishing the World Trade Organization," http://www.wto.org/english/docs_e/legal_e/27-trips_01_e.htm.
34. For a good discussion of how treaties and trade agreements affect Canadian copyright policy, see Tawfik, "International Copyright Law," 66–85.
35. Http://www.wipo.int/treaties/en/ip/wct/trtdocs_wo033.html; http://www.wipo.int/treaties/en/ip/wppt/.

3. Copyright's Scope

1. For an accessible overview of Canadian intellectual property laws, see Kratz, *Canada's Intellectual Property Law in a Nutshell*; and Vaver, *Intellectual Property Law*. There are other intellectual property laws besides the "big four." In Canada, federal acts that deal with special instances of intellectual property include the Industrial Design Act (1985), Plant Breeders' Rights Act (1990), and Integrated Circuit Topography Act (1990).
2. Recent Canadian cases indicating controversy over the balance between owners' rights and users' rights in the area of patents include *Monsanto Canada Inc. v. Schmeiser* and *Harvard College v. Canada (Commissioner of Patents)*. In the area of trademarks, see *Mattel, Inc. v. 3894207 Canada Inc.* and *Veuve Clicquot Ponsardin v. Boutiques Cliquot Ltée*.
3. Hayhurst, "Copyright Subject Matter," 31.
4. *Canadian Admiral Ltd. v. Rediffusion Inc.*, 91.
5. This determination was ultimately reversed by the Appeals Court and the Supreme Court of Canada.
6. *Tele-Direct v. American Business Information Inc.*, para. 28. Leave to appeal to the Supreme Court was denied.
7. *CCH v. Law Society of Upper Canada*, para. 16.
8. Ibid., para. 23. Later in the decision, the court grounded its placement of the originality standard in policy terms, stating: "When an author must exercise skill and judgment to ground originality in a work, there is a safeguard against the author being overcompensated for his or her work. This helps ensure that there is room for the public domain to flourish as others are able to produce new works by building on the ideas and information contained in the works of others."
9. Ibid., para. 25.
10. The U.S. statute does spell out the fixation requirement. It grants protection to "original works of authorship fixed in any tangible medium of expression, now known or later developed, from which they can be perceived, reproduced, or otherwise communicated, either directly or with the aid of a machine or device" (section 102), and states that "a work is 'fixed' in a tangible medium of expression when its embodiment in a copy or phonorecord, by or under the authority of the author, is sufficiently permanent or stable to permit it to be perceived, reproduced, or otherwise communicated for a period of more than transitory duration" (section 101).

11. Vaver, *Copyright Law*, 65.

12. When Jana Sterbak's *Vanitas: Flesh Dress for an Albino Anorectic* (1987) was exhibited in Ottawa's National Gallery, it caused quite a controversy as it slowly decayed. For more information, see http://art-history.concordia.ca/eea/artists/sterbak.html.

13. The right to the first fixation of a performance belongs to the performer, as section 15(1)(a)(iii) gives the performer the right to fix a performance in any material form where it is not yet fixed—but also grants copyright protection to the unfixed performance.

14. For the linguist Ferdinand de Saussure, language structures our very experience of reality, an idea elaborated by psychoanalyst Jacques Lacan, Marxist scholars of ideology, including Louis Althusser, and various anthropologists and feminist scholars. With different emphases, these and other scholars argue that language is not a label for underlying facts or ideas (or for an underlying "self"), but rather brings these into being. See Schleifer and Rupp, "Structuralism."

15. A similar conclusion was reached in the classic U.S. case *Baker v. Selden* (1879). In that case the court allowed copyright in a book describing accounting methods, but not in the methods themselves or the particular forms devised to facilitate them: "The very object of publishing a book on science or the useful arts is," the court said, "to communicate to the world the useful knowledge which it contains. But this object would be frustrated if the knowledge could not be used without incurring the guilt of piracy of the book." Quoted in Litman, "Public Domain," 981.

16. *Anne of Green Gables Licensing Authority Inc. v. Avonlea Traditions Inc.*, para. 100, 121. The copyright terms in the works of L.M. Montgomery ended in 1993, but the case concerned some uses dating back before that time.

17. *Delrina Corp. v. Triolet Systems Inc.*, para. 52.

18. The lack of a formality requirement is a significant difference between copyright and patents. Patents are only issued after an application and formal examination process.

19. Copyright Act, section 39(2); see chapter 7 here.

20. Canadian Intellectual Property Office, "Guide to Copyrights."

21. The dates for the transitional periods are calculated somewhat differently in Canadian Intellectual Property Office, "Guide to Copyrights." While an attempt was made in 2004 to extend the phase-out period for an unpublished work of an author who died before Jan. 1, 1949, in what came to be known as the "Lucy Maud Montgomery Act" provisions of Bill C-8, this effort ultimately failed. See Legislative Summary, Bill C-8: The Library and Archives of Canada Act, prepared by Sam Banks and Monique Hébert, Law and Government Division, Feb. 18, 2004, http://www.parl.gc.ca/common/Bills_ls.asp?lang=E&source=library_prb&Parl=37&Ses=3&ls=C8#7end); and Howard Knopf, "Mouse in the House: A New Bill in Ottawa Appears to Adopt U.S.-Style Copyright Term Extension," *National Post*, June 7, 2003, FP 11.

4. Owners' Rights

1. Reproduction is also a highly problematic concept with regard to computer use. Abraham Drassinower, "Taking User Rights Seriously," 473, states:

   > Digital technology ruptures the continuity between copyright theory and copyright doctrine, such that the concept of reproduction no longer adequately separates infringing from non-infringing use. Applied in the digital environment, the right of reproduction grants owners the exclusive right to view their works where such viewing requires—as it does in the case of "browsing"—the making of temporary copies. Thus, to insist on reproduction as the central organizing category of copyright law is to upset the copyright balance so as to grant owners a new and unprecedented control of access to copyrighted works.

2. "Licence Application by Pointe-a-Callière, Montreal Museum of Archeology and History for the Reproduction of Quotations," Copyright Board, March 29, 2004, http://www.cb-cda.gc.ca/unlocatable/other/1-b.pdf; "Re: Breakthough Films," Copyright Board, March 6, 2006, http://cb-cda.gc.ca/unlocatable/156r-b.pdf.
3. Although broadcast law and technology have changed since this case, it remains appropriate for its thinking on what is meant by "public" performance.
4. The definition does get more complex, as section 2.2(1) provides:

   > For the purposes of this Act, "publication" means
   > (a) in relation to works,
   > (i) making copies of a work available to the public,
   > (ii) the construction of an architectural work, and
   > (iii) the incorporation of an artistic work into an architectural work, and
   > (b) in relation to sound recordings, making copies of a sound recording available to the public,
   > but does not include
   > (c) the performance in public, or the communication to the public by telecommunication, of a literary, dramatic, musical or artistic work or a sound recording, or
   > (d) the exhibition in public of an artistic work.

5. The majority of the Federal Court of Appeal agreed, and the Supreme Court of Canada declined to review the case. The case on appeal dealt with a host of issues; here we focus only on translation rights.
6. While there are no cases on this point, it would seem that conversion rights should also be applicable to new media: for example, in a situation where a work is "translated" into a multimedia presentation or a video game.
7. *CCH v. Law Society of Upper Canada*, para 38.
8. The Visual Artists Rights Act of 1990 (Pub. L. No 101–650) added section 106A to

the U.S. Copyright Act, setting forth certain moral rights for visual arts and adding a definition of visual arts to section 101:

> to include (1) a painting, drawing, print or sculpture, existing in a single copy, in a limited edition of 200 copies or fewer that are signed and consecutively numbered by the author, or, in the case of a sculpture, in multiple cast, carved, or fabricated sculptures of 200 or fewer that are consecutively numbered by the author and bear the signature or other identifying mark of the author; or (2) a still photographic image produced for exhibition purposes only, existing in a single copy that is signed by the author, or in a limited edition of 200 copies or fewer that are signed and consecutively numbered by the author.

Among the limitations to the definition are "works for hire."

5. Determining Ownership

1. The Reproduction of Federal Law Order (SI/97-5) states: "Anyone may, without charge or request for permission, reproduce enactments and consolidations of enactments of the Government of Canada, and decisions and reasons for decisions of federally-constituted courts and administrative tribunals, provided due diligence is exercised in ensuring the accuracy of the materials reproduced and the reproduction is not represented as an official version." See http://laws.justice.gc.ca/en/otherreg/si-97-5/189099.html. Similar orders also pertain to most of the provinces.

2. For a thorough analysis of arguments for abolishing Crown copyright, see Judge, "Crown Copyright and Copyright Reform in Canada," 550–94. For the United States, S.C. section 105 provides: "Copyright protection under this title is not available for any work of the United States Government, but the United States Government is not precluded from receiving and holding copyrights transferred to it by assignment, bequest, or otherwise."

3. For a complete list, see the Copyright Board website, www.cb-cda.gc.ca.

4. See Tariff 1A (for commercial radio) and Tariff 1B (for non-commercial radio), http://www.socan.ca/jsp/en/resources/tariffs.jsp.

5. Lorinc, "Creators and Copyright in Canada," 52–53.

6. See Copyright Board of Canada website, www.cb-cda.gc.ca. See also chapter 4, p.56, for an example of a Copyright Board ruling on unlocatable owners. The application process is described on the Copyright Board website.

7. See U.S. Copyright Office, "Report on Orphan Works," January 2006, http://www.copyright.gov/orphan/.

6. Users' Rights

1. *CCH Canadian Ltd. v. Law Society of Upper Canada (C.A.)*, para. 48.
2. See, for example, *Basic Books, Inc. v. Kinko's Graphics Corp.*(1991); *American Geophysical Union v. Texaco, Inc.*; *Princeton University Press v. Michigan Document Services*; *BMG Music v. Gonzalez*. For a summary of these and other fair use cases from the United States, along with links to the full-texts, see http://fairusenetwork.org/reference/refs-cases.php.
3. Vaidhyanathan, "Copyright Law and Creativity." For information about U.S. fair use, see the encyclopedic website, http://fairuse.stanford.edu/.
4. Howell, Vincent, and Manson, *Intellectual Property Law: Cases and Materials*, 351.
5. *Bishop v. Stevens* (1990), citing *Performing Right Society, Ltd. v. Hammond's Bradford Brewery Co.*, 1 ch. 121, 127.
6. *Compagnie Générale des Établissements Michelin-Michelin & Cie v. National Automobile, Aerospace, Transportation and General Workers Union of Canada (CAW-Canada)*, part II.iii, part III.A.ii.
7. For a thorough critique of the *Michelin* case on this grounds, see Bailey, "Deflating the Michelin Man," 125–66.
8. *Théberge v. Galerie d'Art du Petit Champlain Inc.*, para. 31, 32.
9. The 1997 amendments to the Copyright Act added section 92, which also indicated that "within five years" the minister would prepare and send to Parliament "a report on the provisions and operation of this Act, including any recommendations for amendments to this Act." This Section 92 Report was tabled in the House of Commons in December 2002. Industry Canada, *Supporting Culture and Innovation*. The departments of Industry and Canadian Heritage also held special consultations on the issue of educational use of the Internet in December 2002, publishing a subsequent working group report, "Copyright and the Educational Use of Internet Content," Dec. 8, 2003. See Industry and Canadian Heritage, Departments of.
10. *CCH Canadian Ltd. v. Law Society of Upper Canada (T.D.)*, para. 2.
11. *CCH Canadian Ltd. v. Law Society of Upper Canada (C.A.)*, para. 126.
12. *CCH Canadian Ltd. v. Law Society of Upper Canada*, para. 48.
13. Ibid.
14. *Society of Composers, Authors and Music Publishers of Canada (SOCAN) v. Canadian Association of Internet Providers*, para. 40. For the specific importance of the SOCAN case with respect to the communication right, see chapter 4.
15. *CCH Canadian Ltd. v. Law Society of Upper Canada*, para. 52.
16. Ibid., para. 54, 51.
17. Ibid., para. 55.
18. Ibid. at para. 56.
19. Ibid., para. 57.
20. Ibid.
21. Ibid., para. 59.

22. Broadcasters are permitted to make ephemeral copies of works, performances, and sound recordings as needed according to the logistics of the situation, with certain conditions (Copyright Act, sections 30.8, 30.9); the Librarian and Archivist of Canada is permitted a series of exceptions for preservation-related uses under section 30.5; section 32.1(1) allows copies or transmission of information for the purpose of complying with the Access to Information Act, Privacy Act, Broadcast Act, and Cultural Property Import and Export Act.

7. Enforcement of Owners' Rights

1. In *Milliken & Co. v. Interface Flooring Systems (Canada) Inc. (T.D.)*, the court said that while the burden of showing knowledge rests with the plaintiff, it can be inferred from the facts. In this case a designer had been retained by the defendant to design a carpet tile on a large project. Even though the designer was not an employee or officer of the corporation, the knowledge was imputed to the defendant because she was given charge of the project, and based on her expertise in the field the court found she should have known she was infringing.

2. The possibility of large statutory damages creates a chilling effect in many institutions. Especially in risk-averse institutions that are serving the public, this potential liability discourages people from asserting the rights that they (or their students or patrons) should be entitled to. See chapter 10, "Education"; and in the final chapter we suggest limiting statutory damages for this reason.

3. In the United States there is a further reduction of damages provision that could in essence be adopted in Canada. Under section 504 of the U.S. Copyright Act, the court is directed to remit damages in cases where the infringer believed and had reasonable grounds for believing that the copyrighted work was a fair use under section 107 (17 USC 107), if the infringer was working for a non-profit educational institution, library, or archives (or under certain circumstances a public broadcasting entity). This section provides employees of institutions that are trying to help members of the public a certain degree of protection against damage awards where their assessment of fair use was wrong but made in good faith. While the Canadian courts have the discretion to reduce the award in such a circumstance, they do not have to.

4. The Crown prosecutor decides, based on the seriousness of the offence, whether to proceed summarily or by indictment.

5. For a forceful argument that piracy is a major problem requiring increased criminal enforcement, see Gayle MacDonald, "Pirates of the Canadians," *Globe and Mail*, Jan. 13, 2007, R1, 9. Michael Geist responds in "U.S. Movie Piracy Claims Mostly Fiction," *Toronto Star*, Feb. 5, 2007; available at http://www.michaelgeist.ca/content/view/1656/159/. Bill C-59, an act to amend the Criminal Code to add new prohibitions against camcording in theatres, received royal assent on June 22, 2007; http://www2.parl.gc.ca/content/hoc/Bills/391/Government/C-59/C-59_31/.pdf.

6. Royal Canadian Mounted Police and Department of Justice, "Copyright

Enforcement Guideline," RCMP Operations Manual, Appendix IV-6-1, June 26, 1998. Cited in "Assessment of Commercial Scale Criminal Copyright Piracy and Trade-mark Counterfeiting in Canada," n.d., http://www.rcmp-grc.gc.ca/crimint/copyright_piracy_e.htm.

7. Some forty-eight countries, including Canada, are on the ISTR's Priority Watch List or the Watch List, or fall under section 306 Monitoring. See http://www.ustr.gov/Document_Library/Reports_Publications/2006/2006_Special_301_Review/Section_Index.html.

8. Craft and Design

1. To find out if a particular industrial design is registered, see the database of registered industrial designs in Canadian Intellectual Property Office, "Guide to Industrial Designs."

2. Public shaming has been used widely of late: for example, an entire blog (http://urbancounterfeiters.com/) exists to track and trace the apparent perfidy of Urban Outfitters, a company accused of stealing the designs of independent creators.

3. For example, Scottish knitting designer Alice Starmore caused a huge furor with amateur knitters when she started to assert intellectual property rights: see Lisa Moricoli Latham, "Copyright Dispute Becomes Quite a Yarn," *Seattle Times*, Dec. 16, 2002, http://archives.seattletimes.nwsource.com/cgi-bin/texis.cgi/web/vortex/display?slug=btknitting16&date=20021216.

4. Robertson, "Craft and Copyright."

5. See Free to Stitch, Free to Bitch, http://www.freetostitchfreetobitch.org/info.htm.

6. See Storey, "Filing Design Applications in Canada and the United States,"123–49.

7. U.S. Copyright Act, 17 U.S.C. § 101.

8. In the United States, there has been considerable discussion about the desirability of offering copyright-like protection to fashion design. Critics of the idea have argued that the current legal situation may actually benefit the commercial producers that it appears to leave "unprotected." As Raustiala, "Fashion Victims," puts it:

> Copying drives the fashion cycle. Unlike areas such as software or cellphones [in which] the more people who use your software or the more callers on your network, the better off you are, fashion designs become progressively less attractive as they saturate a market…. The hunger for design distinctiveness drives fashion lovers back into Barneys, Bergdorfs, and the boutiques on a regular (and ever-quickening) basis.

See also the 2006 report of the U.S. Copyright Office on the question, http://www.copyright.gov/docs/regstat072706.html; and further critiques by Art Brodsky and Laurie Racine, http://www.publicknowledge.org/node/568 and http://www.publicknowledge.org/node/576.

9. Digital Rights Management

1. For example, the company Readex specializes in digitizing public domain sources; see http://www.newsbank.com/readex/. While Readex is not reducing the public's access to the original documents—most are available in special collections at research libraries—it is preserving a certain inequity of access, because the price for subscription is steep. A different approach is represented by public access digitization projects such as Project Gutenberg (www.gutenberg.org).

2. The right of resale is codified in the United States as the "first sale doctrine." While it is not codified in Canadian law, it is equally established in custom and commerce. See Reese, "First Sale Doctrine in the Era of Digital Networks," 577.

3. eBooks.com, "Purchase License," http://www.ebooks.com/information/purchase-license.asp.

4. When you rip open the shrink wrap that encloses a software package, or click through an agreement online, you may be giving your assent to an enforceable contract. It's important, therefore, to read and understand the terms. However, the Canadian law on this topic is still emerging and is not always consistent. See Morgan, "I Click, You Click, We all Click ... But Do We Have a Contract?" 109–18; and Sigel et al., "Validity of Webwrap Contracts."

5. See Doctorow, "Sony Anti-Customer Technology Round-up and Time-Line."

6. *Théberge v. Galerie d'Art du Petit Champlain Inc.*, paras. 31, 32. For more on the court's statement, see p.78 here.

7. Digital Millennium Copyright Act, Pub. L. no. 105–304, 112 Stat. 2860 (1998), http://www.copyright.gov/legislation/dmca.pdf.

8. Section 1201 (a)(1)(A) prohibits the act of circumventing "a technical measure that effectively controls access to a [copyrighted] work." Sections 1201(a)(2) and 1201(b)(1) dictate that no person shall "manufacture, import, offer to the public, provide, or otherwise traffic in any technology, product, service, device, component, or part thereof" that makes circumvention possible. Although the Library of Congress announced some mitigating rules in November 2006 (see http://www.copyright.gov/1201/), these are limited and temporary.

9. The Electronic Frontier Foundation has provided a compelling collection of examples of how the DMCA has stifled innovation, hampered scientific research, and otherwise chilled the exercise of legitimate expression: http://www.eff.org/IP/DMCA/unintended_consequences.php.

10. Education

1. Section 2 defines "educational institution" as:

> (a) a non-profit institution licensed or recognized by or under an Act of Parliament or the legislature of a province to provide pre-school, elementary, secondary or post-secondary education,

(b) a non-profit institution that is directed or controlled by a board of education regulated by or under an Act of the legislature of a province and that provides continuing, professional or vocational education or training,

c) a department or agency of any order of government, or any non-profit body, that controls or supervises education or training referred to in paragraph (a) or (b), or

(d) any other non-profit institution prescribed by regulation.

2. Section 2 states: "'premises' means, in relation to an educational institution, a place where education or training referred to in the definition 'educational institution' is provided, controlled or supervised by the educational institution." This definition creates difficulties for institutions that are trying to conduct outreach beyond their campuses, for instance through distance education programs.

3. Section 2 states that "commercially available," in relation to a work or other subject matter, means that the item is "(a) available on the Canadian market within a reasonable time and for a reasonable price and may be located with reasonable effort," or is one "(b) for which a licence to reproduce, perform in public or communicate to the public by telecommunication is available from a collective society within a reasonable time and for a reasonable price and may be located with reasonable effort." This definition allows the publisher, in essence, to control the applicability of the exception.

4. Many educational institutions have licences with the collectives Criterion and Audio Ciné to cover the "public performance" of film materials. The very necessity of having such a licence is not at all clear given that a classroom might not be seen as a truly public space (see chapter 3). To add to the confusion around treatment of various media, the act features a few other exceptions that may be used by educational institutions along with religious, charitable, and fraternal organizations (see Table 8, p.88).

5. Vaver, *Copyright Law*, 213.

6. These licences are not mandatory. The Supreme Court said in *CCH Canadian Ltd. v. Law Society of Upper Canada* (2004) that "the availability of a licence is not relevant to deciding whether a dealing has been fair" (70), but the general feeling seems to be that protection from liability is worth the price. Quebec institutions deal with the collective COPIBEC (Société québécoise de gestion collective des droits de reproduction).

7. See Access Copyright, "Incidental Photocopying," http://www.accesscopyright. ca/ca/Default.aspx?id=93.

8. Access Copyright will arrange licences for digital reproduction of some individual items. See Access Copyright, "Digital Licensing," http://www.accesscopyright.ca/ licenses.asp?a=10.

9. The answer to our rhetorical question is simple enough: textbook manufacturers have a lot to lose if schools and teachers can produce their own teaching resources,

especially drawing from material available on the Internet.

10. *CCH Canadian Ltd. v. Law Society of Upper Canada* (2004), para. 49.

11. Ibid., para. 55.

12. See Bill C-60, section 18 (adding new sections 30.01 and 30.02), available online at http://www2.parl.gc.ca/content/hoc/Bills/381/Government/C-60/C-60_1/C-60_1. pdf. If the intention of these sections was to permit activities associated with technology-enhanced learning, it might have been simpler to just expand the definition of "premises." In any event, we think the complexity of proposed sections 30.01 and 30.02 rises to the level of absurdity. For a discussion about how to address the needs of technology-enhanced learning initiatives, see Hirshhorn, "Assessing the Economic Impact of Copyright Reform in the Area of Technology-Enhanced Learning."

13. Canada, Standing Committee on Canadian Heritage, *Interim Report on Copyright Reform*, May 2004, recommendations nos. 5, 18. The Committee also noted (p.17) "that collective licensing regimes that are already in place are capable of providing the same broad service in a digital environment that they do in the paper-based environment" and that "such a regime would protect rights holders' economic interests by ensuring fair and reasonable compensation for access to material."

14. See, for example, the AUCC media release of April 15, 2005, http://www.aucc.ca/publications/media/2005/04_15_e.html; and their letter of April 13, 2005, to Ministers Emerson and Frulla, http://www.aucc.ca/_pdf/english/media/copyright_letter_04_15_05_e.pdf. For commentary, see Murray, "Protecting Ourselves to Death." For the CIPPIC/PIAC response to the Standing Committee on Canadian Heritage's report, see http://www.cippic.ca/en/news/documents/Response_to_Bulte_Report_FINAL.pdf.

II. Film and Video

1. See http://www.youtube.com. Nobody who has posted allegedly infringing material on YouTube has yet been sued by copyright holders, but Google, its new owner, has promised to police copyright more carefully. See Bogatin, "Google, YouTube: Multi-Billion Dollar 'Fair-Use' Risky Bets." It remains to be seen whether the new rules will distinguish between infringement and the exercise of users' rights. See Electronic Frontier Foundation, "Unfairly Caught in Viacom's Dragnet: Let Us Know"—and its accompanying video at http://www.youtube.com/watch?v=OAd_vpsufRU (viewed Feb. 9, 2007).

2. Walter Forsberg, remark in discussion at Copycamp, an "Unconference" sponsored by the Creators' Rights Alliance and others at Ryerson University, Toronto, Sept. 30, 2006.

3. See *Mattel, Inc. v. 3894207 Canada Inc.*, and *Veuve Clicquot Ponsardin v. Boutiques Cliquot Ltée.*

4. For more on art as criticism, see chapter 16. In a discussion of Conservative ads using clips of television shots of Liberal leadership candidates, Bob Tarantino contends that only criticism of the reproduced work itself—rather than cultural phenomena

represented in it— "counts" in Canadian fair dealing provisions as they stand: see "Would've Said No," http://bobtarantino.blogs.com, Jan. 29, 2007.

5. Kevin McMahon, interview with Laura Murray, Toronto, Nov. 16, 2006.

6. "Canada's Documentary Film Heritage and Its Future in Jeopardy," press release, Dec. 4, 2006, http://www.docorg.ca/.

7. See "Dyke to Open up BBC Archive," Aug. 24, 2003, http://news.bbc.co.uk/2/hi/entertainment/3177479.stm; the test period ended in October 2006 and the project is now being evaluated. See http://creativearchive.bbc.co.uk/archives/the_bbcs_plans/. For the Canadian animated shorts, see www.nfb.ca. The NFB also initiated Citizenshift, designed to be an online forum for activist filmmaking; the success of this project is at the moment unclear, perhaps partly because of the NFB's caution in vetting materials for copyright infringement.

8. In an excellent white paper commissioned by the Department of Communications in December 2006, copyright lawyer and activist Howard Knopf offers other suggestions for appropriate copyright reform—including reform of the unlocatable copyright owner regime, which frustrates much use of archival materials, penalties in the Act for "overclaiming" of rights, and legal constraints on digital rights management in materials and equipment. These provisions have advantages for other Canadians as well. (See our chapter 19 policy recommendations.)

12. Journalism

1. See Vaver, *Copyright Law*, 83–90. Employees might argue that some work done on their own time or initiative belongs to them.

2. "Where the work is an article or other contribution to a newspaper, magazine or similar periodical," Section 13(3) reserves "to the author a right to restrain the publication of the work, otherwise than as part of a newspaper, magazine or similar periodical." Historically, this might have been something like a moral right, protecting the writer's reputation from unwanted associations. But *Robertson v. Thomson Corp.* suggests that the right is economically valuable in an environment in which publishers can make money from republishing in electronic formats—then again, this confirmation of its value probably means that employers will be even more likely to clear it away by contract.

3. See Vaver, *Copyright Law*, 84–86, 89–90, 95–97.

4. See "How to Free the Culture," posting to Blog This (*This Magazine*), Nov. 5, 2004, http://blog.thismagazine.ca/archives/2004/11/as_paul_wells_p.html.

5. Canadian Professional Writers Survey, May 2006, http://www.pwac.ca/PWACsurveyFINALweb.pdf; posting to Canadian Magazines discussion, by D.B. Scott, May 29, 2006, http://canadianmags.blogspot.com/2006/05/freelancers-life-and-earnings.html.

6. *Toronto Star*, "Pages of the Past," http://thestar.pagesofthepast.ca.

7. "Intellectual Property: A Balance. The British Library Manifesto," Sept. 25, 2006, http://www.bl.uk/news/pdf/ipmanifesto.pdf.

8. Professional Writers Association of Canada, http://www.pwac.ca/about/faqanswers2.

9. *Robertson v. Thomson Corp.*, 70.

10. This decision may also hamper digitization of small periodicals—the arts magazines and local papers that form the cutting edge or grassroots of Canadian culture. These publications don't have the staff or budget to track down past contributors. But perhaps it is mainly a matter of choosing the right software: the *Robertson v. Thomson* case suggests that if a publisher emphasizes the integrity of the publication as a whole, clearance from authors is not necessary. Or perhaps a royalty or revenue-sharing arrangement for digital uses unimagined at the time of original publication could work, along with special grants for small magazines and small publishers to "migrate" their materials to electronic archives. The challenge will be to find a mechanism that will fairly and productively accommodate not only the megapublishers and their contributors, but also the small publishers and their contributors, while allowing preservation of Canada's literary and journalistic heritage.

11. Brad Wheeler, "Look, It's Trying to Pop out of My Bra Right Now!" *Globe and Mail*, Oct. 23 2006, R1.

12. *Compagnie Générale des Établissements Michelin-Michelin & Cie v. National Automobile, Aerospace, Transportation and General Workers Union of Canada.* In this case the Federal Court said that unionization posters using the "Michelin Man" were not "protected expression" under the Charter because they used "private property" without permission. The court also said that the Canadian Auto Workers could have expressed the same idea without using the Michelin Man image. This case has been the subject of much criticism and seems now to be of questionable validity (see chapters 6 and 16).

13. Libraries and Museums

1. According to section 2 of the Copyright Act:

> Library, archive or museum' means
> (a) an institution, whether or not incorporated, that is not established or conducted for profit or that does not form a part of, or is not administered or directly or indirectly controlled by, a body that is established or conducted for profit, in which is held and maintained a collection of documents and other materials that is open to the public or to researchers, or (b) any other non-profit institution prescribed by regulation.

2. See, for example, McAnanama, "Copyright Law: Libraries and Their Users Have Special Needs," 225.

3. See testimony of Graham Hill for the Canadian Association of Research Libraries before the Standing Committee on Canadian Heritage, 2nd Session, 35th Parliament, Oct. 29, 1996, http://www.carl-abrc.ca/projects/copyright/testimony_Hill-e.html.

4. The bill as first tabled provided a clear exception in matters of liability arising from the operating of public, self-service photocopiers. The Heritage Committee weakened the exception by tying it to the existence of a contract with a collective society. The amended version also expanded instances of "commercial availability" in such a way as to limit the effectiveness of various exceptions that would not apply if the material was commercially available. The Canadian Association of Research Libraries also objected to a new clause providing that even further restrictions on the limited rights granted to libraries could be enacted by regulation. For the withdrawal of support, see Canadian Association of Research Libraries, "Brief to the Senate Committee on Transport and Communication Concerning Bill C-32 (an Act to amend the Copyright Act), 16 April 1997," http://www.carl-abrc.ca/projects/copyright/senate_brief-e.html.

5. See Exception for Educational Institutions, Libraries, Archives and Museums Regulations [S.O.R./99-325], http://www.canlii.org/ca/regu/sor99-325/. Thankfully, the onerous record-keeping provisions have since been withdrawn.

6. Vaver, *Intellectual Property Law*, 201. For a more detailed discussion about the 1997 amendments, see Wilkinson, "Filtering the Flow from the Fountains of Knowledge," 331–74; and Trosow, "Changing Landscape of Academic Libraries and Copyright Policy," 375–407.

7. The CCA's resolution is quoted in Wilson, "CLA Condemns Captain Copyright." For the text of the letter sent from CLA to Access Copyright, see http://www.cla.ca/Access_Copyright_CptCopy_let_Final_.pdf. For Access Copyright, see its "Statement Regarding Captain Copyright," http://www.accesscopyright.ca/resources.asp?a=201.

8. See Liblicense: Licensing Digital Information: A Resource for Librarians, Yale University, http://www.library.yale.edu/~llicense/.

9. Wikipedia usefully defines the phrase "serials crisis" as "common shorthand for the runaway cost increases of many scholarly journals. The crisis is a result of the cost rising much faster than the rate of inflation, the number of such journals proliferating, and the funds available to the libraries is decreasing"; http://en.wikipedia.org/wiki/Serials_crisis.

10. Panitch and Michalak, "Serials Crisis."

11. For a directory of open access journals, see http://www.doaj.org/. For examples of open access journals, see the Public Library of Science, http://www.plos.org/; and BioMed Central, http://www.biomedcentral.com/. See also *SPARC Open Access Newsletter* (maintained by Peter Suber), http://www.earlham.edu/~peters/fos/.

12. According to the American Library Association, ILL service "is intended to complement local collections and is not a substitute for good library collections" and "is based on a tradition of sharing resources between various types and sizes of libraries." Interlibrary Loan Code for the United States Explanatory Supplement (section 2), http://www.ala.org/ala/rusa/rusaprotools/referenceguide/interlibraryloancode.htm. See also the *Canadian University Reciprocal Borrowing Agreement*, http://www.coppul.ca/rb/rbindex.html.

13. Compare the complexity of this section with the simplicity of the fair dealing section, which provides that "fair dealing for the purpose of research or private study does not infringe copyright": in recent years, legislators have embraced a micromanaging style of legislative drafting that becomes mindboggling for practitioners.

14. *CCH v. Law Society of Upper Canada* (2004), para 49. The court also ruled that while the Law Society did not need to rely on the library exemption, were it necessary it would have been entitled to do so (para 84).

15. Bill C-60 (see http://www2.parl.gc.ca/content/hoc/Bills/381/Government/C-60/C-60_1/C-60_1.pdf) would have amended section 30.2(5) to permit digitization of printed matter but only if the library took measures "to prevent the making of any reproduction of the copy other than a single printing, its communication, or its use for a period of more than seven days." Obviously, this clause would hamper research: people might not be able to use an item in the given time, would want to share it with a co-worker, and so on. For a more complete analysis of Bill C-60's library provisions, see Trosow, "Changing Landscape of Academic Libraries and Copyright Policy," 375, 390–96.

16. *CCH v. Law Society of Upper Canada* (2004), para 39. The Supreme Court's decision made no mention as to whether the library even had a blanket licence with CanCopy for photocopying, probably because the facts and incidents that gave rise to the case occurred prior to the 1997 amendments coming into force.

17. Ibid., para 43. The court also stated that while section 30.3 explicitly permits libraries to offer self-service copiers, the Law Society library did not even need this specific exception to stay within the bounds of non-infringing practice. Although the regulations associated with section 30.3 specify precise wording for copyright notices to be posted above copy machines (see this chapter, note 5), the court left the clear impression that the less alarmist wording sufficed.

18. See http://www.virtualmuseum.ca; and http://www.alouettecanada.ca

19. The 2002 resource paper "An Analysis of Economic Models for Administering Museum Intellectual Property," CHIN website (published April 27, 2002), http://www.chin.gc.ca/English/Intellectual_Property/Economic_Models/index.html, states: "By assembling photographs of the items in its collection, a museum is able to compile a series of potentially valuable intellectual property rights in such items" (Section II). The U.S. case *Bridgeman Art Library, Ltd. v. Corel Corp.* (1999) held that a photograph of a two-dimensional work was not sufficiently original for copyright to subsist.

20. Bielstein, *Permissions, A Survival Guide*, 101.

21. Zorich, "Developing Intellectual Property Policies." Of course, insofar as collections include works under copyright, would-be users must set the price of reproduction with the actual copyright owner, and museums have to negotiate terms for online exhibition. See chapter 16 for related issues. Our focus here is on the public domain, the easiest place for LAMs to start with a renewed strategy for cultural public service.

14. Music

1. As of January 2007, sales of recorded music online are up 122 per cent in Canada from the previous year. See Michael Geist, "Canada a World Leader in Digital Download Sales Growth," Jan. 19, 2007, http://www.michaelgeist.ca/content/view/1621/125; Howard Knopf, "The Sky Isn't Falling," Jan. 18, 2007, http://excesscopyright.blogspot.com/2007/01/sky-isnt-falling.html.

2. "Sound recording maker" is defined in the Copyright Act as "the person by whom the arrangements necessary for the first fixation of the sounds are undertaken," with the elaboration that such arrangements may "include arrangements for entering into contracts with performers, financial arrangements and technical arrangements." Note that the maker is not the engineer, the person at the soundboard, but rather the person who makes the recording happen. In many cases, the "maker" may be the performer; in other situations it is a label. Like performers' rights, makers' rights are limited to those associated with Rome Convention countries; see Copyright Act 18(2).

3. For information on specific collectives and tariffs, see http://www.cb-cda.gc.ca/societies/index-e.html and http://www.socan.ca/jsp/en/resources/tariffs.jsp.

4. Since 1997 Canadian law provides performers and sound-recording makers from Rome Convention countries with an equitable right to remuneration with composers. The International Convention for the Protection of Performers, Producers of Phonograms, and Broadcasting Organizations was negotiated at Rome in 1961; it is administered by the World Intellectual Property Organization. For the details of Rome's conditions and members, see Copyright Act 15(2) and http://www.wipo.int/treaties/en/ip/rome/. Canada is a party to this treaty, but the United States is not, so performers there do not hold rights except by individual contract.

5. Sections 14.1, 28.1, and 28.2 by their terms apply only to "works."

6. See CMRRA's brochure "Mechanical Licensing and Other Mysteries," http://www.cmrra.ca/cmrradocs/mlbe06.pdf.

7. For the full decision and musical works at issue, see http://www.columbia.edu/ccnmtl/projects/law/library/cases/case_grandwarner.html. While U.S. precedents do not necessarily hold in Canada, the recording industry is dominated by U.S.-based labels, so the normal practice is founded in U.S. case law.

8. See Kelefa Sanneh, "With Arrest of DJ Drama, the Law Takes Aim at Mixtapes," New York Times, Jan. 18, 2007, E1.

9. http://www.musiccreators.ca.

15. Photography

1. Brito and Dooling, "Orphan Works Affirmative Defense to Copyright Infringement Actions."

2. Alex Cameron offers a compelling critique and alternative to this approach in his "Lights, Camera, ... Harmonize: Photography Issues in Copyright Reform."

3. Stéphane Baillargeon,"Hauteurs et bassesses du droit d'auteur," *Le Devoir*, Aug. 31, 2006, A1.
4. *Mattel, Inc. v. 3894207 Canada Inc.; Veuve Clicquot Ponsardin v. Boutiques Cliquot Ltée.*
5. *Les Editions Vice-Versa & Gilbert Duclos v. Pascale Claude Aubry.*
6. Kristian Gravenor, "Shot without Consent," *Montreal Mirror*, Aug. 4, 2005, http://www.montrealmirror.com/2005/080405/news1.html. See also Duclos's film on the experience and related issues: *La Rue zone interdite* (Productions Virage, 2005).

16. Visual Arts

1. Status of the Artist Act [S.C. 1992, c. 33], http://www.canlii.org/ca/sta/s-19.6/.
2. Emphasis added.
3. *Théberge v. Galerie d'Art du Petit Champlain Inc.*
4. Ibid., para 31.
5. A letter to Ministers of Canadian Heritage and Industry, June 2006, Appropriation Art website, http://www.appropriationart.ca/?page_id=3.
6. Roberta Smith, "When One Man's Video Art Is Another's Copyright Crime," *New York Times*, May 6, 2004, E1, E5.
7. *Suntrust v. Houghton Mifflin.* Randall did not in fact use any character names or words from Mitchell's novel—but whether or not she would have been infringing outside of fair use was never resolved because the case was settled out of court. It might also be noted that as Margaret Mitchell died in 1949, *Gone with the Wind* has been in the Canadian public domain since 2000, so there was never a copyright issue in Canada; in the United States *Gone with the Wind* will not enter the public domain until 2020.
8. *Rogers v. Koons* (1990). See also Jaszi, "On the Author Effect: Contemporary Copyright and Collective Creativity," 29–56.
9. *CCH v. Law Society of Upper Canada*, para 57.

17. Websites

1. Wikipedia, "Wikipedia: Copyrights," http://en.wikipedia.org/wiki/Wikipedia: Copyrights#Reusers.27_rights_and_obligations.
2. *The Globe and Mail* Online, "Terms and Conditions," www.theglobeandmail.com. If you are inclined to dig through a mass of jargon, compare these terms and conditions with those provided in Geist, ed., *In the Public Interest* (see p.181 here).
3. See www.creativecommons.ca.
4. Exxon Mobil, "Terms and Conditions," http://www2.exxonmobil.com/siteflow/ Notices/SF_MS_LegalNotice_TC.asp, para. 2(I); New York Stock Exchange, Inc.,

"World Wide Web Site Terms and Conditions of Use," http://www.nyse.com/home/copyrightr.html.

5. Michael Geist, "Links to Friends, Foes Fair Game in the Internet," *Toronto Star*, June 12, 2006, http://www.michaelgeist.ca/index.php?option=com_content&task=view&id=1296. Geist reports that the prohibition on the Access Copyright website was changed a few times, and read (at the time of the story) that they have "the right to withhold permission to link from any site that in its opinion may be damaging to its reputation, particularly sites featuring the objectionable content." The Access Copyright page, http://www.accesscopyright.ca/ipn.asp, states:

> Permission is expressly granted to any person who wishes to place a link in his or her own web site to www.accesscopyright.ca or any of its pages with the following exception: permission to link is explicitly withheld from any web site the contents of which may, in the opinion of the Access Copyright, be damaging or cause harm to the reputation of, Access Copyright. In the event we contact you and request the link be removed, you agree to comply with that request promptly. If you link to or otherwise include www.accesscopyright.ca on your website, please let us know and create any link to our home page only.

6. Geist, "Links to Friends."
7. Wikipedia, "Deep Linking," http://en.wikipedia.org/wiki/Deep_linking.
8. An excellent resource on deep linking was maintained by Stefan Bechtold, http://www.jura.uni-tuebingen.de/bechtold/lcp.html. While the page was frozen in July 2004, it remains a useful resource on this issue, and it includes a compilation of cases that have arisen from deep-linking controversies (none of which were from Canada).

18. Copyright's Counterparts

1. For resistance to pharmaceutical and biotech commodification, see Indigenous Peoples Council on Biocolonialism website, http://www.ipcb.org. The World Intellectual Property Organization has also been a focus of international activism: see http://www.wipo.int/tk/en/. For a range of discussion of cultural matters, see Ziff and Rao, eds., *Borrowed Power: Essays on Cultural Appropriation*.
2. Caroline Anawak, "Indigenous Knowledge and Artistic Expression," for example, writes: "Indigenous artists must take great care not to interpret what they are given. They must be true to the bond and deliberately refrain from changing that which is not changeable."
3. This is, of course, a generalization. There are as many distinct customary laws as there are First Nations; First Nations people in Canada have been subjected to Canadian law for several generations; cultures have changed; and Aboriginal individuals live and work in the city and participate in the art world or the marketplace.

Tension sometimes arises over the authority to make decisions about use of cultural traditions. But there is a broad consensus in Aboriginal circles about the idea of responsibility to the history and future of the people, and a widespread frustration and anger at non-Aboriginal appropriation of Aboriginal culture.

4. Robert Bringhurst, quoted in entry for Ghandl, BC Bookworld, http://www.abc-bookworld.com/?state=view_author&author_id=7605.

5. Jusquan, "Yew Wood to Bringhurst: A Story of Indigenous Knowledge," *Redwire*, Spring 2005; reproduced in Koebel, "Aboriginal Youth and Traditional Knowledge."

6. "Copyleft" entry, Wikipedia, http://en.wikipedia.org/wiki/Copyleft.

7. For the full annotated text of the definition along with its history of amendments, see http://opensource.org/docs/definition.html. For other information and software, see http://www.ubuntu.com and http://opensource.org.

8. Johan Söderberg, "Copyleft vs. Copyright: A Marxist Critique," states: "The distinguishing and most promising feature of free software is that it has mushroomed spontaneously and entirely outside of previous capital structures of production. It has built a parallel economy that outperforms the market economy."

9. Creative Commons Canada, "'Some Rights Reserved.'"

10. Because of the independent but overlapping nature of citation and copyright economies, you can infringe copyright without plagiarizing (if you cite your source but you don't ask permission), and you can plagiarize without infringing copyright (if, for example, you take from a source in the public domain).

11. Bakhtin, *Dialogic Imagination*, 293.

12. This is the name of the leading academic "citation index," a way in which influence can be quantified by the number of times a given paper has been cited. Thus the rather romantic metaphor of a "web" is turned into a "productivity indicator": our point being that citation systems are not necessarily "nicer" than market systems—just different.

13. The Ministry of Canadian Heritage has sponsored various studies on the subject of educating children about copyright; see http://www.pch.gc.ca/progs/ac-ca/progs/pda-cpb/neuf-new/awareness_e.cfm. Access Copyright unveiled Captain Copyright, an education resource, in 2006, but withdrew the site's content the same year after a wave of criticism at the biased nature of the information. See Geist, "Captain Copyright"; and a letter from the Canadian Library Association to the Ministers of Industry and Canadian Heritage, http://www.cla.ca/Access_Copyright_CptCopy_let_Final_.pdf.

14. Quoted by Susan Crean, Copycamp, Toronto, September 2006. Also see Lorinc, "Creators and Copyright in Canada."

15. See their websites dedicated to this goal: http://www.forumonpublicdomain.ca; and http://onthecommons.org.

16. Documentary Organization of Canada, "Canada's Documentary Film Heritage and Its Future in Jeopardy," press release, Dec. 5, 2006, http://www.docorg.ca. On museum copyright policies, see chapter 13.

17. Holden, "Cultural Value and the Crisis of Legitimacy."
18. Along with grants, the Canadian government has developed mechanisms such as the Public Lending Right and a now-eliminated requirement that new government-funded buildings spend a certain percentage of their budget on art; it could explore new approaches such as tax incentives for artists. See http://www.plr-dpp.ca/PLR/about.asp, and for a timeline that indicates a wide range Canadian cultural policy ideas over the years, http://culturescope.ca/policy-timeline/time-line-2000_en.htm.
19. Michael Schrage, "Why Giveaways Are Changing the Rules of Business," *Financial Times*, Feb.6, 2006.

19. Copyright's Future

1. See http://www.parl.gc.ca (Select Bills, 38th Parliament, and C-60); Standing Committee on Canadian Heritage, *Interim Report on Copyright Reform: Report of the Standing Committee on Canadian Heritage* (May 2004), http://cmte.parl.gc.ca/cmte/committeepublication.aspx?sourceid=80836. This report generated a massive amount of response; see, for example, the CIPPIC/PIAC response, June 2004, http://www.cippic.ca/en/news/documents/Response_to_Bulte_Report_FINAL.pdf); Canadian Federation Students Member Advisory, "Renewal of the Copyright Act," November 2004, http://www.cfs-fcee.ca/html/english/research/factsheets/MemAdv-2004Copyright-e.pdf).
2. Websites and blogs centrally dedicated to discussion of copyright issues include www.digital-copyright.ca; www.cippic.ca; www.michaelgeist.ca; www.faircopy-right.ca; www.copyrighttalk.ca; excesscopyright.blogspot.com; www.xanga.com/publicdomain; www.onlinerights.ca; and www.forumonpublicdomain.ca.
3. See Kady O'Malley, "A Copycat Campaign," *Maclean's*, Jan. 17, 2007.
4. For example, see http://www.creatorscopyright.ca; http://www.musiccreators.ca; and http://www.appropriationart.ca/.
5. Bill C-60 was twenty-eight pages of single-spaced dense text, and many of its clauses were as confusing to lawyers as they were to laypeople. See http://www.parl.gc.ca (Select Bills, 38th Parliament, and C-60).
6. Our section 29(1) merely includes the existing categories of research, private study, criticism, review, and news reporting as now found in the existing sections 29, 29.1 and 29.2, with the addition of the words "such as."
7. Similarly, usage of the word "shall include" indicates an intention to be open-ended such that the enumerated categories on the list are illustrative rather than exclusive. With two exceptions, this listing is taken directly from the Supreme Court's decision in *CCH v. Law Society of Upper Canada*, which in turn adopted the criteria from J. Linden's decision in the Federal Court of Appeal. First, the words "or other subject matter" are added to subsections (d) and (f) to clarify that fair dealing is applicable to other subject matter as well as works. Second, subsection (f) replaces the attribution requirements in current sections 29.1 and 29.2 because it

seems sufficient that proper attribution should rise only to the level of being one of many factors to consider and not a means for disqualification itself.

8. The sector-by-sector approach was taken in 1997, with poor results for users' rights, as we saw in chapters 10 and 13. An additional risk to this approach would be that a specific provision might be included in a first and second reading version of a bill but later removed in committee, thereby creating a legislative history that shows an intention *not* to include that particular provision.

Legal Citations & Cases

A Note on Understanding Legal Citation and Finding Cases

LEGAL WRITERS use a system of case citation to locate and identify cases. While the exact content of the citation may vary from court to court, or even over time, certain general rules apply. For example:

Allen v. Toronto Star Newspapers Ltd (1997) 36 O.R. (3d) 201.

- Citations begin with the name of the case. When used in prose, case names are usually underlined or italicized.

- The *Allen* case was decided in 1997. The next number is the volume number of the "reporter" containing the case, followed by the abbreviated name of the reporter, followed by the edition (if beyond the first), and then by the page number. This case is found in volume 36 of Ontario Reports, in its third series or edition. Within volume 36, the case starts on page 201.

Another example:

Apple Computer v. Mackintosh Computer Ltd [1988] 1 F.C. 673; rev den [1990] 2 S.C.R. 209.

- In this citation, the date is in square brackets instead of parentheses to indicate that the volume numbers flip back to 1 every year. This case is found on page 673 of the first volume of Federal Court Reports issued in 1988. If you look for 1 F.C. 673 without starting with the [1988], you will never find the case. In *Apple*, the losing party sought to have the case reviewed in the Supreme Court, but the application for review was denied (and this was reported in the second volume of the Supreme Court Reports issued in 1990 at page 209).

- In general, if you find a series of dates in a legal citation, it means the case was appealed up through the courts. The last part is the highest court ruling.

The next step is finding the case. A law library at a nearby university can help you. But you can start with the Canadian Legal Information Institute (CanLII) website, a collection of cases online. CanLII is part of an international "open law" movement including sites in various other countries. It does not require a subscription and is open to the public. Some downsides: it is not (yet) complete, and not all the older cases have page or paragraph numbering so it can be hard to find precise parts of the judgments. But because of CanLII's accessibility, we have used CanLII citations where they are available.

Thus *CCH v. Law Society of Upper Canada* is cited two ways: [2004] 1 S.C.R. 339 and 2004 SCC 13 (CanLII). It is found in the first volume of the Supreme Court Reports issued in 2004 beginning at page 339, but the 2004 SCC 13 notation simply means it is the thirteenth case from the Supreme Court of Canada issued in 2004; it can be found online at http://www.canlii.org/ca/cas/scc/2004/2004scc13.html.

Canadian Supreme Court cases are also available online from Lexum at the University of Montreal, where the url for the *CCH* case is http://scc.lexum.umontreal.ca/en/2004/2004scc13/2004scc13.html.

The U.S. LII is run out of Cornell Law School: http://www.law.cornell.edu/.

Legal Cases Cited

Allen v. Toronto Star Newspapers Ltd. (1997) 36 O.R. (3d) 201(Div.Court).

American Geophysical Union v. Texaco, Inc., 60 F.3d 913 (2d Cir. 1995).

Anne of Green Gables Licensing Authority v. Avonlea Traditions Inc. (2000) 6 C.P.R. (4th) 57, 2000 CanLII 5698 (ON C.A.), http://www.canlii.org/en/on/onca/doc/2000/2000canlii5698/2000canlii5698.html.

Apple Computer v. Mackintosh Computer Ltd. 10, C.P.R. (3d) 1 (Fed Trial Court, 1986); [1988] 1 F.C. 673; [1990] 2 S.C.R. 209.

Basic Books, Inc. v. Kinko's Graphics Corp., 758 F.Supp. 1522 (S.D.N.Y. 1991).

B.C. Jockey Club v. Standen (1986) 8 C.P.R. (3rd) 2883 (B.C.C.A.).

Bishop v. Stevens [1990] 2 S.C.R. 467, 1990 CanLII 75 (S.C.C.), http://www.canlii.org/en/ca/scc/doc/1990/1990canlii75/1990canlii75.html.

BMG Canada v. Doe, 2004 FC 488.

BMG Canada Inc. v. Doe, 2005 FCA 193 (CanLII), http://www.canlii.org/ca/cas/fca/2005/2005fca193.html.

BMG Music v. Gonzalez, 430 F.3d 888 (7th Cir. 2005), http://www.ca7.uscourts.gov/tmp/5B1C0T6N.pdf.

Bridgeman Art Library, Ltd. v. Corel Corp. 36 F. Supp. 2d 191 (S.D.N.Y. 1999), http://www.law.cornell.edu/copyright/cases/36_FSupp2d_191.htm.

Campbell v. Acuff-Rose Music (1994) 510 U.S. 596, http://www.law.cornell.edu/supct/html/92-1292.ZS.html.

Canadian Admiral Ltd. v. Rediffusion Inc. [1954] Exchequer Court Rep. 382, 20 C.P.R. 75.

CCH v. Law Society of Upper Canada 2 C.P.R. (4th) 129 (1999).

CCH Canadian Ltd. v. Law Society of Upper Canada (T.D.), [2000] 2 F.C. 451, 1999 CanLII 7479 (F.C.).

CCH Canadian Ltd. v. Law Society of Upper Canada (C.A.), [2002] 4 F.C. 213, 2002 FCA 187 (CanLII).

CCH Canadian v. Law Society of Upper Canada [2004] 1 S.C.R. 339, 2004 SCC 13, http://www.canlii.org/ca/cas/scc/2004/2004scc13.html.

Compagnie Générale des Établissements Michelin-Michelin & Cie v. National Automobile, Aerospace, Transportation and General Workers Union of Canada (CAW-Canada) (T.D.), [1997] 2 F.C. 306, 1996 CanLII 3920 (F.C.), http://www.canlii.org/ca/cas/fct/1996/1996fct10133.html.

Cuisenaire v. South West Imports Ltd. [1969] S.C.R.208.

Delrina Corp. v. Triolet Systems Inc. (2002) 58 O.R. (3d) 339, 2002 CanLII 11389 (ON C.A.), http://www.canlii.org/en/on/onca/doc/2002/2002canlii11389/2002canlii11389.html.

Feist Publications v. Rural Telephone Service, 499 U.S. 340 (1991).

Glenn Gould Estate v. Stoddart Publishing Co. Ltd.(1998), 39 O.R. (3d) 545, 1998 CanLII 5513 (ON C.A.), http://www.canlii.org/en/on/onca/doc/1998/1998canlii5513/1998canlii5513.html.

Hager v. ECW Press Ltd. [1999] 2 F.C. 287, 1998 CanLII 9115 (F.C.), http://www.canlii.org/en/ca/fct/doc/1998/1998canlii9115/1998canlii9115.html.

Harvard College v. Canada (Commissioner of Patents), [2002] 4 S.C.R. 45, 2002 SCC 76 (CanLII), http://www.canlii.org/en/ca/scc/doc/2002/2002scc76/2002scc76.html.

Les Editions Vice-Versa & Gilbert Duclos v. Pascale Claude Aubry, SCC 1998, http://www.canlii.org/ca/cas/scc/1998/1998scc31.html.

Mattel, Inc. v. 3894207 Canada Inc., [2006] 1 S.C.R. 772, 2006 SCC 22 (CanLII), http://scc.lexum.umontreal.ca/en/2006/2006scc22/2006scc22.html.

Michelin v. CAW (1997). See *Compagnie Générale des Établissements Michelin*.

Milliken & Co. v. Interface Flooring Systems (Canada) Inc. (T.D.), [1998] 3 F.C. 103, 1998 CanLII 9044 (F.C.)(aff'd at 2000 CanLII 14871 (F.C.A.).

Monsanto Canada Inc. v. Schmeiser, [2004] 1 S.C.R. 902, 2004 SCC 34 (CanLII).

Princeton University Press v. Michigan Document Services, 99 F.3d 1381 (6th Cir. 1996), cert. denied 520 U.S. 1156 (1997).

Prise de Parole Inc. v. Guérin (1995) 66 C.P.R. (3d) 257 (Federal Court Trial Div), aff'd (1996) 73 C.P.R. (3d) 557 (Fed. C.A.).

Prism Hospital Software v. Hospital Medical Records Institute 57 C.P.R. (3d) 129 (B.C.S.C., 1994).

Robertson v. Thomson Corp., 2006 SCC 43, Oct. 12, 2006, http://scc.lexum.umontreal.ca/en/2006/2006scc43/2006scc43.html.

Rogers v. Koons, 751 F. Supp. 474 (S.D.N.Y. 1990), upheld at 960 F.2d 301 (2d Cir. 1992).

Society of Composers, Authors and Music Publishers of Canada (SOCAN) v. Canadian Association of Internet Providers. 1 C.P.R. (4th) 417 (Copyright Board, 1999); [2002] 4 F.C. 3 (Federal Court of Appeal, 2002); [2004] 2 S.C.R. 427, 2004 SCC 45 (Supreme Court of Canada, 2004), http://www.canlii.org/en/ca/scc/doc/2004/2004scc45/2004scc45.html.

Snow v. Eaton Centre Ltd. 70 C.P.R. (2d) 105 (Ontario High Court of Justice).

Sony Corp. of America v. Universal City Studios, Inc., 464 U.S. 417 (1984).

Stowe v. Thomas, 23 F. Cas. 201 (C.C.E.D. Pa. 1853) (No. 13,514).

Suntrust Bank v Houghton Mifflin, 268 F.3d 1267(11th Cir. 2001), http://www.ca11.uscourts.gov/opinions/ops/200112200.ORD.pdf.

Tele-Direct (Publications) Inc. v. American Business Information, Inc. 1997 CanLII 6378 (F.C.A.), [1998] 2 F.C. 22, http://www.canlii.org/en/ca/fca/doc/1997/1997canlii6378/1997canlii6378.html.

Théberge v. Galerie d'Art du Petit Champlain Inc. 2002 SCC 34, [2002] S.C.R. 336, www.canlii.org/ca/cas/scc/20002/2002scc34.html.

Veuve Clicquot Ponsardin v. Boutiques Cliquot Ltée, [2006] 1 S.C.R. 824, 2006 SCC 23 (CanLII), http://scc.lexum.umontreal.ca/en/2006/2006scc23/2006scc23.html.

Bibliography

Anawak, Caroline. "Indigenous Knowledge and Artistic Expression." Discussion paper prepared for National Gatherings on Indigenous Knowledge, Department of Canadian Heritage, 2005, http://www.traditions.gc.ca/docs/docs_disc_anawak_e.cfm.

Aoki, Keith, Jennifer Jenkins, and James Boyle. *Bound by Law? Tales from the Public Domain*. Durham N.C.: Center for the Study of Public Domain, Duke Law School, March 2006, http://www.law.duke.edu/cspd/comics/index.html.

Austin, John. *The Province of Jurisprudence Determined*. Introduction by H.L.A. Hart. New York: Humanities Press, 1965 [1832].

Avalon Project, Yale University, www.yale.edu/lawweb/avalon.

Bailey, Jane. "Deflating the Michelin Man: Protecting Users' Rights in the Canadian Copyright Reform Process." In *In the Public Interest*, ed. Geist.

Bakhtin, Mikhail. *The Dialogic Imagination*. Ed. Michael Holquist. Trans. Caryl Emerson and Michael Holquist. Austin: University of Texas Press, 1981.

Benkler, Yochai. "From Consumers to Users: Shifting the Deeper Structures of Regulation Towards Sustainable Commons and User Access." *Federal Communications Law Journal*, 52,3 (May 2000).

Bentham, Jeremy. *Introduction to the Principles of Morals and Legislation* [1823]. Jeremy's Labyrinth website, www.la.utexas.edu/labyrinth.

Bielstein, Susan M. *Permissions, A Survival Guide: Blunt Talk about Art as Intellectual Property*. Chicago: University of Chicago Press, 2006.

Bogatin, Donna. "Google, YouTube: Multi-Billion Dollar 'Fair-Use' Risky Bets," http://blogs.zdnet.com/micro-markets/?p=451.

Boswell, James. *Boswell's Life of Johnson*. London: Oxford University Press, 1961.

Boyle, James. *Shamans, Software, and Spleens: Law and the Construction of the Information Society*. Cambridge, Mass.: Harvard University Press, 1996.

—. "The Second Enclosure Movement and the Construction of the Public Domain." *Law and Contemporary Problems*, 66 (2003).

Bollier, David. *Silent Theft: The Private Plunder of Our Common Wealth*. New York and London: Routledge, 2002.

Brito, Jerry and Bridget Dooling. "An Orphan Works Affirmative Defense to Copyright Infringement Actions." *Michigan Telecommunications and Technology Law Review* 12, 75 (2005), http://www.mttlr.org/voltwelve/brito&dooling.pdf.

Cameron, Alex. "Lights, Camera, ... Harmonize: Photography Issues in Copyright Reform." In *In the Public Interest*, ed. Geist.

Canada, Department of Canadian Heritage. "Music Is My Business." www.music.gc.ca.

—, Industry Canada/Canadian Heritage, Copyright Policy Branch. "A Framework for Copyright Reform." Ottawa, 2001, http://strategis.ic.gc.ca/epic/site/crp-prda.nsf/en/rp01101e.html.

—, Standing Committee on Canadian Heritage. *Interim Report on Copyright Reform: Report of the Standing Committee on Canadian Heritage* (known as the *Bulte Report*, after Sarmite Bulte, the chairperson of the committee). Ottawa, May 2004, www.parl.gc.ca/InfocomDoc/Documents/37/3/parlbus/commbus/house/reports/herirp0 /herirp0 -e.pdf.

Canadian Federation of Students. "Copyright for the Public Interest." Spring 2006, http://www.cfs-nl.ca/mysql/Factsheet-2006-Copyright.pdf.

Canadian Intellectual Property Office. "A Guide to Copyrights: Registration of Copyright." http://strategis.gc.ca/sc_mrksv/cipo/cp/copy_gd_regis-e.html#1.

—. "A Guide to Industrial Designs." http://strategis.ic.gc.ca/sc_mrksv/cipo/id/idguide-e.pdf.

Cohen, Julie E. "Constitutional Issues Involving Use of the Internet: Intellectual Property and Censorship of the Internet." *Seton Hall Constitutional Law Journal*, 8 (1998).

Coombe, Rosemary J. *The Cultural Life of Intellectual Properties: Authorship, Appropriation, and the Law*. Durham, N.C.: Duke University Press, 1998.

Creative Commons Canada. "'Some Rights Reserved': Building a Layer of Reasonable Copyright." http://creativecommons.ca/index.php?p=history.

Davies, Gillian. *Copyright and the Public Interest*. London: Sweet and Maxwell, 2002.

DeBeer, Jeremy F. "The Role of Levies in Canada's Digital Music Market." *Canadian Journal of Law & Technology*, 4,3 (2005), http://papers.ssrn.com/sol3/papers.cfm?abstract_id=877191.

Doctorow, Cory. "Sony Anti-Customer Technology Round-up and Time-Line." Nov. 14, 2005, http://boingboing.net/2005/11/14/sony_anticustomer_te.html.

Drassinower, Abraham. "Taking User Rights Seriously." In *In the Public Interest*, ed. Geist.

Electronic Frontier Foundation. "Unintended Consequences: Seven Years Under the DMCA." http://www.eff.org/IP/DMCA/unintended_consequences.php.

—. "Unfairly Caught in Viacom's Dragnet: Let Us Know," http://www.eff.org/deep-links/archives/005109.php.

Feather, John. "From Rights in Copies to Copyright: The Recognition of Authors' Rights in English Law and Practice in the Sixteenth and Seventeenth Centuries." In *The Construction of Authorship: Textual Appropriation in Law and Literature*, ed. Martha Woodmansee and Peter Jaszi. Durham, N.C.: Duke University Press, 1994.

Fisher, William W. "Theories of Intellectual Property." In *New Essays in the Legal and Political Theory of Property*, ed. Stephen R. Munzer. Cambridge and New York: Cambridge University Press, 2001, http://www.law.harvard.edu/faculty/tfisher/iptheory.html.

—. *Promises to Keep: Technology, Law, and the Future of Entertainment*. Palo Alto, Cal.: Stanford University Press, 2004.

Fisk, C. "Credit Where It's Due: Attribution Rights without Intellectual Property Rights." Oxford Intellectual Property Research Centre Working Paper, Series no. 1, January 2006, http://www.oiprc.ox.ac.uk/EJWP0106.html.

Frye, Northrop. *Anatomy of Criticism*. Princeton, N.J.: Princeton University Press, 1957.

Geist, Michael. "Anti-Circumvention Legislation and Competition Policy: Defining a Canadian Way?" In *In the Public Interest*, ed. Geist.

—, ed. *In the Public Interest: The Future of Canadian Copyright Law*. Toronto: Irwin Law, 2005, http://209.171.61.222/PublicInterest/two_4_geist.htm.

—. "Captain Copyright." June 1, 2006, http://michaelgeist.ca/component/option,com_content/task,view/id,1275.

Ginsburg, Jane C. "A Tale of Two Copyrights: Literary Property in Revolutionary France and America." *Tulane Law Review*, 64 (1990).

Hatch, Sen. Orrin. "Toward a Principled Approach to Copyright Legislation at the Turn of the Millennium." *University of Pittsburgh Law Review*, 59, 719, 720 (1998).

Hayhurst, William L. "Copyright Subject Matter." In *Copyright and Confidential Information Law in Canada*, ed. Gordon Henderson, Howard Knopf, and John Rudolph. Scarborough, Ont.: Carswell, 1994.

Hesse, Carla. *Publishing and Cultural Politics in Revolutionary Paris, 1789–1810*. Berkeley: University of California Press, 1991.

—. "The Rise of Intellectual Property, 700 B.C.–A.D. 2000: An Idea in the Balance." *Daedalus* 131, 2 (2002), http://www.forumonpublicdomain.ca/node/23.

Hirshhorn, Ronald. "Assessing the Economic Impact of Copyright Reform in the Area of Technology-Enhanced Learning." Prepared for Marketplace Framework Policy Branch, Industry Canada, 2003, http://strategis.ic.gc.ca/epic/site/ippd-dppi.nsf/

en/ip01098e.html.

Holden, John. "Cultural Value and the Crisis of Legitimacy: Why Culture Needs a Democratic Mandate." *Demos*, March 29, 2006, http://www.demos.co.uk/publications/culturallegitimacy.

Holmes, Oliver Wendell. "The Path of the Law." *Harvard Law Review*, 10, 457 (1897).

Howell, Robert G., Linda Vincent, and Michael D. Manson. *Intellectual Property Law: Cases and Materials*. Toronto: E. Montgomery, 1999.

Hughes, Justin. "Locke's 1694 Memorandum (and More Incomplete Copyright Historiographies)." Cardozo Legal Studies Research Paper no. 167 (October 2006); Social Sciences Research Network website, www.ssrn.com.

Industry Canada. *Supporting Culture and Innovation: Report on the Provisions and Operation of the Copyright Act* (Section 92 Report). Ottawa, October 2002, http://strategis.ic.gc.ca/epic/internet/incrp-prda.nsf/en/rp00863e.html.

Industry and Canadian Heritage, Departments of. "Copyright and the Educational Use of Internet Content." Working Group report, Dec. 8, 2003, http://strategis.ic.gc.ca/epic/internet/incrp-prda.nsf/en/rp01114e.html.

Jaszi, Peter. "On the Author Effect: Contemporary Copyright and Collective Creativity." In *The Construction of Authorship: Textual Appropriation in Law and Literature*, ed. Martha Woodmansee and Peter Jaszi. Durham, N.C.: Duke University Press, 1994.

Jefferson, Thomas. *The Writings of Thomas Jefferson*. Constitution Society website, www.constitution.org.

Judge, Elizabeth F. "Crown Copyright and Copyright Reform in Canada." In *In the Public Interest*, ed. Geist.

Koebel, Jaime. "Aboriginal Youth and Traditional Knowledge: Honouring the Past and Acknowledging the Future." Discussion paper prepared for the National Gatherings on Indigenous Knowledge, Department of Canadian Heritage, 2005, http://www.traditions.gc.ca/docs/docs_disc_koebel_e.cfm.

Knopf, Howard. "Excess Caution." Feb. 6, 2006, http://excesscopyright.blogspot.com/2006/02/excess-caution.html.

—. "The Copyright Clearance Culture and Canadian Documentaries: A White Paper on Behalf of the Documentary Organisation of Canada ("DOC")." Nov. 22, 2006, http://www.docorg.ca.

Kratz, Martin P.J. *Canada's Intellectual Property Law in a Nutshell*. Toronto: Carswell, 1998.

Kusek, David and Gerd Leonhard. *The Future of Music: Manifesto for the Digital Music Revolution*. Boston: Berklee Press, 2005, http://www.futureofmusicbook.com/.

Lessig, Lawrence. *Free Culture: How Big Media Uses Technology and the Law to Lock Down Culture and Control Creativity*. London: Penguin, 2004, http://www.free-culture.cc/.

Litman, Jessica. "The Public Domain." *Emory Law Journal*, 39, 965 (1990).

Locke, John. *Second Treatise of Government* [1690]; Project Gutenberg website, www. gutenberg.org.

Loewenstein, Joseph. *The Author's Due: Printing and the Prehistory of Copyright.* Chicago: University of Chicago Press, 2002.

Lorinc, John. "Creators and Copyright in Canada." Prepared for the Creators Copyright Coalition, November 2004, http://www.creatorscopyright.ca/documents/lorinc. html.

Macdonald, Roderick Alexander. *Lessons of Everyday Law.* Law Commission of Canada and School of Policy Studies, Queen's University (Kingston and Montreal: McGill-Queen's University Press, 2002).

Maruca, Lisa. "The Plagiarism Panic: Digital Policing in the New Intellectual Property Regime." Paper presented at the AHRB Copyright Research Network: 2004 Conference on New Directions in Copyright, June 30, 2004, http://www.copy-right.bbk.ac.uk/contents/publications/conferences/2004/lmaruca.pdf.

McAnanama, Judith. "Copyright Law: Libraries and Their Users Have Special Needs." *Intellectual Property Journal*, 6 (1991).

McGill, Meredith. "The Matter of the Text: Commerce, Print Culture, and the Authority of the State in American Copyright Law." *American Literary History*, 9, 1 (1997).

—. *American Literature and the Culture of Reprinting, 1834–1853*. Philadelphia: University of Pennsylvania Press, 2003.

McKeon, Michael. *The Secret History of Domesticity: Public, Private, and the Division of Knowledge*. Baltimore: John Hopkins University Press, 2005.

Milton, John. "Areopagitica" (1644); http://www.uoregon.edu/~rbear/areopagitica. html.

Morgan, Charles. "I Click, You Click, We all Click … But Do We Have a Contract? A Case Comment on Aspencerl.com v. Paysystems." *Canadian Journal of Law and Technology* 14,2 (July 2005), PERLINKhttp://cjlt.dal.ca/vol4_no2/pdfarticles/morgan.pdfhttp://cjlt.dal.ca/vol4_no2/pdfarticles/morgan.pdf.

Murray, Laura J. "Protecting Ourselves to Death." *First Monday* 9, 10 (2004), http://www.firstmonday.org.

—. "Copyright Talk: Patterns and Pitfalls in Canadian Policy Discourses." In *In the Public Interest*, ed. Geist.

Nadel, Ira B. "Copyright, Empire and the Politics of Print: The Case of Canada." Unpublished manuscript, 2006.

Netanel, Neil Weinstock. "Copyright and a Democratic Civil Society." *Yale Law Journal* 106 (1996).

Office of the United States Trade Representative. *Special 301 Report*, 2006, http://www.ustr.gov/Document_Library/Reports_Publications/2006/2006_Special_301_Review/Section_Index.html.

Panitch, Judith M. and Sarah Michalak. "The Serials Crisis: A White Paper for the UNC-Chapel Hill Scholarly Communications Convocation." University of North Carolina,

January 2005, http://www.unc.edu/scholcomdig/whitepapers/panitch-michalak. html.

Parker, George L. *The Beginnings of the Book Trade in Canada*. Toronto: University of Toronto Press, 1985.

Patterson, Lyman Ray. *Copyright in Historical Perspective*. Nashville, Tenn.: Vanderbilt University Press, 1968.

Raustiala, Kal. "Fashion Victims," *The New Republic Online*, March 15, 2005, http://www.tnr.com/doc.mhtml?i=w050314&s=raustiala031505.

Reese, R. Anthony. "The First Sale Doctrine in the Era of Digital Networks." *Boston College Law Review* 44 (March 2003).

Reports of Sir Edward Coke. *English Reports* 638 (Common Pleas, 1610); http://plaza. ufl.edu/edale/Dr%20Bonham's%20Case.htm.

Richardson, Henry S. "The Stupidity of the Cost-Benefit Standard." In *Cost Benefit Analysis: Legal, Economic, and Philosophical Perspectives*, ed. Matthew D. Adler and Eric A. Posner. Chicago: University of Chicago Press, 2001.

Robertson, Kirsty. "Craft and Copyright." Unpublished manuscript, December 2006.

Rose, Mark. "The Author as Proprietor: Donaldson v. Becket and the Genealogy of Modern Authorship." *Representations* 23 (Summer 1988).

—. *Authors and Owners: The Invention of Copyright*. Cambridge, Mass.: Harvard University Press, 1993.

Saint-Amour, Paul K. *The Copywrights: Intellectual Property and the Literary Imagination*. Ithaca, N.Y.: Cornell University Press, 2003.

Samuels, Edward. *The Illustrated Story of Copyright*. New York: Thomas Dunne Books, St. Martin's Press, 2000, http://www.edwardsamuels.com/copyright/index.html.

Sanderson, Paul E. *Musicians and the Law in Canada*, 3rd ed. Toronto: Carswell, 2000.

Schleifer, Ronald and Gabriel Rupp. "Structuralism." *The Johns Hopkins Guide to Literary Theory and Criticism*, 2nd ed., http://litguide.press.jhu.edu/cgi-bin/view. cgi?eid=247&query=structuralism.

Sigel, Skip et al. "The Validity of Webwrap Contracts." Paper prepared for the Uniform Law Conference of Canada, http://www.ulcc.ca/en/cls/index. cfm?sec=4&sub=4i.

Söderberg, Johan. "Copyleft vs. Copyright: A Marxist Critique." *First Monday* 7, 3 (March 4, 2002), http://www.firstmonday.dk/issues/issue7_3/soderberg/.

Stearns, Laurie. "Copy Wrong: Plagiarism, Process, Property, and the Law." In *Perspectives on Plagiarism and Intellectual Property in a Postmodern World*, ed. Lise Buranen and Alice M. Roy. Buffalo: State University of New York Press, 1999.

Stein-Sacks, Shelley. "The Canadian Independent Music Industry: An Examination of Distribution and Access." Prepared for the Department of Canadian Heritage, September 2006, http://www.pch.gc.ca/pc-ch/pubs/music_industry/index_ e.cfm.

Stokes, Simon. "Some Reflections on Art and Copyright," 2004, http://www.oiprc. ox.ac.uk/EJWP0604.html.

Storey, R.B. "Filing Design Applications in Canada and the United States." *University of Baltimore Intellectual Property Law Journal* 10, 2 (2002).

Tawfik, Myra J. "Copyright as Droit d'Auteur." *Intellectual Property Journal*, 17 (2003).

—. "International Copyright Law: W[h]ither User Rights." In *In the Public Interest*, ed. Geist.

Trosow, Samuel E. "The Changing Landscape of Academic Libraries and Copyright Policy: Interlibrary Loans, Electronic-Reserves, and Distance Education." In *In the Public Interest*, ed. Geist.

Vaidhyanathan, Siva. *Copyrights and Copywrongs: The Rise of Intellectual Property and How It Threatens Creativity*. New York: New York University Press, 2001.

—. "Copyright Law and Creativity." Presentation at Originality, Imitation, and Plagiarism, University of Michigan conference, Sept. 23–25, 2005.

Vaver, David. *Intellectual Property Law: Copyright, Patents, Trade-Marks*. Toronto: Irwin Law, 1997.

—. *Copyright Law*. Toronto: Irwin, 2000.

Wells, Pete. "New Era of the Recipe Burglar." *Food & Wine*, November 2006, http:// foodandwine.com/articles/new-era-of-the-recipe-burglar.

Wilkinson, Margaret Ann. "Filtering the Flow from the Fountains of Knowledge: Access and Copyright in Education and Libraries." In *In the Public Interest*, ed. Geist.

Wilson, Drew. "CLA Condemns Captain Copyright." *Slyck News*, June 27, 2006, http:// www.slyck.com/story1236.html.

Woodmansee, Martha and Peter Jaszi, eds. *The Construction of Authorship: Textual Appropriation in Law and Literature*. Durham, N.C.: Duke University Press, 1994.

Young, Edward. "Conjectures on Original Composition." London: Millar and Dodsley, 1759. Representative Poetry Online, http://rpo.library.utoronto.ca.

Ziff, Bruce and Pratima V. Rao, eds. *Borrowed Power: Essays on Cultural Appropriation*. New Brunswick, N.J.: Rutgers University Press, 1997.

Zimmerman, Diane Leenheer. "The Story of Bleistein v. Donaldson Lithographic Company: Originality as a Vehicle for Copyright Inclusivity." In *Intellectual Property Stories*, ed. Jane C. Ginsburg and Rochelle Cooper Dreyfuss. New York: Foundation Press, 2006.

Zorich, Diane M. "Developing Intellectual Property Policies: A How-to Guide for Museums." http://www.chin.gc.ca/English/Intellectual_Property/Developing_ Policies/index.html.

Illustration Permissions

p.78, CAW Michelin Man poster. *Federal Court of Canada Reports*, [1997] 2 F.C. 390, Appendix II.

No permission sought. Reproducing this image is, we believe, a necessary part of our discussion and criticism of the case. The image was published in the decision, and while the court reporter is covered by Crown Copyright we believe that reproducing one page is reasonable under the Federal Reproduction Order (P.C. 1996–1995 19 December, 1996), according to which "Anyone may, without charge or request for permission, reproduce enactments and consolidations of enactments of the Government of Canada, and decisions and reasons for decisions of federally-constituted courts and administrative tribunals, provided due diligence is exercised in ensuring the accuracy of the materials reproduced and the reproduction is not represented as an official version."

As for permissions we might seek from CAW or Michelin, it is not clear given the court ruling that CAW owns copyright in the poster. Michelin owns copyright only in the image of the Michelin Man. Given too that we consider our use a strong instance of fair dealing, we have opted not to ask permission.

p.97, Condom Country advertisement.
Reproduced with permission of the Aids Committee of Toronto (ACT).

p.167, photo of *La Joute*, a sculpture by Jean-Paul Riopelle, Montreal, 1969. Photo by Kirsty Robertson, reproduced with permission.

p.189, Logo, Vancouver Olympics, 2010.
Reproduced without permission from the Vancouver Olympic website, http://www.vancouver2010.com/en/LookVancouver2010/Protecting Brand/OlympicBrandFAQs.

We hope it is obvious from the context that we are using this image to critique the enclosure of images, particularly those based on existing images in the public domain and in this instance of First Nations origin; reproduction of the logo is necessary to make our critical point. Within the terms of the tailor-made legislation giving extraordinary protection to this logo (Olympic and Paralympic Marks Act, 2007), our use is acceptable because we are not using this image to direct readers to a business, ware, or service, nor are we misleading the public to believe that a business, ware, or service is approved, authorized, or endorsed by the Canadian Olympic Committee or the Canadian Paralympic Committee.

Index